The Conjugal Act as Personal Act

DONALD P. ASCI

The Conjugal Act as Personal Act

A Study of the Catholic Concept of the Conjugal Act in the Light of Christian Anthropology

IGNATIUS PRESS SAN FRANCISCO

Nihil Obstat: The Very Reverend Gerald D. Coleman, S.S.

Imprimatur: † His Excellency William J. Levada
Archbishop of San Francisco

This nihil obstat and imprimatur are official declarations that a book or pamphlet is free of doctrinal or moral error. No implication is contained therein that those who have granted the nihil obstat and imprimatur agree with the contents, opinions or statements expressed.

Cover design by Riz Boncan Marsella

ISBN 0-89870-844-3
Library of Congress Control Number 2001094783
Printed in the United States of America ♾

CONTENTS

ACKNOWLEDGMENTS

My current reflection on the conjugal act and Christian anthropology represents the fruit of the two main academic projects that have occupied me for the past four years: my doctoral studies at the Pontificia Università della Santa Croce in Rome and the courses that I have taught in Gaming, Austria. Here I wish to acknowledge those who have assisted and encouraged me in both of these endeavors.

I was fortunate enough to write my doctoral dissertation at Santa Croce under the generous and patient direction of the Reverend Professor Robert A. Gahl, Jr. I remain grateful for Fr. Gahl's sincere dedication to the success of this project and for his many valuable insights and suggestions.

My studies at Santa Croce would have been impossible without the encouragement and support of numerous friends and benefactors. To all those who helped me during my time in Rome I remain truly grateful. Among those who provided crucial assistance at several key moments in my program of studies, I must mention the following: Dr. William E. May, Fr. Marcel Guarnizo, Adrian Tomlinson of the Venerable English College, the Hartley family, Helene Sigler, Joseph Ferguson and the Abbeystore Faithful, Brent and Tina West, and the Roman Athenaeum Foundation.

I am also indebted to the late Ramón García de Haro, under whom I had the privilege to study at Santa Croce. Unfortunately, I knew him only a very short time, yet his teaching and writings have been not only intellectually enlightening for me but also personally inspiring as I have worked in the field of moral theology.

Though the ideas expressed in these pages comprise the substance of my doctoral dissertation, everything written here has found its way into the courses that I have given both at the Austrian Program of Franciscan University of Steubenville and at the International Theological Institute for Studies on Marriage and the Family in Gaming, Austria. The teaching opportunities afforded me by these institutions have been an important factor in the development of my ideas regarding marriage and family life. I am thankful for the many students who have asked insightful questions that have brought me to a clearer understanding of my own thoughts and for the encouragement offered by my colleagues. In particular, Dr. Michael Waldstein has demonstrated unmerited faith in me and true kindness toward me, and for this I am sincerely grateful.

For their support in my academic endeavors and many others in life, I am above all grateful to my family. In both word and deed, my parents have provided constant support and encouragement, even in the face of seemingly impossible odds. In the light of their appreciation of my achievements, the toil and hardship have been a small price to pay.

Finally, I must honor my dear wife, Michelle, who, with heroic self-sacrifice, has been my constant companion and faithful friend throughout a cascade of joys and sorrows. Without her encouragement and strength I surely would have abandoned my course years ago. For the sake of my studies and teaching, Michelle has graciously endured nearly incessant pacing, blank stares in the place of lively conversation, and a maddening degree of forgetfulness on my part. I could never repay Michelle or adequately express my gratitude for the love she has shown me, so I leave that to God and his infinite blessings.

January 1, 2001
Solemnity of Mary the Mother of God

INTRODUCTION

A simple survey of the contemporary cultural landscape reveals a great interest in the sexual relationship between man and woman, with many books, articles, and programs dedicated to this subject. However, the energy spent seeking new ways to "improve" modern man's sexual experience betrays an almost equally great dissatisfaction. Though modern man's discontentment with sexuality undoubtedly derives from multiple factors, one cannot avoid suspecting that the contemporary approach to sexuality produces so little satisfaction because it sees sexuality in the most superficial of terms. Anytime we judge something profound by superficial standards we fail to grasp not only its significance but also its value for our lives.[1]

In contrast to the popular view of human sexuality, the Catholic Church promotes an understanding that not only includes unique considerations on the ethical level but that also appreciates the most profound aspects of sexuality without neglecting any genuinely human aspect of the sexual relationship. The Catholic concept of sexuality and sexual intercourse articulates the ethical norms by which these profound realities are preserved and promoted. Consequently, the teachings of the Church open the path to a joy and fulfillment

[1] Thus, for example, some people are bored at the Holy Sacrifice of the Mass, blaming the length of the homily or the quality of the music. In fact, the second Person of the Trinity is becoming sacramentally present on the altar during Mass, an event that could never fail to excite and to produce joy if properly understood and appreciated.

that only the deepest aspects of sexuality can supply. Beyond the moral norms of the Church's sexual ethics lies a theology of sexuality that recalls what is at stake in the realm of sexual activity. Thus, the Church not only affirms marriage as the only morally acceptable context for sexual intercourse but also develops a specific concept of the conjugal act, recalling all that sexual intercourse can and should be for husband and wife.

I have undertaken this study of the Catholic concept of the conjugal act in order to investigate and present the deeper significance of the conjugal act, that is, the profound and sacred significance that the Church's theology of sexuality recognizes in sexual intercourse between husband and wife. In light of the contemporary situation, I see a great many people whose minds and hearts (and cultures) need to encounter these profound truths if they are ever to appreciate and value sexuality to its full potential. Thus, the opportunity to contribute to such an encounter in any small manner is worth taking. However, I am further motivated to study the Catholic concept of the conjugal act by the larger, more fundamental theological framework from which this concept of the conjugal act emerges. Within this theological framework, the Church's teaching becomes a true theology of the conjugal act, drawing upon fundamental theological principles, especially those related to theological anthropology. Thus, a study of the conjugal act provides a window or an opening to this greater theological framework and enables us to see how the Church's anthropological vision finds its way into the life of the person. In other words, the value of studying the conjugal act derives from the opportunity it affords to consider the Church's vision of man and the implications this anthropological vision has for our lives.

Throughout my consideration of the conjugal act and its related fields of study I seek to examine and present the "Catholic position" by focusing principally, though not exclusively, on the Magisterium's official pronouncements. In one sense, the Catholic position admits of various interpretations, so identifying such a position in a definitive manner seems nearly impossible. Yet, when we examine what is said by those who attack or dissent from the Catholic position on the conjugal act as well as by those who defend and promote it, several core, indispensable, and identifiable elements emerge that possess certain presuppositions and implications, the further details of which admit of various interpretations. Consequently, in the course of my consideration I concentrate on identifying the core elements of the Church's theology of the conjugal act while also forwarding the most reasonable presuppositions and implications of the explicit teachings or pronouncements. In accomplishing this task I rely on the official teachings of the Church and the writings of those authors who explore and promote these teachings,[2] while I

[2] Regarding these secondary sources, I concentrate my attention on the writings of those authors who demonstrate a clear effort to support or develop the official teachings of the Magisterium or whose work possesses a clear correspondence to the ideas articulated in the official teachings of the Magisterium. Though a great many theologians and philosophers fulfill this criteria, I mention (in alphabetical order) the following as authors who have done exemplary work in this repect and who represent significant sources for the development of my study: Carlo Caffarra, Ramón García de Haro, Francisco Gil Hellín, Alain Mattheeuws, William E. May, Martin Rhonheimer, Janet Smith, Dionigi Tettamanzi, and Karol Wojtyla. Additionally, regarding certain concepts, I make substantial reference to the writings of St. Augustine of Hippo and St. Thomas Aquinas as two authorities explicitly incorporated into the teachings of the Magisterium (for example, in Pius XI's *Casti connubii* and John Paul II's *Veritatis splendor*). The specific books and articles from these authors (as well as other relevant sources) that have been instrumental in the development of my ideas are cited throughout the text and contained in the bibliography. For a more comprehensive bibliography of the relevant work published in this area of study, consult Janet Smith, "*Humanae Vitae*", *a Generation Later* (Washington, D.C.: Catholic University of America Press, 1993), and Alain Mattheeuws, *Union et procréation* (Paris: Les Éditions du Cerf, 1989), both of which contain extensive bibliographies.

mention only rarely those who take exception to these teachings. The dissenting position deserves serious consideration, but in another context.[3]

An examination and summary of the Church's position proves challenging precisely because it has been unfolding over a great number of years and in vastly diverse circumstances or contexts. Because the Church's position develops in this manner, certain elements in it receive greater or lesser emphasis according to the purpose and context of a particular teaching. However, though this manner of unfolding

[3] By "dissenting position" I mean the writings of those theologians and philosophers who, though working in a Christian context, do not fully accept the official teachings of the Church regarding the sexual relationship of husband and wife. For a simplified but classic example of this line of thought, see Anthony Kosnik et al., *Human Sexuality, New Directions in American Catholic Thought: A Study*, commissioned by the Catholic Theological Society of America (New York: Paulist Press, 1977). Although this position is usually expressed with regard to particular moral conclusions affirmed by the Magisterium, such as the Church's condemnation of contraception, the dissenting position amounts to an understanding of human sexuality and human action and, consequently, a concept of the conjugal act that differ fundamentally from the Catholic understanding of the same issues. The difference between the dissenting position and the doctrine of the Magisterium, then, cannot be reduced to a simple disagreement about certain sexual acts. Instead, those who dissent from the Church's teaching on the conjugal act invariably espouse, in one form or another, concepts of the human person and moral theories that are incompatible with the teachings of the Church. In simple terms, those who reject the teaching of *Humanae vitae* usually find themselves at odds with the teaching of *Veritatis splendor*. Prominent examples of this line of thought can be found in the writings of Charles Curran, Josef Fuchs, Bernard Häring, Louis Janssens, and Richard McCormick. The ideas and positions of these authors and others, often described as "revisionists", have been given serious consideration. For an analysis and critique of the dissenting position, including relevant bibliographical information, consult William May, *An Introduction to Moral Theology*, rev. ed. (Huntington, Ind.: Our Sunday Visitor, 1994), pp. 109–53; Martin Rhonheimer, "Intentional Acts and the Meaning of Object: A Reply to Richard McCormick", *Thomist*, vol. 59, no. 2 (1995), pp. 279–311; and Smith, "*Humanae Vitae*", pp. 161–229.

begins as a challenge, it ultimately becomes an advantage precisely because it allows each core element of the Church's position to receive an adequate prominence or emphasis. In other words, each core element receives adequate treatment because it eventually comes to the center of discussion by virtue of the vast circumstances in which the Church's position has been reiterated or deepened. For that reason, emphasis on one core element in one context should not be taken as a denial or dislodging of a core element that has been affirmed in a different context. In order to navigate the situation we cannot reduce the Catholic position to any one particular teaching, otherwise core elements of the position that are emphasized elsewhere will be lost. The Church diligently avoids a reductive approach in her theology of marriage and her theology of the conjugal act by preserving a multi-faceted unity across many years and differing circumstances. For this reason, I approach the diverse teachings, each representing a particular context and purpose, as a unified and coherent whole and prescind from speculation about the competition that each teaching poses to the others. The resulting summary provides a profound view of marriage and the conjugal act from diverse yet harmonious perspectives.

As a consequence of the Church's multi-faceted approach to the conjugal life of husband and wife, her theology of marriage considers this sacred relationship from three principal perspectives: marriage as a natural institution, marriage as an intimate friendship, and marriage as a sacrament. As a natural institution, marriage possesses a specific content in terms of its structure, purposes, blessings, and laws. The institution of marriage finds its origin in God, in the very creation of man as male and female, ordering masculinity and femininity to marriage. The institution of marriage bestows certain rights on husband and wife while also imposing obligations on them toward each other and toward God the Creator. The conjugal friendship "gives life" to the institution of marriage, confirming it as a loving personal communion. As an intimate friendship that embraces the good of the whole person, marriage demands the personal energy and emotion of the spouses as well as their firm commitment and selfless sacrifice. For its part, the institution of marriage protects and promotes spousal love, directing husband and wife to the goods upon which their personal communion is based. The sacramental dimension of marriage enables the relationship of husband and wife to share in and signify the mystery of God's love for humanity and Christ's love for the Church. Thus, marriage acquires a sacred role or purpose in the world insofar as the relationship of husband and wife should announce and manifest God's covenantal love. Moreover, because spouses fulfill this sacred role only when the essence of marriage as an institution and a loving communion remains intact, husband and wife discover in the sacramental dimension of marriage a serious motivation for conforming their daily life to God's plan for the conjugal life.

The Church's theology of the conjugal act emerges from this multi-faceted theology of marriage and relates intimately to each dimension of marriage as an institution, an intimate friendship, and a sacrament. These various dimensions of marriage harmoniously converge in the conjugal act, just as they do in the whole of conjugal life. Therefore, the conjugal act cannot be reduced to an obligation of the institution or to an expression of love. Instead, the conjugal act embraces each of these dimensions as the consummation of marital consent and the embodiment of conjugal love, sharing the sacramental signification of the conjugal covenant. It does so through a specific use of human freedom that relies upon the potential of human sexuality. Consequently, the Church's theology of the conjugal act advances along with greater insights into Christian anthropology, insights that clarify the nature of human freedom and the place of sexuality in the human body/soul composite. The Church's vision of the human person provides the necessary theological framework for the concept of an act that embraces the various dimensions of marriage and also supports the Church's broader teachings on marriage itself.

On the foundations of the Church's teaching on marriage and within the framework of Christian anthropology, a theology of the conjugal act emerges in which sexual intercourse between husband and wife is a particular human act (issuing from reason and will), a symbolic act (expressing love in the language of the body), and a sacramental act (sharing in the sacramentality of the conjugal covenant). Each of these various dimensions of the conjugal act confirms the conjugal act as a *personal act*, an act that depends upon the specifically personal characteristics of man and woman and that allows them to fulfill their fundamental vocation to love and communion. Thus, the Church's view of the conjugal act far surpasses the level of momentary erotic pleasure or the satisfaction of an urge. The Church's theology of the conjugal act affirms the wealth of significance and beauty inherent in the sexual relationship of husband and wife. The Church's theology of the conjugal act imbues the act with the dignity proper to husband and wife as persons and also exhorts husband and wife to preserve the dignity and beauty of their love by approaching the marital embrace precisely as a personal act.

The course of this study of the conjugal act proceeds along the thought that in order to understand the conjugal act we must grasp what the Church means by *conjugal* and what she means by *act*. In turn, these terms are intelligible only in the light of a vision of the *person* because only persons marry and only persons act. I begin my study with a review of Catholic magisterial teaching on marriage from 1930 through 1968, in which marriage is presented as an institution of fruitful love. The teachings from this period provide a foundation for understanding the conjugal life and the goods to which it is ordered as an institution and as a friendship. I next consider the manner in which the Church develops her theology of the conjugal act in the framework of Christian anthropology by examining magisterial teaching from 1968 to the present, focusing on the encyclical *Humanae vitae* and the teachings of Pope John Paul II. Because the Church's theology of the conjugal act centers on the doctrine of an indissoluble connection between the procreative and unitive meanings of the act, I dedicate the third chapter of the work to a consideration of procreation and union and the manner in which they enter into the conjugal act. In the fourth and final chapter of the work I consider the various dimensions of the conjugal act, the anthropological vision that underlies this concept of the conjugal act, and the manner in which the conjugal act is a personal act. Throughout my study I focus on two overlapping and converging areas as they arise in the teachings of the Church: the conjugal relationship and Christian anthropology. Consequently, this consideration of the conjugal act bears a threefold fruit insofar as it investigates the conjugal act itself, the nature of the conjugal relationship, and the Church's vision of man.

Chapter One

An Institution of Fruitful Love

God's Plan for Marriage in Catholic Magisterial Teaching from 1930 to 1968

In and through the conjugal act spouses consummate their marital consent and express their abiding love in an utterly unique fashion. As the consummation of matrimonial consent and as the embodiment of conjugal love, the conjugal act is inseparable from conjugal love and marriage. Consequently, the Catholic concept of the conjugal act depends and builds upon the larger theological context provided by the Church's doctrine on marriage and conjugal love, and an accurate understanding of the nature and significance of the conjugal act requires an understanding of the conjugal life itself. A review of the Church's teaching on marriage and sexuality during the first half of the twentieth century provides a comprehensive view of the conjugal life of husband and wife because during this time period the Church examined marriage and conjugal love from a variety of perspectives, seeking to emphasize each of the aspects of the married life in turn according to the respective pastoral concerns and the purposes of each document or discourse. Drawing upon the evidence of Scripture and that found in the nature of man and woman themselves, the magisterial pronouncements of this period articulate a theology of marriage in which man and God cooperate in the fulfillment of God's plan for human love and the transmission of human life. Within the context of this theology of marriage, the various pronouncements treat of issues such as the role of human freedom in marriage, the limitations of man's dominion over the human body, and the proper understanding of procreation. The resulting image of marriage harmonizes its ontological and juridical aspects with the personal love that the institution of marriage confirms and protects.

In *Casti connubii*, Pope Pius XI focuses on the divine origin of marriage, its sacred character, and the role of human freedom in the married life. Concentrating primarily on the institutional aspect of marriage, Pius XI confirms the procreation and education of children and conjugal fidelity as goods and ends of marriage to which God directs spouses in the married life. While God determines the nature of the institution of marriage and its ends and blessings in the very creation of man and woman, husband and wife cooperate with God in the birth of each particular marriage and in the loving development of its intrinsic nature.

In the context of his various discourses, Pope Pius XII reaffirms the Church's doctrine on the institution of marriage and its primary end of procreation, and the Pope also promotes an appreciation of the so-called "personal values" of marriage, those pertaining to and experienced by the spouses themselves. Rather than inserting tension between the intrinsic ends of marriage and these personal values, Pius XII presents the personal values as the fruit of marital love when it conforms to the requirements of the institution inscribed by God in the very nature of man and woman.

The Second Vatican Council seeks to clarify these fundamental teachings in the light of Christian anthropology. By drawing out the inherent relationship between conjugal love and the institution of marriage, the Council Fathers create an image of marriage as the institution of a love that embraces the good of the whole person, is founded upon the reciprocal self-donation of the spouses, is ordered to the procreation and education of children, and develops according to the nature of the human person and his acts. In addition to being a natural institution and a unique friendship, in light of the Council's doctrine on the universal call to holiness, marriage is confirmed as a "vocation", a call and a path to holiness.

Throughout my review of these teachings from 1930 through 1968, I concentrate on the harmony and continuity that exists between the diverse approaches to marriage taken in the various pronouncements. Clearly, a certain development of doctrine took place between *Casti connubii* and the Second Vatican Council. However, the principal value of the later pronouncements derives from their ability to synthesize and harmonize the fundamental truths present in the earlier teachings and to put these into new light by relating them to equally fundamental ideas that had yet to be emphasized. To insert opposition or tension between the various pronouncements would not only be contrary to the nature of doctrinal development but also would obscure the whole truth about marriage, reducing marriage to one of its essential elements without seeing the intrinsic and organic relationship between them. The respective approaches to marriage adopted in the various pronouncements represent diverse ways of viewing the same sacred reality of holy matrimony. Moreover, each approach supports the view of married life as man's participation in an institution of fruitful love that is divinely inscribed in the very being of man and woman.

1. THE ENCYCLICAL *CASTI CONNUBII*

Casti connubii was promulgated on December 31, 1930, by Pope Pius XI. Though the encyclical explicitly responds to certain modern misconceptions of marriage, the encyclical entails a comprehensive and concise summary of the Church's teaching on marriage up until that time rather than merely reactionary statements.[1] Drawing upon both magisterial and non-magisterial works, *Casti connubii* is divided into three areas of concern: the nature of marriage, vices opposed to marriage, and the necessary remedies. Throughout the encyclical Pius XI relies upon the fundamental idea that God has authored marriage with a particular content (that is, structure, purposes, blessings, and laws). In light of this fundamental idea, man's role in marriage becomes one of a cooperator with God in fulfilling the divine plan for marriage. Thus, in the course of his presentation, Pius XI establishes the proper role of human freedom within the conjugal community. While each particular marriage depends on human freedom for its existence, the nature of marriage derives from laws inscribed in the being of man and woman at their very creation. These laws govern the entire conjugal community, including the pursuit of the goods of marriage, the order between husband and wife, and the expression of conjugal love in the conjugal act. Therefore, in order to live faithfully the married life, husband and wife must conform their activity to creative intentions of God reflected in human nature and confirmed in Scripture.

[1] Regarding the motivations behind the encyclical, consult: Ramón García de Haro, *Marriage and Family in the Documents of the Magisterium*, trans. William May (San Francisco: Ignatius Press, 1993), pp. 107–10.

Casti connubii contributes to the foundations of a theology of the conjugal act precisely by its clarification of the manner in which God and man cooperate in the married life. According to the encyclical, God directs husband and wife to the pursuit of specific goods according to laws inscribed in human nature. These laws of marriage guide husband and wife in their pursuit of the goods of marriage in the conjugal act. The conjugal act possesses an intrinsic structure, ordered principally to the procreation of children and secondarily to the preservation of conjugal fidelity. The rationale behind such a concept of the conjugal act depends upon the notion that man and woman are free to contract marriage while the nature of marriage remains independent of human will; it depends on a notion of freedom in which man is not wholly autonomous. In its teaching on the divine institution of marriage, on the goods of marriage, and on conjugal morality, the encyclical promotes just such a notion of human freedom within marriage.

Human Freedom within the Divine Institution of Marriage

The first teaching and the fundamental principle of the encyclical concerns the divine authorship of marriage.[2] The encyclical clearly rejects the idea of marriage as an institution of human origin, or as a convention of human society. Rather, marriage was instituted by God through divine decree. Pius XI states, "it is an immutable and inviolable fundamental doctrine that matrimony was not instituted or restored by man but by God."[3] As a divine institution with a specific nature and

---

[2] Holy Scripture serves as the basis for the long-standing teaching of the divine institution of marriage. Pius XI cites specifically: Genesis 1:27–28, 2:22–23; Matthew 19:3ff., and Ephesians 5:33ff.

[3] Pius XI, encyclical letter *Casti connubii*, *AAS* 22 (1930): 541.

ends, the conjugal life is governed by God's law. Yet, when we look to the scriptural sources of the divine institution of marriage, we discover no mention of the word "marriage" at all. Instead, the creation accounts of man and woman serve as the scriptural references for the institution of marriage. This is a subtle yet important point: the origins of marriage are to be found at the very origins of humanity, and what it means to be man and woman is intrinsically linked to marriage. Creating "them male and female" is God's manner of instituting marriage. Through his reference to Genesis 1:27–28 and 2:22–23, Pius XI affirms marriage as the finality of masculinity and femininity. God instituted marriage precisely through his creation of the human person as male and female. God does not create man and then institute marriage; rather by creating man male and female, God establishes the basis for marriage in the spousal communion of man and woman. Marriage finds its origin in human nature inasmuch as human nature embraces both masculinity and femininity. If we look further into the reference from Genesis chapter 1 we see also that the creation of man "male and female" relates directly to man's being created in the image and likeness of God, for it is when "God created man in his own image, in the image of God" that he created them "male and female".[4]

The institution of marriage is found in the creation of man and woman, and the structure and ends of marriage can be discerned in the very nature of man and woman. This design, evidenced in human nature, manifests the nature of marriage and determines the content of matrimonial consent. Man participates in marriage through his authentic use of freedom and determines the coming to be of his partic-

[4] Gen 1:27–28.

ular marriage bond by his act of consent. However, since God determines the nature of marriage, man consequently only brings a marriage into existence if his consent conforms to God's will for marriage (that is, the nature of marriage).[5] Man consents to marry, but he cannot of himself define, limit, or expand the institution of marriage. Marriage, as an institution of divine origin, corresponds to the nature of man himself. The nature and structure of marriage are therefore independent of man's volition.[6]

Marriage requires human volition insofar as man and woman must choose and consent to marry, but the divine intention for marriage determines the structure and content of marital consent. Thus, the free act of marital consent must conform to God's law, or else a marriage does not take place. In this doctrine, Pius XI does not embrace a type of voluntarism, nor does he lessen the dignity of man by pointing out this proper view of the role of human freedom in marriage. The Pope does, however, set an important tone and articulate a key theme that recurs prominently in the Church's teaching on marriage: the authentic exercise of human freedom in the area of marriage (and more broadly in the area of sexuality) makes man a *cooperator* with God. In turn the capacity to cooperate with God manifests human dignity.

Man's rational nature allows him to cooperate with God. Rationality allows him to come to know God's design for marriage, to recognize its ends and purposes, and to accept the laws that govern the actualization of the institution of marriage. Upon perceiving these truths about marriage, man can act in accord with this knowledge by a free choice. Unlike animal unions, which proceed from "blind instinct" according to the

---

[5] *Casti connubii*, p. 541.

[6] Ibid.

nature of the animal, marriage requires of man "a firm and deliberate act of the will".[7] This act of the will is neither instinct nor blind, for an authentic matrimonial consent conforms to what man knows to be the nature of marriage. Here God's intentions as they are manifested both in human nature and also revelation direct man's action. This direction does not impede man's freedom but, rather, makes possible its authentic use. Marriage results then from "both the will of God and the will of man" through a form of cooperation that establishes the standard for all of man's actions regarding his sexuality.[8] Man makes particular choices and effects particular acts of a sexual nature, but he is always guided by Divine Wisdom manifesting itself to him in his own nature.

The idea of headship in marriage offers an example of how husband and wife conform their conjugal life to God's intention while also contributing their own particular creativity. Basing himself on Ephesians 5 and following the example of Leo XIII, Pius XI affirms that we can speak of a certain headship that is to be exercised by the husband and a corresponding subjection on the part of the wife. According to the Pope, this order within the family is part of the structure of the family flowing from the nature of marriage as authored by God. However, he also clearly indicates that this subjection of the wife to the husband "in its degree and manner may vary according to the different conditions of persons, place and time".[9] Headship and subjection will perhaps differ for each couple according to the particulars of each family situation. In other words, this order between the spouses is determined by God, yet the concrete realization

[7] Ibid., p. 542.

[8] Ibid., pp. 542–43.

[9] Ibid., pp. 549–50.

of this order will be lived out according to the reasonable discretion of the spouses, with the possibility of variety among the forms that it takes in diverse families. Thus, as the spouses live out the married life, they make this divine institution their own, and the universal of marriage and family becomes this particular marriage and family.

This example provides the basic pattern for the whole married life; the nature and structure of marriage are objective and universal, yet particular marriages may vary "according to the different conditions of persons, place and time". This variety never denies the objective nature and structure of marriage. Such variety in the conjugal life derives from man's rationality and freedom, from man's capacity to *cooperate* with God. Moreover, the goodness of each particular marriage and its conduciveness to the happiness of the spouses depend on the faithfulness of the spouses with regard to the objective nature of marriage. Ramón García de Haro has developed this line of thought in his analysis of the encyclical.[10] His analysis rests fundamentally on the idea that marriage essentially entails God's plan for marriage and man's response to this plan. God has a "plan" for marriage insofar as he has authored marriage in the very nature of man and woman, and man for his part must respond to this plan either by accepting it or by neglecting or rejecting it. The true and fruitful development of marriage requires man to acknowledge this plan and accept it by conforming his actions to it. Man must live according to the laws that govern the married life if he is to have a fruitful marriage and strive for his own happiness. As García de Haro points out, "Man can refuse to obey

[10] Cf. García de Haro, *Marriage*, pp. 110–14.

them [God's laws for marriage], but he cannot arrange matters such that this disobedience will render him happy. Denying them does not remove them from his own nature, but rather leads it to ruin and in this way damages society also."[11] Indeed, as the fundamental remedy to combat errors in the area of marriage and sexuality, Pius XI exhorts spouses to adhere to the divine plan and to subject themselves to God.[12]

The Goods and Ends of Marriage

In order to conform his actions and intentions to the divine plan for marriage, man must recognize and pursue the ends for which marriage was instituted and seek to reap those goods and blessings to which marriage tends by its nature. *Casti connubii*'s teaching concerning the goods or ends of marriage comprises an excellent summary of the Christian position regarding this aspect of the theology of marriage. In his exposition, Pius XI clearly follows St. Augustine's thought on this matter and does well to place this tradition in its most positive light.[13] Thus, the encyclical affirms that there are three goods of marriage: procreation, conjugal fidelity, and the sacrament. Here I examine only Pius XI's treatment of the goods of procreation and conjugal fidelity. In the Pope's presentation of these goods we again have examples of how man cooperates with God in order that marriage may yield its proper fruit and achieve its appointed ends.

---

[11] Ibid., p. 112.

[12] *Casti connubii*, p. 577.

[13] Pius XI refers explicitly to St. Augustine's *On the Good of Marriage*. Cf. ibid., p. 543.

Among the goods of marriage the child holds the first place.[14] The Pope uses Scripture to give foundation to this long-held teaching of the Church.[15] By the good of the child, or *proles*, Pius XI does not intend the physical replication of man and woman, the biological consequence of a sexual encounter, or the mere propagation of the species. Instead, the Pope views the child primarily as a gift given by God to the couple through their cooperation. The child is the fruit of the spouses' cooperation with the omnipotent power of God.[16] The human person finds his source in the Divine Goodness, which calls him into being, not simply in biology, which represents one aspect of his personhood. The couple fundamentally relates to the child, not as creators or generators, but rather as the recipients of a gift, whose coming to be results from their cooperation with each other and God. Procreation, then, is primarily the cooperation of man and woman with God through their sexuality and the reception of the gift that God bestows upon them through their sexuality. The gift of the child, once received, places upon the couple a responsibility that they have not only toward the child but also to God, who has given the child to them.[17]

Among their responsibilities, the parents bear that of educating the child in religious truth as well as in secular knowledge. The proper education of children is provided for in the best possible way in the institution of marriage because

[14] Ibid.: "Itaque primum inter matrimonii bona locum tenet proles." The doctrine of the procreation and education of children as the primary end of marriage appears in the theological tradition and the 1917 *Code of Canon Law*.

[15] Cf. *Casti connubii*, p. 543. Again Pius XI refers to Genesis as well as St. Paul's First Letter to Timothy.

[16] Cf. ibid., p. 544.

[17] Cf. ibid., p. 545.

the parents are bound to each other by an indissoluble bond. Marriage as an institution is consistently dedicated to the good of the child, and therefore "every use of the faculty given by God for the procreation of new life is the right and privilege of the married state alone, by the law of God and of nature, and must be confined absolutely within the sacred limits of that state alone."[18]

With this concept of procreation in mind, what does the Pope mean by saying that this good holds the first place, or is the primary good of marriage? The primacy of the child, or the procreation of the child, follows from procreation's relationship to the institution of marriage and its relationship to the other goods of marriage, as well as the dignity and significance of the reality in question.[19] God's design for marriage has the procreation and education of children as its primary end, and this affects every aspect of what marriage is. In other words, the "final cause" of marriage is manifest in its formal cause. The nature and properties of the conjugal friendship itself derive from its ordination to the good of procreation. The indissolubility of marriage and the properties of unity and exclusivity proper to the conjugal relationship correspond to marriage's ordination to procreation. Its ordination to procreation specifies the conjugal

[18] Ibid., p. 546.

[19] García de Haro summarizes well the significance of the encyclical's affirmation of the primacy of the child among the goods of marriage. He writes, "The encyclical emphasizes that this good holds the 'first place,' precisely because it is the 'primary end' of marriage; and it is always the end that determines the characteristics of any plan. The grandeur of the objective—the transmission of life and care for its development—is the first cause of the properties and excellence of the conjugal community. . . . The centrality of the service of life both deepens and expands the other goods of marriage" (*Marriage*, p. 119).

relationship, distinguishing marriage from all other human relationships. The characteristics and the activities of the marital friendship exist precisely because its primary end is procreation, for it is always the end that determines the characteristics of any plan.

The primacy of procreation also derives from the grandeur of this good itself, that is, from the grandeur of the human person. As the transmission of human life, procreation is a "higher good" than the other goods of marriage. The grandeur of this good results from the final end of man: to enter the Life of the Trinity for eternity. With the transmission of human life comes the creation of an immortal soul. The union of the spouses, or the marital bond, is not immortal. Marriage does not endure after the death of one of the spouses. While man was made for eternity, the marital friendship was not.[20] Nonetheless, the primacy of procreation in no way lessens the goodness of conjugal fidelity or the friendship of the spouses; it still remains a good or end of marriage in itself and never merely a means to procreation.

Pius XI also includes the good of conjugal fidelity in his teaching on the goods of marriage. The essence of conjugal fidelity is the complete union of the spouses, a union characterized by its unity, exclusivity, and permanence. The principle of this union is conjugal love. In biblical terms this union is expressed in the notion of man and woman becoming "one flesh". While the chaste sexual intercourse of husband and wife effects and manifests their becoming one flesh, the unity of husband and wife must extend to every aspect of the conjugal community. Conjugal fidelity represents the complete union of life among the man and woman, not just

[20] Cf. Mt 22:24–30; Mk 12:18–27; Lk 20:27–40.

sexual union. Their union results from their mutual giving and receiving of each other, with the relation between Christ and the Church as its model.

Conjugal fidelity regards the union of the spouses that results from their gift or surrender of themselves to each other and their reception by the other.[21] Conjugal union consists essentially in the total and unreserved surrender of one's whole person to the other, while receiving the other's gift of self. Giving oneself in this way comes not from a passing desire, nor is it a mere matter of words or promises. Rather, it is an "attachment of the heart" that finds its expression in action.[22] Furthermore, this gift of man and woman to each other enables them to aid in the perfection of each other. In their joining they become mutual aids to each other not only in the affairs of earthly life but also on the way to perfection. More than a cooperation in daily tasks, conjugal fidelity pertains to the interior perfection of each spouse in cooperation with the other.[23]

What, then, does it mean that this good of conjugal fidelity is secondary to the good of procreation? This terminology expresses the fact that the good of conjugal fidelity does not relate to the structure of marriage in the same way that procreation relates to marriage. The encyclical's terminology reflects a belief that procreation as a good or end of marriage determines the characteristics and activities proper to marriage in a way that the unity or the communion of the spouses does not. The uniqueness of the marital friendship is not due to the fact that it entails forming a communion of persons. Rather, the uniqueness of the marital friendship lies

[21] *Casti connubii*, p. 542.

[22] Ibid., p. 548.

[23] Cf. ibid.

in marriage's ordination to procreation, which determines the form of marriage and the marital friendship. By putting conjugal fidelity in the second place among the goods of marriage, this encyclical does nothing to discount the value of this good; it only draws out the proper metaphysical relation of each good to marriage as an objective reality authored by God.[24]

Although the most prominent aspect of Pius XI's presentation of these two goods of marriage is an affirmation of the hierarchy among them, some of the minor points of this presentation contain ideas in seminal form that will later be more fully and more clearly articulated by the Magisterium. For example, in his analysis of the immorality of sterilization, Pius XI acknowledges an essential connection between these goods of marriage, stating, "Every sin committed as regards the offspring becomes in some way a sin against conjugal faith, since both these blessings are essentially connected."[25] Additionally, Pius XI acknowledges that even when for reasons beyond the will of the spouses the good of the transmission of life cannot be achieved in its fullness, spouses can pursue the other secondary ends of marriage and the conjugal act, such as "mutual aid, the cultivating of mutual love, and the quieting of concupiscence".[26] Thus, the Pope emphasizes the worth of the other goods of marriage and the value of their honest pursuit as ends (ends that are ordered to

[24] Concerning the good of fidelity, García de Haro writes, "It is put in the second place, not because it is to be considered secondary, but in accordance with a traditional custom that finds its explanation in the fact that, metaphysically, the end determines the form: the ordination to the generation and education of human life defines the requirements, and unique characteristics of conjugal love" (*Marriage*, p. 123).

[25] *Casti connubii*, pp. 565–66.

[26] Ibid., p. 561.

the procreation and education of children without being merely means to this end), even while insisting on the primacy of the transmission of life.

The Intrinsic Structure of the Conjugal Act

The encyclical locates the root of errors against marriage in the denial of the encyclical's fundamental teaching that God instituted marriage with a specific nature and laws. Similarly, errors in the area of sexual morality result from man's denial of God's intention for human sexuality, an intention expressed in the nature of human sexuality itself. The encyclical's fundamental principle of sexual morality could be summarized as: That which is in accordance with the nature of human sexuality is good, and that which is contrary or against that nature is intrinsically evil. Having nature as the moral reference point may seem biologistic to some. Yet, as John Gallagher notes, "In the context of the whole encyclical, however, it seems that what is 'according to nature' is to be determined not by considering the physical aspect by itself but by looking at the nature and purposes of matrimony." [27]

The encyclical's condemnation of fornication, contraception (and sterilization), abortion, and adultery illustrates the encyclical's fundamental moral principle. God has ordered the sexual faculty to specific goods, and the sexual act has a structure and purpose in and of itself, independent of the intention of man. Thus, Pius XI writes,

> But no reason, however grave, may be put forward by which anything intrinsically against nature may become conform-

[27] J. Gallagher, "Magisterial Teaching from 1918 to the Present", in *Human Sexuality and Personhood* (St. Louis: Pope John Center, 1981), p. 196.

able to nature and morally good. Since, therefore, the conjugal act is destined primarily by nature to the begetting of children, those who in exercising it deliberately frustrate its natural power and purpose sin against nature and commit a deed which is shameful and intrinsically vicious.[28]

God wills for the marital act a specific structure, one that man is not free to dismantle. According to its fundamental structure, the conjugal act is intrinsically ordered to procreation. Procreation is not merely the biological side effect of the couple's coming together or simply one among many of the possible effects of the act. Instead, procreation constitutes the primary end to which the marital act is ordered by its nature, and as such it cannot be set aside without the disintegration of the marital act. Just as it gives "form" to marriage as an institution, procreation distinguishes the marital act from all other actions that the couple undertake together. Aware of the other goods to which the act is ordered, Pius XI recognizes the value of engaging in the marital act even at times when conception cannot occur, stating:

> Nor are those considered as acting against nature who in the married state use their right in the proper manner although on account of natural reasons either of time or of certain defects, new life cannot be brought forth. For in matrimony as well as in the use of matrimonial rights there are also secondary ends, such as mutual aid, the cultivating of mutual love, and the quieting of concupiscence which husband and wife are not forbidden to consider so long as they are subordinated to the primary end and so long as the intrinsic structure of the act is preserved.[29]

---

[28] *Casti connubii*, p. 559.

[29] Ibid., p. 561.

The Integrity of the Human Body

Within his discussion of sterilization and its immorality, Pius XI articulates a fundamental principle of Catholic sexual ethics regarding the integrity of the body and man's limited dominion over his own body. The Pope condemns actions on the part of public authority that would entail the forced sterilization of persons within a society, denying that public authority has such a right over the body of an innocent person. In fact, he says that in the case of an innocent person, public authorities "can never directly harm, or tamper with the integrity of the body, either for reasons of eugenics or for any other reason".[30] Thus, the Pope accords to the body a certain integrity that must be respected and maintained. Public authority is limited in what it can do regarding the body of one of its subjects.

Furthermore, the limitations on what can and cannot be done to or with the human body extend to the individual, not simply to public authority. Pius XI declares:

> Christian doctrine establishes and the light of human reason makes it most clear, that private individuals have no other power over the members of their bodies than that which pertains to their natural ends, and they are not free to destroy or mutilate their members, or in any other way render themselves unfit for their natural functions, except when no other provision can be made for the good of the whole body.[31]

This declaration articulates two fundamental principles of the Church's understanding of marriage and sexuality: (a) Man

[30] Ibid., p. 565.

[31] Ibid.

has a limited dominion over his own body; (b) man is free to do that which is in accord with his own nature. Man must not destroy or mutilate the body. Man must not render the body unfit for its natural functions, except when the good of the whole body requires it.

Man does exercise a certain dominion over his body, but this dominion is limited by the nature of the body itself and the nature of human freedom in general. The human body and its structure and its functions are the fruit of God's creative power; they come to man as the result of Divine Wisdom. The finalities of the human body are "objective" in the sense that the body's structure and functions are determined independently of the will of man. God, not man, has given the body its form and has ordered its members to certain ends. Man can discover the truth of this structure and can recognize the ends to which it is ordered, but he cannot determine them. Again, human freedom allows man to be a cooperator with God; it allows man freely to choose to actualize God's plan, which he recognizes in himself. Man's dominion over the body finds its boundaries in God's plan for the body. As such, this limited dominion possesses the character of a "stewardship" in which man cultivates that aspect of God's garden which is himself. Some of these points are present here only implicitly, but their significance should not be underestimated both because they follow from and are congruous with the explicit positions of the encyclical and because they recur with greater prominence in subsequent documents of the Magisterium.[32]

---

[32] These points are further developed, for example, in *Humanae vitae*, *Persona humana*, *Donum vitae*, and the *Catechism of the Catholic Church*.

2. THE SACRA ROMANA ROTA ON THE ENDS OF MARRIAGE

In 1944 the Sacra Romana Rota issued a statement (as part of a judgment) reaffirming the previous teachings of the Church on the purposes of marriage and the marital act, specifically on the primacy of procreation.[33] The need for such a statement on the issue arose because "some authors"[34] explained the end of *mutuum adiutorium* in a different manner from the Church, resulting in a denial of the Church's teaching on procreation as the primary end of marriage. Throughout his pontificate, Pope Pius XII defended the traditional teaching of the Church and clarified the Church's position on procreation as the primary end of marriage. This statement of the Sacra Romana Rota represents an example of the Church's efforts to defend and clarify the Church's position on the ends of marriage and to combat those theologians, whom the document calls "newcomers to matters matrimonial", who would deny the hierarchy among the ends. García de Haro points out that although the document "does not properly constitute the Magisterium, it enjoys a certain authority—as an authorized opinion—both having been inserted into the *Acta Apostolica Sedis* and by the use it has received in the documents of the Magisterium."[35] Thus, this document can be included in a review of the Church's position, especially because it strictly agrees with the teachings of Pope Pius XII on this same matter.

[33] Cf. Sacra Romana Rota, *AAS* 36 (1944).

[34] Ibid., p. 188.

[35] García de Haro, *Marriage*, p. 192.

The value of the document lies in the fact that it: (a) clarifies the meaning of the term *finis*, or end; (b) distinguishes between the ends of the institution and the ends of the agents (spouses) and discusses the relationship between these two types of ends; (c) concisely presents the Church's understanding of each end; and (d) clarifies the relation of each end to the institution of marriage and to the other ends.

"Finis Operis" *vs.* "Finis Operantis"

According to the document, it is evident from magisterial sources, from the common doctrine of theologians, canonists, and moralists, and from the explicit words of canon law that marriage has a primary end and a secondary end.[36] Within this context, the term "end" (*finis*) is employed in a technical sense and means a good (*bonum*) that is meant to be obtained both on the part of nature and by the deliberate intention of the agent.[37] An end is a good to which a thing or agent tends or to which a thing or agent is ordered. Thus, in the very definition of the term "end" as it is used in the context of the Church's teaching on marriage, we discover two important aspects of the term: its relation to the concept of good (*bonum*) and the idea of end as the terminus of intention on the part of nature and on the part of the agent(s).

In order to clarify this last point, the document employs the distinction between *finis operis* and *finis operantis*. The *finis operis* of marriage is that benefit to which marriage tends by its very nature and which God the Creator gave to

[36] Sacra Romana Rota, p. 184.

[37] Cf. ibid.: "Verbum 'finis' in fontibus allegatis sumitur sensu technico et significat bonum in quod obtinendum tenditur, sive ex indole naturae sive ex intentione deliberate agentis."

marriage.[38] The idea of a *finis operis* follows from the fundamental principle that states that God is the author of marriage. In other words, God, being intelligent (indeed, supremely wise), could not but institute marriage with some end(s) being proper to it, some good(s) to which the institution of marriage tends by its very nature. That to which marriage has been ordered by God (thus, by its nature) is the *finis operis* of marriage. In contrast, the *finis operantis* is that end which is intended by the agent or agents. The *finis operantis* of marriage is the good that the spouses intend and pursue in marrying. Spouses, being intelligent creatures (though not supremely wise), must have some end in mind in their very act of marrying. In marrying, man and woman pursue some good or goods that they have apprehended as being caused by or related to the institution of marriage. If the case were otherwise, the spouses would be acting in a truly irrational manner. Thus, the document establishes a two-dimensional manner of viewing the ends of marriage: from the perspective of the institution itself and from the perspective of the man and woman who marry.

Certainly in the everyday course of events the *finis operantis* may or may not coincide with the *finis operis*. A man and a woman entering marriage may have grasped the natural ends of marriage and may have made these their own, entering marriage precisely for the pursuit of these ends. However, this is not always (perhaps not commonly) the case. Sometimes they marry for reasons other than the ends to which marriage is ordered by its nature. Then the *finis operantis* may simply be *extra* or *praeter* to the *finis operis*; the

[38] " 'Fines operis' in matrimonio est illud bonum in quod obtinendum matrimonium tendit ex natura sua, quam Deus Creator instituto matrimonii indidit" (ibid., p. 184).

finis operantis may be different from the *finis operis*, without however negating or contradicting the *finis operis*.[39] However, it is also possible for the *finis operantis* to oppose or be incompatible with the *finis operis*. According to the statement, "this happens every time that a person contracting matrimony has in mind a benefit or an end which is repugnant to one or all of the *fines operis* of matrimony."[40] When a couple attempts to contract marriage while intending something that opposes the natural ends of marriage, no marriage takes place by virtue of a fault in their consent. Thus, there are three possible relationships between the intention of the agents and the *finis operis*: this intention may coincide with the *finis operis*, it may be *extra* or *praeter* to the *finis operis*, or it may be repugnant to the *finis operis*. In order faithfully to contract marriage, the *finis operantis* must at least accord with the *finis operis*, respecting the natural order of the married state itself. Ultimately, by intending "marriage", spouses intend its natural ends, for by intending the whole they intend its essential parts.

Ordered by God to specific ends, the conjugal relationship of husband and wife stands apart from all other human relationships. Though there are many types of intimate friendship, marriage possesses a uniqueness by virtue of its ordination to a specific *finis operis* that distinguishes marriage from other types of friendships and associations. According to the statement from the Sacra Romana Rota, as a natural society marriage must have "a natural *finis operis*, one and indivisible, specifically proper and distinct from every other end".[41] Furthermore, the text states that when there are several ends

[39] Ibid., pp. 184–85.

[40] Ibid., p. 185.

[41] Ibid.

of one society or institution one of these must be "prime or principal" to which the other *fines operis* are subordinate.[42] This principal *finis operis* of marriage is the procreation and education of children. John Gallagher writes, "In summary, the Rota seems to have rejected the notion that marriage has two primary ends, because this would destroy the essential relationship between the ends and leave the way open for marriage with no procreative orientation."[43]

In addition to the primary *finis operis* there are two secondary *fines operis* of marriage: *mutuum adiutorium* and *remedium concupiscentiae*. From the descriptions of these two secondary ends contained in the statement, it is evident that mutual help and the remedy of concupiscence cannot be separated from procreation. It is possible to distinguish between these various ends, yet each of them is interrelated. For example, concupiscence is only remedied through the lawful use of the generative faculty; that is, as ordained to procreation. Concupiscence is remedied when the sexual faculty is ordered to its proper use and purposes, primary of which is procreation. Likewise the end of mutual help is related intrinsically to procreation. Mutual help is meant to include the common life of the spouses that they share on the basis of the marital friendship. This common life is *marital*, or *conjugal*, inasmuch as it includes and is ordered to the procreation and education of children. As the statement points out, "even outside of marriage there can be a reciprocal help and

---

[42] Cf. ibid.: "Unde provenit, quod ubi plures unius eiusdemque societatis assignantur 'finis operis,' ex iis unus debeat primus et principalis, rationem causae formalis habens, in quo alii fines contineantur vel ad quem alii accedant ut ipse facilius, securius, plenius obtineri queat. Necesse igitur est ut inter matrimonii fines determinatus sit ordo, secundum quem fini principali, qui naturam specificam matrimonii determinat, alii finis operis subordinentur."

[43] Gallagher, "Magisterial Teaching", p. 198.

common life between two persons of different sex", such as the case of a brother and sister living together.[44] However, the common life of spouses is distinguished by its "internal relation to the primary end, which differentiates the conjugal union from every other human association".[45] Mutual help in marriage is distinguished from other communions of persons by its ordination to procreation. Indeed, the Rota sees the right to engage in generative acts (acquired by marital consent) as the source of the couple's right to a common life.[46] *Mutuum adiutorium* and *remedium concupiscentiae* are ends of marriage inasmuch as marriage is ordered to both of these as secondary *fines operis*, and each of these is specified as "conjugal" insofar as it relates intrinsically to the procreation and education of children.

Procreation

While confirming the primacy of procreation among the *fines operis* of marriage throughout, the Rota statement contains an important section in which the authors explain how this end is to be understood and in what it consists. The statement contains a multi-dimensional concept of procreation. The primary end of marriage can be considered: (1) from the perspective of the activity of the couple; (2) from the perspective of the offspring inasmuch as they are procreated and educated; (3) in terms of both the activity of the wedded couple and the offspring considered

[44] Sacra Romana Rota, p. 188

[45] Ibid.

[46] Cf. ibid., p. 190: "Ex dictis sequitur, ius ad consortium vitae mutuumque auxilium non oriri in contrahentibus nisi ex primario iure generandae prolis."

together.[47] As the primary *finis operis* of marriage, procreation is more than adding persons to the human family. The very notion of the transmission of human life contains both the activity of the couple in the use of their generative faculty and the person who is the fruit of their generative faculty. Thus, the statement expounds an understanding of procreation devoid of a biologistic approach to procreation. Recognizing the multi-dimensional character of the Church's concept of procreation is essential in understanding the true nature of procreation and how all marriages can be ordered to procreation.

Many fail to recognize the essence of the first dimension of "procreation" and therefore fail to see how procreation is present in all true marriages (and indeed in every conjugal act). Yet, the statement clearly explains how we should understand procreation viewed from the perspective of the activity of the married couple. In essence, it consists in completing the conjugal act in accordance with its natural structure without adopting any end that is contrary to the *finis operis* of the act. According to the Rota, the naturally completed conjugal act is all that is required of the couple in order to fulfill their role in procreation.[48] If the couple has not done anything to dismantle the natural structure of the act, then its completion is sufficient for the first dimension of procreation. The procreative activity of the couple does not require the actual conception of a child. Therefore, it is not necessary for conception to occur for the couple to have fulfilled their role and for the first dimension of procreation to exist. No defect of nature, therefore, can prevent this dimension of procreation even while it prevents

[47] Cf. ibid., p. 185.
[48] Cf. ibid., pp. 185–86.

the second dimension, namely, the coming to be of the offspring itself. Even the marriages of those who are sterile include this first dimension of procreation.[49] Furthermore, it would seem that a man and woman can intend the primary *finis operis* of marriage so long as they intend to complete the conjugal act according to its natural structure, without necessarily intended the conception of a child.

3. DISCOURSES OF POPE PIUS XII

Pope Pius XII did not write an encyclical on marriage or sexual morality. He did, however, give several discourses on various occasions that contributed greatly to the Church's understanding of marriage and sexuality. Throughout his discourses, Pius XII affirms the previous teachings of the Church on marriage and sexual morality by reaffirming the primacy of procreation among the ends of marriage and condemning contraception and sterilization. He also addressed new questions such as those surrounding medical interventions in the area of human generation and the systematic use of periodic continence for the purpose of spacing births. Throughout his analysis of questions old and new, Pius XII demonstrated a profound sense of what it means for man to be a creature as well as a clear sense of what it means to be a person. Always aware that questions of marriage and sexuality involve agents who are human persons, Pius XII provided the Church with teachings that are sensitive to the need to cultivate and protect the personal values of human sexuality while always recognizing the objective, metaphysical context in which these

[49] Cf. ibid., p. 186.

values are situated. The backbone of his teaching is the conviction that as a creature man subjects himself to God his Creator, but as a rational, personal creature his subjection is free and conscious. The resulting teaching on marriage views man as a creature who freely and consciously submits to God's plan for human sexuality in order to pursue and realize its most profound and personal values.

Man as Creature and Person

Man is great. Pius XII reaffirms the greatness of man and reminds us that his greatness endures even after the fall.[50] According to Pius XII, the greatness of man is manifest in the dominion that God has given him over the visible world, the fact that man was placed "on the topmost rung of the ladder of the living".[51] In part man's greatness derives from his possession of intellect and will, the ability to know and choose, which makes man responsible before himself, before others, and before God. Yet, the greatness of man, with his rational abilities and earthly dominion, does not negate the subjection of man to God, who "is the sole commander and legislator of the universe".[52] Man was created in the image and likeness of God, but in order to preserve this image and likeness undistorted man must follow the law impressed in him by God. Even after deviating from this law through original sin, man is given the opportunity to return to his original path, and even surpass it, through God's gift of grace. In this

[50] "Allocution to the Members of the Pontifical Academy of Sciences, November 30, 1941", in *The Teachings of Pius XII* (New York: Pantheon Books, 1957), p. 18.

[51] Ibid., p. 17.

[52] Ibid., p. 19.

context of free subjection, man and woman live out the meaning of sexuality and express and experience conjugal love.

Every creature is the fruit of Divine Love because God the Creator is Love, but man alone among all the visible creatures has been given the ability to love. While animals are attracted to each other through blind instinct, man's love is "personal, that is to say conscious; free, that is to say, subject to the control of his responsible will".[53] Human love is possible because man can know and choose. However, according to Pius XII, human love is more than rational; it is also "personal, that is to say conscious". In the case of authentic human love, the lover and the beloved are conscious (aware) of the love between them. They are conscious of the goodwill they bear toward each other. When it is a question of conjugal love, in addition to goodwill there is a mutual gift of self between the lover and beloved, a gift of self that is "total, exclusive, irrevocable".[54] This mutual gift of self between spouses "becomes a principle of expansion and a source of life".[55]

The Conjugal Act and Its Various Ends

The spousal gift of self entails a "spiritual union" such that "the two beings who love each other identify themselves in all that is most intimate in them, from the unshaken depths of their beliefs to the highest summit of their hopes."[56] However, as human, spousal love also entails a bodily union, the

[53] "Address to Newlyweds, October 23, 1940", in *Teachings of Pius XII*, p. 21.

[54] Ibid.

[55] Ibid., p. 22.

[56] Ibid., p. 21.

conjugal act. This union of bodies maintains its full spousal significance when it is "a principle of expansion and a source of life" and when the intrinsic structure of the act is maintained.[57] Pius XII's teaching on the conjugal act rests principally on four fundamental ideas: (1) the conjugal act is a simultaneous cooperation of the spouses with each other and with God; (2) there is a hierarchy among the various ends of the act that is determined by God and is manifested in the intrinsic structure of the act; (3) the act is an expression of the spousal gift of self; and (4) the morality of the act is to be judged both according to its substance and the circumstances of the act.

The proper use of the sexual faculty entails both the cooperation of each spouse with the other and also the cooperation of the couple with God and his design as it is manifest in nature. Thus, for example, Pius XII speaks of the "admirable collaboration of the parents, of nature, and of God, from which a new human being in the image and likeness of the Creator comes to light".[58] For his part man cooperates by performing a specific or "determined" role, a role that God establishes and inscribes into the very nature of the transmission of life.[59] Nature does not oblige man to act, rather, it "puts at man's disposal the whole chain of causes giving rise to a new human life: it is man who has to release the living force."[60] The sexual faculty is for man a power, a potential that he must actualize by freely cooperating with God's design for this faculty. "Hence it is not a question here of

[57] Ibid., p. 22.

[58] "Address to Midwives", in *Major Addresses of Pius XII* (St. Paul: North Central Publishing, 1961), p. 161.

[59] Ibid.

[60] Ibid.

simple physical or biological laws which agents without reason and blind forces necessarily obey, but of laws whose execution and whose effects are entrusted to the free and voluntary cooperation of man."[61] In the conjugal act, spouses cooperate not only with God and nature but also with each other. Pius XII describes the simultaneous cooperation of the spouses as an expression of the mutual self-gift of the spouses and as a manifestation of the personal nature of the conjugal act. The Pope writes, "The conjugal act, in its natural structure, is a simultaneous and immediate cooperation of the spouses which by the very nature of the agents and of the act is the expression of a reciprocal donation."[62]

The sexual faculty and the sexual act receive their form or structure and their ends from God, the author of nature, and spouses pursue and realize these ends by freely cooperating with this design. In order freely to choose to pursue the intrinsic ends of the conjugal act, spouses must know and recognize these ends. Yet, there are many and varied goods and values associated with the conjugal act that all compete for man's recognition and attention. A notable aspect of Pius XII's teaching on marriage is the manner in which he discusses the relationship between these various goods and values, the so-called "personal values" of the conjugal act, and procreation, the primary end of the conjugal act. Pius XII was compelled to clarify this relationship because "some authors" had exalted the personal values of the conjugal act so as to deny the value of procreation whatsoever. According to Pius XII, the result is not simply an appreciation for the personal values of the act, but rather a "serious inversion of the order of values and ends established by the Creator

[61] Ibid.

[62] Ibid., p. 173.

Himself . . . the propagation of a host of ideas and sentiments directly opposed to the clarity, depth and seriousness of Christian teaching".[63] Pius XII aims, then, not to dissuade the authentic appreciation of the personal values. Instead, he exhorts spouses to preserve the order among the goods of the conjugal act that God himself has established.

Within this proper order, the procreation and education of children is the primary end of marriage. Pius XII explains:

> The truth is that matrimony as a natural institution, by virtue of the will of the Creator, does not have as its primary, intimate end the personal improvement of the couples concerned but the procreation and education of new life. The other ends though also connected with nature are not in the same rank as the first, still less are they superior to it. They are subordinated to it. This holds true for every marriage, even if it bear not fruit.[64]

Reaffirming the doctrine of marriage as a natural institution endowed with ends by its Creator, Pius XII states that among the ends there is a certain order or hierarchy, with procreation primary among them. The other ends are true ends of the institution insofar as they are "connected with nature", but they are not of the "same rank" as procreation. The Pope goes to some lengths to clarify that this formulation does not "deny or diminish what there is of good and right in the personal values arising from marriage and its carrying out".[65] Marriage by its nature tends to various goods, and the hierarchy among them does not diminish or undermine the value of any of them, yet it does reflect God's plan for marriage.

---

[63] Ibid., p. 171.

[64] Ibid., p. 172.

[65] Ibid.

Along with an insistence on the primacy of procreation among the ends of marriage, the Church can recognize the value of those ends which are secondary. According to Pius XII, "these personal values, whether they belong to the sphere of the body and the senses or to the spiritual sphere, are genuine in themselves, but in the scale of values the Creator has put them not in the first but in the second place."[66]

This doctrine on the ends of marriage (and their hierarchy) also applies to the conjugal act. Pius XII describes the generative faculty as:

> a natural power, of which the Creator himself has determined the structure and the essential forms of activity, with a precise purpose and with corresponding duties, to which man is subject in every conscious use of that faculty. Nature's primary purpose (to which the secondary ends are essentially subordinated) in this use is the propagation of new life and the education of the offspring.[67]

God has endowed man with the generative faculty and has determined the structure, essential form, and end of its exercise. God has given this faculty a "precise purpose", which, according to the intimate structure of the conjugal act, is primarily procreation and secondarily the other so-called personal values that arise from the act. Again, these secondary ends are of real value, and they are proper to the act inasmuch as they have been connected to the nature of the act by the Creator. However, they always remain subordinated to the primary end of procreation because "these secondary values in the generative sphere and activity come within the

[66] Ibid., p. 173.

[67] "Address to the Micro-biological Union of San Luca, November 12, 1943", in *Teachings of Pius XII*, p. 115.

scope of the specific office of husband and wife, which is to generate new life and educate it."[68] According to Pius XII,

> if nature had aimed exclusively, or even primarily, at a reciprocal gift and possession of couples in joy and delight, and if it had ordered this act only to make their personal experience happy in the highest possible degree, and not to stimulate them to the service of life, then the Creator would have adopted another design in the formation and constitution of the natural act.[69]

Procreation as a Personal Value

Procreation is the primary purpose of the sexual faculty and the primary end of the conjugal act, but what is procreation according to Pius XII? In the teachings of Pius XII procreation and biological reproduction differ greatly, principally because of the personal nature of procreation. Procreation involves more than the physical elements entailed in the transmission of life because it results from a specific free choice of a man and a woman. In procreating man and woman choose to cooperate with God and nature precisely as persons, as "human beings made of flesh and blood, endowed with minds and hearts".[70] The primary end of the conjugal act, then, is that two human persons with "minds and hearts" cooperate with each other and with God in releasing the force of life. Pius XII affirms the personal character of procreation in his condemnation of artificial fecundation. Due to advances in medical technology, Pius XII was faced with the question of the moral

[68] "Address to Midwives", p. 161.
[69] Ibid., p. 175.
[70] Ibid., p. 172.

licitness of artificial fecundation, and his analysis of this question reveals the truly personal nature of procreation and the conjugal act. Physically, the conjugal act is fundamentally the union of two bodily organs and the transmission of seed from the man to the woman, but considered in its entirety the conjugal act is more than the union of two organs or two cells; the conjugal act is "a personal cooperation".[71] Artificial fecundation is unacceptable because it does not involve this personal cooperation, but rather is a reduction of the transmission of life to its physical elements. If procreation were simply the physical encounter of sperm and egg or merely the coming to be of a human person, and if the conjugal act were merely the encounter of two bodily organs, then artificial fecundation would be an acceptable way of achieving the primary purpose of marriage, and the conjugal act would be a dispensable means to this end. However, according to God's design, procreation is multi-dimensional and involves spiritual aspects that are present only in the conjugal act.

While Pius XII distinguishes between procreation and the personal values of the conjugal act in certain passages of his discourses, the overall sense of his teaching points to a harmonious hierarchy between the various ends of the conjugal act precisely because procreation is a "personal" good to which the act is ordered. Here *personal* signifies that which is proper to persons and not to animals or other creatures. Man experiences certain aspects of the conjugal act (such as union, emotional and spiritual closeness, or tenderness) because he is a conscious being. When procreation is reduced to its physiological elements (the union of sperm and egg), it remains

[71] Ibid., p. 173.

outside the consciously experienced because man and woman are not aware of this union or whether it has even happened as a result of their bodily union. However, when it is understood in its proper and full significance, procreation is indeed truly personal because it is more than the "union of two seeds" and because it requires a personal (that is, conscious) cooperation between husband and wife and God. For this reason, persons procreate while animals reproduce. Animals are not aware that they are fulfilling the plan God has decreed for their multiplication, but spouses are "called as men, not animals without reason, to be united".[72] The transmission of human life does not pertain merely to instinct or the realm of biology. Rather, human life should be transmitted in a human act in which the spouses freely and consciously choose to cooperate with each other and God. All the other ends and goods of the conjugal act come within the sphere of this specific office of husband and wife.[73]

The secondary ends of the conjugal act, because they belong to the nature of the act itself, can not only be enjoyed but can also be sought as personal goods in conformity with the natural structure of the act itself. Pius XII's analysis of the place of pleasure in the conjugal act illustrates his position on the significance of these secondary ends, demonstrating his appreciation for the full range of goods to which the conjugal act is ordered. According to Pius XII, the Creator has ordained that in the transmission of life "husband and wife should experience pleasure and happiness both in body and soul."[74] God has ordained the conjugal act to be an act in which man and woman expe-

[72] Ibid., p. 172.
[73] Ibid., p. 173.
[74] Ibid., p. 174.

rience joy of both a bodily and spiritual character. "In seeking and enjoying this pleasure, therefore, couples do nothing wrong. They accept that which the Creator has given them."[75] Nevertheless, their pursuit and enjoyment of this pleasure must be ordered and within the limits of moderation. In order to do so, couples must concern themselves with "not only the substance of the act but also the circumstances of the act" because though "the substance of the act be unimpaired, one may sin in the manner of performing it".[76] Here Pius XII introduces an important distinction between the substance of the conjugal act and the circumstances of the act. By substance we are to understand the structure of the act, what he calls "the essence of the instinctive act"[77] (genital intercourse between husband and wife), but the circumstances of the act designate "the manner of performing it". The manner in which the act is performed will depend in large part on the interior disposition of the spouses, how the spouses experience the act and each other in the act. It is possible to err by either excess or defect with regard to this interior disposition: the spouses may focus too much on the joy experienced in the act, or they may engage in the act devoid of any such pleasure.

Pius XII's analysis of the question regarding the use of marriage exclusively during the so-called infertile period of the woman's cycle (periodic continence, or what we now call natural family planning) further illustrates his teaching on the conjugal act. In *Casti connubii* Pius XI stated that there was no objection to those who engaged in the marital

[75] Ibid.

[76] Ibid.

[77] Ibid., p. 175.

act at times when conception was thought impossible. He did not, however, address the question of use of the marital act solely when conception was thought impossible in a systematic attempt to avoid conception. Pius XII addresses the question from two perspectives: (1) whether in the act of marital consent husband and wife can restrict the marital right to the so-called infertile period; (2) whether the use of marriage and not the marital right can be restricted to infertile periods. Regarding the first question, the answer is clearly no. If one of the parties were to adopt this intention in making the marital consent, the marriage would be invalid due to "an essential defect in the consent to marry".[78] However, when it is a question of restricting the *use* of the marital right to the infertile period, it must be judged whether such an intention is "based on sufficient and secure moral grounds".[79]

According to Pius XII, "The reason for this is that marriage obliges a state of life which, while conferring certain rights also imposes the fulfillment of a positive work in regard to the married state itself."[80] The married state, once freely entered, obliges husband and wife to fulfill that duty which is proper to the state itself. The positive fulfillment of this duty "may be omitted when serious reasons, independent from the will of those obliged by it, show that this action is not opportune, or prove that a similar demand cannot reasonably be made of human nature".[81] There are various "serious reasons" that can be the basis for setting aside the positive fulfillment of this duty, and a couple may

[78] Ibid., p. 168.
[79] Ibid.
[80] Ibid., p. 169.
[81] Ibid.

be "exempt for a long time, perhaps even the whole duration of the marriage, from the positive and obligatory carrying out of this act".[82] However, "The mere fact that the couple do not offend the nature of the act and are prepared to accept and bring up the child which in spite of their precautions came into the world would not be sufficient in itself to guarantee the rectitude of intention and the unobjectionable motives themselves."[83] Instead, there must be serious reasons for avoiding conception, and these reasons must motivate the couple's intention to abstain. However, in the absence of a serious reason, a married couple has a duty to cooperate with God in the transmission of life, for this is the "characteristic activity" of the married state. "Therefore, to embrace the married state, continuously to make use of the faculty proper to it and lawful in it alone, and on the other hand, to withdraw always and deliberately with no serious reason from its primary obligation, would be a sin against the very meaning of conjugal life."[84]

Not every conjugal act will result in conception; sometimes a couple will engage in the conjugal act with full knowledge that conception will not result; and sometimes circumstances may make the avoidance of conception the prudent course of action. None of these facts, however, alters the truth that procreation is the primary end of the act. There are many physical reasons why conception would not occur in a given sexual encounter, either reasons that are consequent upon a free action committed by one or both of the spouses to render themselves infertile or reasons that are

[82] Ibid.

[83] Ibid., pp. 168–69.

[84] Ibid., p. 169.

not consequent upon such action.[85] Periodic continence does not deny the procreative aspect of the marital act because the couple still exercises a procreative cooperation with God in accordance with the nature of their sexuality. Contraception, on the other hand, is not a cooperation with God, but rather a denial of his authorship of sexuality.

The married couple is obliged to use the generative faculty in accord with its nature and purpose not only because of the duties of the married state but also because of a more general principle regarding man's use of his faculties and his dominion over his body. In the teachings of Pius XII, man is a creature whom God has fashioned and ordered. Indeed, God has given man each of his faculties and has "fixed, prescribed, and limited the use of each".[86] Divine Wisdom determines the design and purpose of each of man's faculties, "therefore, man is not permitted to order his life and the functions of his organs according to his desire, in a way contrary to the internal and inherent purposes assigned to them."[87] More explicitly, Pius XII states, "Actually, man is not the owner and absolute lord of his body, but only its usufructurary."[88] Man does not possess his body as a piece of property, and from this fact is derived "a whole series of principles and rules which regulate the use and the right to dispose of organs and members of the body."[89] This funda-

[85] This second category is sufficient to describe both permanent or prolonged sterility and the temporary infertile times of the woman's cycle. On the distinction between the freely willed privation of the proper ordering of the conjugal act to procreation and that which occurs independently of the intention of man, consult: García de Haro, *Marriage*, pp. 162–63.

[86] "Address to the Micro-biological Union of San Luca", p. 110.

[87] Ibid.

[88] Ibid.

[89] Ibid.

mental principle concerning man's stewardship over the body underlies Pius XII's teaching on sexuality and the use of the generative faculty: Man "is not the absolute master of himself, of his body or of his soul. He cannot, therefore, freely dispose of himself as he pleases." Rather, he is "bound to the immanent teleology laid down by nature. He has the right of use, limited by natural finality, of the faculties and powers of his human nature."[90] In the use of his faculties man is bound by the inherent structure and the immanent finalities of the faculties themselves. Man cannot freely dispose of himself as he pleases because he is not the absolute master of either his body or his soul. Yet, he does exercise a certain limited dominion over his body, as it is his body and no one else's. According to Pius XII, "Though it is limited, man's power over his members and organs is a direct power, as they are constitutional parts of his physical being."[91] Thus, without possessing an absolute sovereignty over his body, man freely exercises his natural faculties, guided always by the divinely inscribed immanent finality of the faculties themselves.

Thus, within the teaching of Pius XII, man's use of his generative faculty is ordered or determined in a twofold manner. Because of man's limited dominion over his body in general, man may not use his sexual faculty as though he were its absolute master, as though he could determine its purposes and proper use. These are determined independently of his will and are manifest in the inherent structure and immanent teleology of the sexual organs. Therefore, the

[90] "Address to the First International Congress on the Histopathology of the Nervous System, September 14, 1952", in *Major Addresses of Pius XII*, p. 228.

[91] "Address to the Micro-biological Union of San Luca", p. 111.

authentic, human use of the generative faculty entails an ordering of such use to the ends assigned to them by the Creator. Moreover, the use of the generative faculty is also ordered by the nature of the married life (or "the very meaning of conjugal life"),[92] which is also determined by God independently of man's will. Why is man, the greatest of all visible creatures, bound by the inherent design of his own body and by his state in life? Simply and only because his body and the married state are of divine origin and are expressions of Divine Wisdom, because "man is great", but "God is the sole commander and legislator of the universe."[93]

The nature of the married state and the inherent finalities of sexuality point to the inseparability of procreation and conjugal love. The idea of the inseparability of procreation and conjugal love runs throughout Pius XII's teaching on marriage and sexuality.[94] The importance of this fundamental idea derives from its ability to resist any sort of false dichotomy between conjugal love and procreation. This principle manifests itself in the Pope's condemnation of artificial fecundation and in his understanding of the marital act as a personal act whose primary end is procreation. He articulates the principle at one point, stating, "Never is it permissible to separate these different aspects so as to exclude positively either the aim of procreation or the conjugal relation."[95] Recognizing the connection of conjugal love to procreation, the Pope condemns the pursuit of either of

[92] "Address to Midwives", p. 169.

[93] "Allocution to the Members of the Pontifical Academy of Sciences, November 30, 1941", pp. 18–19.

[94] Cf. García de Haro, *Marriage*, p. 158.

[95] "Address to the Second World Congress on Fertility and Sterility, May 19, 1956", *AAS* 48 (1956): 470.

these two realities in isolation from the other. Neither the procreative aspect nor the unifying love of the spouses is dispensable in the marital act. Neither is dispensable by the very nature of the realities themselves; true conjugal love is always at the service of life.

4. VATICAN COUNCIL II

The most significant pronouncements of the Council regarding marriage are found in *Gaudium et spes*, the Pastoral Constitution on the Church in the Modern World. This document concerns very much the state of man in the modern world, and so it is fitting that it contain a discussion of marriage. In affirming and clarifying previous doctrines, the Council's teaching on marriage builds upon and accords with the Council's overall anthropological teaching. Therefore, in order to present properly the Council's teaching on marriage, it must be set within this larger anthropological context. In my review of the Council teaching, I first summarize its basic anthropological vision of man as the image of God endowed with freedom and guided by conscience. Next I consider the teaching on marriage and love, focusing particularly on the Council Fathers' clarification of the role of conjugal love in marriage and their affirmation of marriage as a vocation.

Man as the Image of God

The description of man presented by *Gaudium et spes* is a collection of fundamental truths that all converge to create a loose whole; it is not a systematic exposition of the Church's concept of the human person.[96] The common themes that bind this whole together are the dignity and vocation of man, for an adequate description of man requires bringing to light his dignity and vocation. An understanding of man's calling is in effect a profound insight into who man is. The foundations for such an understanding rest on two fundamental ideas: man as the image of God and the revelation of man in Christ.

At the center of Christian anthropology lies the recognition that man has been created in the "image of God", a truly biblical concept found at the very beginnings of salvation history. This fundamental scriptural concept is essential to Christian anthropology, yet its full significance is often difficult to grasp. Man images God in various, interrelated ways, and *Gaudium et spes* recalls the most fundamental of these. First, man's imaging of God seems to be found in his ability "to know and love his Creator".[97] Endowed with an intellect and will, man possesses the ability to enjoy a loving relationship with the Creator. Secondly, man images God as a representative of the Creator among the other creatures. In the world, man exercises dominion over all the other creatures, and God has bestowed on him a certain honor as the Creator's representative here on earth.[98] Furthermore, when

---

[96] Cf. J. Ratzinger, "The Dignity of the Human Person", in *Commentary on the Documents of Vatican II*, ed. H. Vorgrimler (New York: Herder & Herder, 1969), pp. 115–63.

[97] *Gaudium et spes*, no. 12 (hereafter referred to as GS). In Austin Flannery, O.P., ed, *Vatican Council II: The Conciliar and Post Conciliar Documents*, new revised ed. 1992 (Grand Rapids, Mich.: William B. Eerdman's, 1992).

[98] Ibid. The text quotes Psalm 8:5–8, "What is man that you are mindful of him, and the son of man that you care for him? Yet, you made him little less than God, and crown him with glory and honor. You have given him dominion over the works of your hands; you have put all things under his feet."

creating man in his image, God "made him male and female" (Gen. 1:27), thus "God did not create man a solitary being."[99] According to the text, "This partnership of man and woman constitutes the first form of communion between persons. For by his innermost nature man is a social being; and if he does not enter into relations with others he can neither live nor develop his gifts."[100] In this manner, GS links both sexuality and the idea of communion between persons to the manner in which man images God.

Man is able to know God because of his spiritual faculties such as intellect and conscience. Through intellectual knowledge, man can know realities encountered initially by the senses, but he can also know "truths of a higher order".[101] According to GS, "Filled with wisdom man is led through visible realities to those which cannot be seen."[102] In his search for truth and goodness, man is guided by his conscience, "his most secret core" or "sanctuary" where "he is alone with God whose voice echoes in his depths".[103] "Deep within his conscience man discovers a law which he has not laid upon himself but which he must obey."[104] This law has been inscribed in man's heart by God, and "his dignity lies in observing this law."[105] Through conscience man encounters God and discovers the truth that becomes for him a law he must obey. Man does not create the truth, nor does he compose the law. Rather, both are objective (whether or not he recognizes them) and are of divine origin, for it is

[99] GS 12.
[100] Ibid.
[101] GS 15.
[102] Ibid.
[103] GS 16.
[104] Ibid.
[105] Ibid.

God who speaks to man in his conscience, who has inscribed the law on his heart.

Man is able to love God because he is free, because he has been left in his own counsel "so that he might of his own accord seek his creator and freely attain his full and blessed perfection by cleaving to him".[106] Through intellect and conscience man can know truth and goodness, "however, only in freedom [can] man ... turn himself towards what is good."[107] Man's dignity "requires him to act out of conscious and free choice, as moved and drawn in a personal way from within, and not by blind impulses in himself or by mere external restraint".[108] The placement of this paragraph is crucial for gaining a full appreciation for the meaning of freedom according to GS. These comments must be read in close connection with what is stated in the previous paragraph on conscience. In the exercise of his freedom, man indeed must be "moved and drawn in a personal way from within", precisely because within himself he finds a law inscribed in his heart by God. Erroneously viewed, GS's paragraph on freedom is somewhat open to attempts to establish a false dichotomy between law and freedom, yet the context of these statements does not lend itself to such a reading because of the clear statements on conscience.[109]

Human freedom, guided by conscience and the law that God has inscribed in man's heart, presents itself to man as the possibility to make a personal response. According to

[106] GS 17.

[107] Ibid.

[108] Ibid.

[109] The intrinsic and harmonious relationship between God's law and human freedom and the human conscience has since been affirmed and clarified by John Paul II in *Veritatis splendor* (August 6, 1993).

GS, "the dignity of man rests above all on the fact that he is called to communion with God."[110] Freedom, then, is man's ability to respond to this call in a personal way so as to maintain and attain his full dignity. The call to communion takes the form of an "invitation to converse with God" and "is addressed to man as soon as he comes into being".[111] In turn, this invitation is spoken out of love, "for if man exists it is because God has created him through love, and through love continues to hold him in existence."[112] In this context, freedom is not only the ability to seek the Creator and to cleave to him; it is the ability to respond to a loving invitation to converse with God. It is the ability to respond to the love of the Creator, and the only adequate response to love is love. On a truly profound level, human freedom, then, is the ability to love "in a personal way from within" precisely as a response to a call or invitation from the Creator.

Man's call or vocation is made known most fully in the Person of Jesus Christ, for "it is only in the mystery of the Word made flesh that the mystery of man truly becomes clear."[113] The hallmark of a *Christian* anthropology is its christological character. Christ, in the very "revelation of the mystery of the Father and of his love, fully reveals man to himself and brings to light his most high calling".[114] This now famous statement has a multifold significance, at the heart of which lies the fact that Christ reveals both *who man is* and *who man is called to be*. Christ reveals man and man's vocation. The two are intimately related, if for no other reason because his vocation

[110] GS 19.

[111] Ibid.

[112] Ibid.

[113] GS 22.

[114] Ibid.

specifies man's very existence. Man is he who is called "as soon as he comes into being" to converse with God, and man can be called to such a "high calling" because of who he is, because he has been created in the image of God, because he is rational and free and can love.

Love and Marriage

Against this anthropological background, the Council Fathers expound a vision of marriage and family in chapter 1 of the second part of *Gaudium et spes* (GS 46–52). Concerned with the dignity of marriage and family, this section "intends to present certain key points of the Church's teaching in a clearer light . . . to guide and encourage Christians and all men who are trying to preserve and to foster the dignity and supremely sacred value of the married state".[115] While some wish to see the Second Vatican Council as a turning point, or even a new beginning, for the Church's teaching on marriage and sexuality, it is much easier to show its continuity with the tradition than to articulate any substantial differences. None of the statements in this section constitutes a substantial change of doctrine or a denial of any of the firmly established doctrines of the Church regarding marriage and sexuality.[116] The text of *Gaudium et*

---

[115] GS 47.

[116] For a thorough discussion of the Magisterium's firmly established doctrines concerning marriage and sexuality at the opening of the Second Vatican Council, consult García de Haro, *Marriage*, pp. 195–210. This chapter includes a detailed bibliography of previous magisterial statements. These so-called "firmly established doctrines" of the Magisterium include: God's authorship of marriage; the primacy of procreation among the ends of marriage; the condemnation of contraception, abortion, sterilization, and artificial fecundation; the inseparability of procreation and conjugal love.

spes is very much in accord with *Casti connubii*. In fact, there are five footnote references to the encyclical, making it the second most cited source, after Scripture. However, the Council Fathers do present this teaching "in a clearer light" by employing less technical language (in keeping with the document's pastoral character) and by attempting to harmonize further the relationship between the institution of marriage and the conjugal friendship upon which it is based.

The Council documents do reflect a change in presentation or language with regard to the teachings on marriage and sexuality, but much of the traditional teaching remains. Certainly the terminology of the document is not juridical, nor is it metaphysical in the sense that it does not refer to "intrinsic structures" or "primary and secondary purposes". Yet, the terminology employed does not serve to deny the value of juridical or metaphysical terminology in teachings on marriage, much less to deny the value of the concepts behind such terminology. Instead, the terminology employed simply accords with the pastoral nature of the document.[117] Furthermore, many of the traditional teachings of the Church are present in the document, in their familiar terms. For example, GS 47 describes marriage as an institution and a state in life with its own ends and laws, all of which are determined by the Creator. This institution is based upon the "mutual surrender" of the spouses to each other, "is ordered to the procreation and education of the offspring", and entails fidelity and unity between the

[117] Cf. for example, *Acta Synodalia Sacrosancti Vaticani II*, vol. 4, pt. 7 (Rome: Typis Polyglottis Vaticanis, 1978), pp. 477–79, and Janet Smith, *"Humanae Vitae," a Generation Later* (Washington, D.C.: Catholic University of America Press, 1991), p. 48.

spouses.[118] These would seem to be the "certain key points of the Church's teaching" that the Council Fathers hoped to present in a clearer light.[119] However, this change in presentation has resulted in disputed questions regarding GS's continuity with the previous magisterial pronouncements of this century.

The most disputed question regarding the Council's continuity with the past concerns the primacy of procreation among the ends of marriage. Since the publication of *Casti connubii*, the Magisterium had resisted attempts to deny the fact that procreation is the primary end (*finis operis*) of marriage as a natural institution. However, some authors see in GS a reversal of this position and a subsequent rejection of the idea of a hierarchy among the ends of marriage. For example, on the hierarchy of ends, James P. Hanigan writes, "the Council refused to rank one purpose above the other, as had been traditionally done. . . . In contemporary terms the unitive and procreative functions of sexuality were accorded equal status." [120]

In light of the chapter as a whole, this claim seems excessive. When the ends of marriage are first mentioned in GS 48, the text cites St. Augustine, St. Thomas Aquinas, and *Casti connubii*, each of which held a clear hierarchy of the ends of marriage with procreation ranked first. While this reference does not signify complete agreement between the Council Fathers and these sources, through this citation the Council Fathers implicitly invoke the traditional teaching of a hierarchy among the ends of marriage. The other teach-

[118] GS 48.

[119] GS 47.

[120] James P. Hanigan, *What Are They Saying about Sexual Morality?* (New York: Paulist Press, 1982), p. 33.

ings of this section of GS are entirely compatible with the traditional teaching on this hierarchy, though none makes direct reference to it. For example, GS 50 states that marriage and conjugal love are ordered to procreation and that children are "the supreme gift of marriage".[121] The text also states that without "intending to lessen the other ends of marriage, it must be said that true married love and the whole structure of married life resulting from it is directed to disposing the spouses to cooperate valiantly with the love of the Creator and Savior" in the transmission of life.[122] Thus, nothing in these statements of GS refutes or contradicts the traditional hierarchy of the ends of marriage, and there does seem to be some support for this traditional formulation because of the manner in which the document distinguishes the procreation and education of children (called the "crowning glory" of marriage)[123] from the other ends of marriage.

One could perhaps say that this section of GS remains "silent" on the issue of a hierarchy among the ends of marriage in that it does not employ this terminology. The language of primary and secondary ends or hierarchy of ends does not appear in the definitive text of GS. By designating procreation as the "most excellent gift of marriage", however, GS does distinguish it from the other ends of marriage in a singular way. Therefore, while some wish to view this silence regarding the hierarchy as a rejection of the traditional teaching, others such as Miralles, García de Haro, W. May, Gil Hellín, and A. Mattheeuws have concluded that this silence is not grounds for a rejection of this long-held

---

[121] GS 50.

[122] Ibid.

[123] GS 48.

doctrine.[124] Instead, within the teaching of GS, procreation remains an "intrinsic end" of marriage and the "primordial end" of marriage as a natural institution.[125] According to Pope John Paul II, within the teaching of GS "the traditional teaching on the ends of marriage (and their hierarchy) is reaffirmed and at the same time deepened from the viewpoint of the interior life of the spouses."[126]

Further continuity between GS and previous magisterial pronouncements appears in the area of conjugal morality. Pius XI stated that married love is fully manifest in deeds and not in mere words. Pius XI developed his moral teaching on the fundamental principle that accepted as morally licit those acts that are in accord with the nature of marriage and human nature. As a result, such acts as contraception, abortion, adultery, and divorce were condemned. Within the framework established by Pius XI, the moral evaluation of an action rests on that action's conformity to human nature and the nature of sexuality.

---

[124] According to Antonio Miralles, "Possiamo dunque ben concludere che il silenzio del concilo Vaticano II sulla gerarchia dei fini del matrimonio non significa che la dottrina tradizionale al riguardo sia stata abbandonata" (*Il Matrimonio* [Milan: Edizione San Paolo, 1996], p. 77). This interpretation is shared by Ramón García de Haro in his *Marriage*, p. 244. Consult also: William May, *Marriage: The Rock on Which the Family Is Built* (San Francisco: Ignatius Press, 1995), pp. 109–15; Francisco Gil Hellín, "Los 'bona matrimonii' en la Constitución pastoral 'Gaudium et spes' del Concilio Vaticano II", in *Scripta Theologica* 11 (1979): 153–61, where he suggests that the absence of the traditional terminology of the hierarchy of the ends of marriage in GS reflects the pastoral nature of the document and not a change in doctrine; also his *Il Matrimonio e la Vita Coniugale* (Vatican City: Libreria Editrice Vaticano, 1996), pp. 101–14; Smith, *"Humanae Vitae"*, p. 48; Alain Mattheeuws, *Union et procréation* (Paris: Les Éditions du Cerf, 1989), pp. 97–102.

[125] See Gil Hellín, *Matrimonio*, pp. 106–10.

[126] Pope John Paul II, General Audience of October 10, 1984, in *The Theology of the Body* (Boston: Pauline Books and Media, 1997).

Although the term "nature" does not play as prominent a role in the conjugal morality of GS, the standards of morality are essentially the same, with human nature as a fundamental reference point. GS 49 reaffirms that married love is "expressed and perfected by the exercise of acts proper to marriage"[127] because conjugal love is not a matter of mere sentiment. Indeed, "the truly human performance of these acts fosters the self-giving they signify and enriches the spouses in joy and gratitude."[128] Upon what criteria would the Council Fathers evaluate the actions of married couples? According to GS 51, there are divine laws that govern the transmission of life and the fostering of married love, so that man is not left to decide for himself the manner in which to express love and transmit life. Following this, the text states that man must carry out his task of transmitting life in a manner worthy of himself, that acts proper to married love are to be ordered according to authentic human dignity, and that in determining the morality of a couple's activity objective criteria must be used, "criteria drawn from the nature of the human person and human action".[129] Here, again, man stands at the center of conjugal morality, his own nature serving as the criterion upon which to judge and order his actions. As with Pius XI, this criterion reveals the immorality of contraception and abortion. In order to "respect the total meaning of mutual self-giving and human procreation in the context of true love", man and woman must strive for the "truly human performance" of the conjugal act as revealed by human nature itself.[130]

[127] GS 49.

[128] Ibid.

[129] GS 51.

[130] GS 51 and 49.

Conjugal Love and Vocation

In addition to maintaining a continuity with past magisterial pronouncements, Vatican II made significant contributions of its own to the Church's understanding of marriage and sexuality. The Council's most relevant contributions to the doctrine of marriage and sexuality relate to its treatment of conjugal love and its recognition of marriage as a vocation. Highlighting the importance of conjugal love, GS recalls the importance of the loving relationship between the spouses for the married life. However, GS does so in such a way as to reject attempts to oppose this loving relationship to marriage as an institution. In addition to being a natural institution and a personal relationship, within the teaching of Vatican II marriage is also a vocation, a response to a call from God and a path to holiness.

The Significance of Conjugal Love

Married love, that is, the love of husband and wife, has always been seen as a unique kind of human love. The marital friendship is recognized as standing apart from other friendships. In the decades after *Casti connubii* some began to assert that this love between man and woman is of such significance that marriage is ordered more, or at least equally, to the perfection of this friendship than to the procreation of children. The Church, however, never considered this friendship to be an end, much less a more primary end of marriage than procreation. Yet, the role of conjugal love in marriage had not been fully expressed by the Church. The task of GS was, then, to articulate the full significance of married love in the theology of marriage, to clarify the relationship of conjugal love to the institution of marriage, and to relate properly this love to procreation. Rather than being done through precise declarations, GS accomplishes this task principally by its overall presentation of the teaching on marriage.

The Council Fathers in no manner designate conjugal love as an end of marriage. Instead, within the framework of GS conjugal love has the same properties and ends as the institution of marriage itself. When the ends and benefits of marriage are mentioned, reference is made to the traditional formulation of the ends of marriage, which did not list conjugal love as an end of marriage. Conjugal love, rather than being an end of marriage, is the love or friendship that the institution confirms and protects. Married love is the friendship, or the type of friendship, that is the foundation and principle of marriage, yet it is neither an end of nor synonymous with this institution. These points are developed well by A. Mattheeuws, F. Gil Hellín, and García de Haro in their analyses of conjugal love in GS.[131] As Mattheeuws explains, conjugal love and the institution of marriage have the same ends and properties because they are integral parts of the one reality which is marriage or the conjugal community. The institution is born out of an act of conjugal love and then the institution confirms and protects the love of the spouses.[132] Thus, for example, in two places (GS 48 and 50) the text describes both marriage and conjugal love as being ordered to the procreation and education of children.

---

[131] See Mattheeuws, *Union*, pp. 88–91; Gil Hellín, *Matrimonio*, pp. 129–65; García de Haro, *Marriage*, pp. 235–57.

[132] Mattheeuws, *Union*, pp. 89–90. Gil Hellín writes, "L'amore coniugale non è fine del matrimonio, ma, come questo, si orienta ai fini essenziali, alla procreazione ed educazione di figli e al mutuo aiuto degli sposi. . . . Però nemmeno l'amore conuigale è una proprietà come l'unità e l'indissolubilità, ma come lo stesso matrimonio, anche l'amore conuigale è uno e indissolubile" (*Matrimonio*, p. 130).

The manner in which GS includes conjugal love in its teaching on marriage possesses a twofold value because the text both reminds the world of the importance of love in marriage and clarifies the relationship between conjugal love and the institution of marriage. It is possible to err either by reducing marriage to a juridical entity or by reducing marriage to the personal relationship between spouses. GS, implicitly rejecting both reductive approaches to marriage, teaches that marriage necessarily entails both a loving friendship and an institution. These two integral parts of marriage can never exist separately because the same act brings each into existence: the act of matrimonial consent. The institution of marriage exists from the moment of consent, a "human act by which the partners mutually surrender themselves to each other".[133] However, this human act is an act of conjugal love and is the beginning of the conjugal friendship; prior to this the spouses have another type of friendship, one that is not ordered to procreation or indissoluble.

Yet, the institution and the conjugal friendship do not just happen to result from the same act, nor do they merely coexist. They are intimately related, because conjugal love is what the institution confirms, protects, and sanctifies. Indeed, the institution and conjugal love are "distinct and complementary aspects"[134] of the one reality marriage, but also they are intrinsically related because the institution is the *institution of conjugal love* and because this institution is brought into existence by an act of conjugal love. As García de Haro writes, "the institution of marriage arises from an act of love, and the institution protects love, for true conjugal love is not limited or impeded by it, but rather both elements mutually

[133] GS 48.

[134] See Gil Hellín, *Matrimonio*, pp. 152–54.

require and complete each other."[135] This relationship is analogous to the relationship of body and soul in the human person. Both body and soul are essential aspects of a human person, but their relationship cannot be reduced to the fact that they are both constitutive elements of the same person. Instead, we can also speak of a direct relationship between the two because the soul animates the body. Likewise, conjugal love and the marriage institution are not simply related by virtue of the fact that they both belong to the greater reality which is the conjugal community. Instead the two also relate directly because conjugal love gives life to ("animates") the institution. The institution is, then, in a sense an embodiment of the love between the spouses.

If these two aspects of marriage were merely distinct and complementary elements of marriage and if there were no direct intrinsic relationship between them, the presence of tension between the two would become a possibility, as would questions of which is more essential to marriage. However, according to the teaching of GS, no such tension exists. Some may wish to posit such tension between conjugal friendship and the institution of marriage, but in doing so they betray a failure to recognize the intrinsic relationship between them. Moreover, once this intrinsic relationship is recognized, it is not reasonable to assert that an emphasis on the institutional aspect of marriage neglects the importance of love. Because the institution is the institution of conjugal love (its "embodiment"), highlighting the institutional dimension of marriage neither denies nor neglects the value of conjugal love. Likewise, a description of marriage that emphasizes the loving relationship between the spouses need not be understood

[135] García de Haro, *Marriage*, p. 240.

as a movement away from the institutional aspect of marriage. The Church need not decide between describing marriage as a community of love and life or as a natural institution; in accordance with Divine Wisdom it is both.

In addition to clarifying the relationship of the institution of marriage and conjugal love, the text of GS also clarifies the relationship between conjugal love and procreation. In developing the intrinsic relationship between the institution of marriage and conjugal love, GS teaches that not only marriage as a whole but conjugal love itself is ordered to the procreation and education of children as an end.[136] Procreation is an end of marriage when viewed as a loving friendship between man and woman as well as when it is considered in its institutional dimension. Echoing GS 48, GS 50 states, "Marriage and married love are by nature ordered to the procreation and education of children." Properly speaking, conjugal love's ordination to procreation makes the friendship between spouses the unique friendship that it is, a conjugal friendship. Considering the fact that conjugal love "embraces the good of the whole person",[137] it could not be other than procreative. In no other friendship is the love such that it includes the lovers' capacity for parenthood, but this is precisely the case with conjugal love. The conjugal communion of persons is always at the service of life, and indeed the ordination to procreation distinguishes the conjugal communion of persons from all other communions of persons. On the basis of this understanding of conjugal love,

[136] According to García de Haro, "the most novel affirmation of GS, and that which signals true theological advance on the issue, is that conjugal love—and not only marriage—has as its end the procreation and education of children" (*Marriage*, p. 244).

[137] GS 49.

the Council Fathers state that there can be no contradiction between the divine laws governing the transmission of life and the fostering of authentic conjugal love.[138]

This love that embraces the good of the whole person is "rooted in the will" and is "experienced in tenderness and action".[139] Conjugal love is not a love of mere sentiment or words. Rather, conjugal love, with both spiritual and physical elements, entails specific and concrete human acts. The text states, "Married love is uniquely expressed and perfected by the exercise of the acts proper to marriage."[140] Those acts that are proper to marriage both express and perfect the love between husband and wife. In the following article of the document the Council Fathers articulate the moral criteria upon which married persons can base their actions, and these have been examined above. The relevance of this statement rests on its declaration of a standard regarding the manner in which husband and wife can increase and express their love for one another: through those acts "proper to marriage" (perhaps one could say proper marital acts).

Marriage as a Vocation

At the turn of the century few questioned the idea of marriage as a "vocation". However, prior to the Council the term *vocation* was principally applied exclusively to a calling to the consecrated life, though this idea was never formalized in the doctrines of the Magisterium. The Council's recognition of marriage as a vocation is a consequence and an extension of *Lumen gentium*'s teaching on the so-called

[138] GS 51.
[139] GS 49.
[140] Ibid.

"universal call to holiness." According to LG 40, "all Christians in any state or walk of life are called to the fullness of the Christian life and to the perfection of love." [141] Within the Church there are different routes or paths to the same goal, because "the forms and tasks of life are many but holiness is one—that sanctity which is cultivated by all who act under God's Spirit and, obeying the Father's voice and adoring God the Father in spirit and truth, follow Christ." [142] Describing marriage as a vocation, the Church teaches that married life is one specific path or way to holiness. The daily actions that comprise married life are actions that can lead to holiness through their performance in charity and in accord with the requirements of marriage as divinely instituted. Therefore, the idea of marriage as a vocation qualifies the married state itself.

However, in the context of this study the designation of marriage as a vocation reveals something more significant, something that concerns man's ontological state and in particular his free use of the sexual faculty. In addition to qualifying marriage as a path to holiness, the term *vocation* denotes a call, a call by God for and to man. God wills for men and women to enter marriage, and thus the concept of vocation takes on a moral significance. God wills something for man. God calls man to do something. Man for his part must choose to accept and act upon this call or to reject (perhaps neglect) this call and act otherwise. Man either acts in accord with the call or does not. Once the call is made by God, man's actions no longer exist as a self-referential series, but rather they are always in relation and reference to this call, as in conformity to or in contradiction to what God wills. Thus,

[141] *Lumen gentium*, 40 (hereafter LG).

[142] LG 41.

when one applies the term *vocation* to marriage, one states that God calls man and wills for him something with regard to his sexuality. It seems that this "something" to which God calls man must be something specific, or better yet, it must entail specific acts. If a divine vocation were not to require specific acts, then it would be more like a noise heard rumbling in the distance than a personal call.

In light of the notion of marriage as a vocation man cannot reflect upon his sexuality as if *he* had to establish some existential reference point from which he should begin or to which he should proceed. Rather, his reflection takes on the nature of a response to God's call. In deliberating the exercise which he will make of his sexual faculty, man must have as his reference point that to which God calls him, that which God wills for him. In this sense, while maintaining his freedom, man does not start with a blank canvas upon which to create the role that his sexuality shall play in his life. Blessed Josemaría Escrivá once said, "Our calling discloses to us the meaning of our existence." [143] As a vocation, marriage discloses to man and woman the meaning of their sexuality. A vocation provides an orientation to and a context for the use of human freedom, and in the case of marriage it provides these for the free use of the sexual faculty.

Even before the Magisterium applied the notion of vocation to marriage, man was not given free reign to determine how to actualize his generative potential. Theologically and philosophically it is possible to speak of the ends to which sexuality is ordained by its nature or the structure that is intrinsic to the marital act, and these have deep significance for man's sexual actions. However, when these considerations

[143] Escrivá, "In Joseph's Workshop", in *Christ Is Passing By* (New Rochelle: Scepter Press, 1974), p. 73.

are combined with the notion of vocation they take on greater significance. In the context of the theology of vocation these ends and this structure become the content of God's call to man as a spiritual being. They become the medium by which man can respond positively to God. In the acceptance of a vocation, man remains free, however the manner in which he should exercise his freedom is disclosed to him by God. The acceptance of a vocation is the conformity of man's will to that of God. In the rejection of a vocation, man rejects God's will for him, and in a very real sense he rejects his true self. Thus, the notion of vocation addresses man's "ontological situation" as a spiritual being.[144] Because marriage is a vocation, man's role in human generation remains a cooperation with nature and God through the fulfillment of a designated role.[145] Now, however, this cooperation takes on greater significance because the designation of man's role comes in the form of a personal call, and the response is recognized as a path to holiness.

CONCLUSION

In the forty years preceding the promulgation of the encyclical *Humanae vitae*, the Magisterium devoted considerable time and effort to articulating a Christian understanding of marriage. Each of the various approaches taken in expounding this understanding reveals something fundamental about the mystery of man and woman bound in marriage. In reviewing the teachings of *Casti connubii* and the 1944 statement of the Sacra Romana Rota, we find an example of the

[144] García de Haro, *Marriage*, p. 224.
[145] Cf. Pius XII, "Address to Midwives".

Magisterium's teaching on marriage as a natural institution, authored by God the Creator. These documents focus on marriage as an objective reality, an institution in which man freely cooperates with God. For the most part, these pronouncements employ technical, metaphysical language in order to convey the clear and objective reality of marriage as an institution, an institution in which man participates according to God's plan. Throughout this presentation of marriage, the Church reaffirms God's role as the author of marriage in order to remind man of marriage's sacred character. Yet, these documents also acknowledge the subjective participation of man in this sacred institution. The Church recognizes that the objective reality of marriage will vary "according to the different conditions of persons, time, and place" [146] and that couples enter the institution of marriage for varied and very personal reasons. Thus, while the focus is on the objective, divinely instituted reality of marriage, the Church never forgets that those who enter marriage are living, personal subjects with minds and hearts of their own. Human freedom is always accorded its proper role, but the concept of human freedom espoused is decidedly Catholic. Against those who would subject marriage to the wishes of men and to the currents of society, these documents are a clear statement of its objective nature and divine origin.

In his statements on marriage and sexuality Pope Pius XII uses a decidedly less technical and juridical terminology, partly because of the circumstances in which his teachings were presented. He explicitly addresses the question of the "personal values" of marriage, those that pertain to the spouses themselves and that are consciously experienced by them,

[146] *Casti connubii*, pp. 549–50.

demonstrating a greater appreciation for these values than was explicitly present in previous magisterial pronouncements. However, Pius XII's greatest contribution to the authentic appreciation and cultivation of these personal values is his recognition of the objective institution that promotes and fosters these goods. Thus, along with his appreciation of these values, Pius XII firmly and clearly defends the natural institution of marriage and the hierarchy among its ends. He reminds his listeners of the divine origin of marriage and the Creator's intention for marriage as it is revealed in Sacred Scripture and human nature. Pope Pius XII confirms the intrinsic link between the objective requirements of the institution of marriage and the personal values available in marriage. They are intrinsically linked by "the very meaning of the conjugal life" [147] and by the nature of the human person. The institution of marriage, the conjugal act, and procreation are personal by their very nature because the subjects of all three are persons.

In proposing a Catholic vision of marriage to the modern world, the authors of *Gaudium et spes* intended "to present certain key points of the Church's teaching in a clearer light".[148] The result is an exposition of the dignity of marriage and family that does not employ juridical or technical terminology. In the context of reaffirming key points of the Church's teaching on marriage, GS places a greater emphasis on the place of conjugal love in marriage than previous magisterial pronouncements. Thus, while recognizing marriage as a natural institution, endowed with laws and ends by the author of nature, GS also describes marriage as a personal, covenantal relationship grounded in a love that "embraces

[147] "Address to Midwives", p. 169.
[148] GS 48.

the good of the whole person".[149] The text presents the traditional view of marriage in non-juridical and pastoral terms, and herein lies its value: by expressing these traditional ideas in pastoral language, GS confirms that they are not solely juridical or metaphysical concepts but have full theological value. The text neutralizes any opposition between the two orders. The juridical and the personal are harmonized within the conjugal community. Again, the Church avoids a vision of marriage that entails an either/or approach to this sacred reality.

Though marriage is both a personal friendship (unique among other friendships) and a natural institution, the consequences of reducing it to either one of these realities are real and significant. Such a reduction produces effects beyond the merely semantic or academic level. When marriage is presented solely as a personal friendship between two people, its structure, content, and meaning become the products of a mutual agreement between the "friends". Since it is their friendship, the couple now decides whether it will be permanent, whether they will have children and how many, or whether it will be an exclusive relationship. These central questions of the married life are subject to the whims of the couple (or in some cases determined by the society in which they reside). The opposite approach to marriage, presenting it solely as a natural institution, has equally damaging though different effects. As a natural institution based upon a binding contract, marriage is reduced to the performance of specific acts and the fulfillment of certain duties, but it does not require of the couple the personal energy and emotion proper to the married state. The external performance of

[149] GS 49.

duty, devoid of emotional involvement, empties marriage of love, its very life. Thus, either reductive approach has dire consequences for marriage, changing the meaning of married life and ultimately, though implicitly, emptying it of its greatest treasure, its sacramental value, its ability to symbolize the love of God for man in the relationship of Christ and the Church.

The Church's theology of the conjugal act emerges in the context of this effort to strike a balance between the nature of marriage as a natural institution and as a personal friendship. The Church's concept of the conjugal act, therefore, encounters the same need to strike a balance between extremes. Immediately after the Second Vatican Council and in anticipation of *Humanae vitae*, the focus of attention in the theology of marriage and sexuality shifts to the conjugal act itself rather than marriage as a whole primarily because of the question of contraception. At this point it is no longer sufficient to clarify the theology of marriage as a whole because the pressing theological question has shifted to the finalities of the conjugal act itself, in particular the finality of procreation. Specifically, it becomes a question of whether the finalities of marriage pertain "to the ensemble of conjugal life, rather than to its single acts".[150] The Church's answer to this question avoids the extremes of reducing the conjugal act to the consummation of a contract or reducing the conjugal act to an expression of personal friendship loosely understood. Like marriage itself, the conjugal act possesses an intrinsic structure and finality yet demands the personal love, energy, and emotion of the spouses. Thus, in the performance of the conjugal act, spouses "are not free to pro-

[150] Paul VI, encyclical letter *Humanae vitae*, 3 (hereafter abbreviated as HV).

ceed completely at will, as if they could determine in a wholly autonomous way the honest path to follow; but they conform their activity to the creative intentions of God."[151]

Just as spouses must incorporate the structure and finalities of marriage into their conjugal friendship according to the creative intentions of God, in the conjugal act spouses must incorporate its intrinsic structure and finalities into their expression of love and conform their activity to the creative intentions of God. While this is the fundamental principle of the Church's theology of the conjugal act, an adequate articulation of this teaching revolves around a very precise understanding of freedom and human autonomy, "a specifically human meaning of the body",[152] and the manner in which the human expression of conjugal love conforms to (or is informed by) the creative intentions of God. Thus, alongside and inherently linked to the Church's theology of the conjugal act we discover "an integral vision of man"[153] that provides this concept of the conjugal act with a coherency as well as an anthropological context.

Within the teaching of *Humanae vitae* and during the Pontificate of Pope John Paul II, the Church presents a theology of the conjugal act that centers upon the doctrine of the indissoluble connection between procreation and union in the conjugal act, a doctrine first articulated in HV 12. This theology of the conjugal act reflects an application of the Church's fundamental principles concerning the conjugal life to the unique act of love between husband and wife. Thus, the notion of man as a cooperator in God's plan for fruitful

---

[151] HV 9.

[152] John Paul II, encyclical letter *Veritatis splendor*, 50 (hereafter abbreviated as VS).

[153] HV 7.

love extends to the conjugal act as well as to the whole of the conjugal life. In its development of a theology of the conjugal act, the Church also articulates the principles of Christian anthropology that serve as the proper context for understanding the conjugal relation of husband and wife. This anthropological vision not only provides coherency to the Church's theology of the conjugal act but also reveals some of the underlying principles of previous magisterial pronouncements on marriage. Therefore, the Church's doctrine since the Second Vatican Council has advanced our understanding of marriage and sexuality in a twofold manner: the more recent pronouncements apply previous principles in a renewed context and bring to light the implicit anthropological principles that support the Church's entire body of doctrine on marriage and sexuality.

Chapter Two

Toward a Theology of the Conjugal Act

Viewing the Conjugal Act in the Light of an Integral Vision of Man

During the time period between 1930 and 1968 the Magisterium of the Church developed a theology of marriage and family life that harmonized the elements of marriage as a natural institution with the requirements of conjugal love. According to the teachings of this period, marriage emerges as an institution of fruitful love in which man and woman cooperate with God in living his plan for marriage, a plan inscribed in their very beings as man and woman. However, by 1968 the "controversy" over the practice of contraception in marriage caused a shift in focus as the need for a more developed theology of the conjugal act increased. Though the issue of contraception is undoubtedly complex and multi-dimensional, its immorality emerges most clearly in the context of a theology of the conjugal act understood as a specific act of conjugal love. Therefore, in order to address questions of sexual ethics, including the immorality of contraception, the Church has developed a theology of the conjugal act that results in a concept of the conjugal act viewed as a specific act of conjugal love by which husband and wife confirm their conjugal union and cooperate with God in the transmission of life.

Beginning with the promulgation of Paul VI's encyclical *Humanae vitae*, the doctrine of an indissoluble connection between the procreative and unitive meanings of the conjugal act has become the centerpiece of the Church's concept of the conjugal act. According to this doctrine, the conjugal act intrinsically possesses a unitive aspect and a procreative aspect that become the "meanings" of the conjugal act in the order of human awareness or consciousness. Thus, the Church describes the conjugal act both in terms of its objective, fundamental structure and in terms of its subjective dimension, which arises from an awareness of the nature of the act on the part of the man and woman who perform it. Because the conjugal act proceeds according to laws inscribed in the very being of man and woman, husband and wife discover within their sexuality a "prescribed" form and manner of expressing conjugal love. Yet, through the function of conscience, this prescribed, objective expression of conjugal love becomes personal and intimate. Thus, guided by laws inscribed in their own being, husband and wife freely love each other in the conjugal act without proceeding in a wholly autonomous manner, thereby fulfilling their role as cooperators in God's plan of fruitful love.

Such a concept of the conjugal act depends greatly upon certain fundamental anthropological tenets for its inner rationale and for its ultimate coherency. In particular, this concept of the conjugal act relies upon a specific understanding of the human body and its sexual dimension, an understanding of freedom as *theonomy* in which freedom is perfected in the acceptance of God's law, and a notion of conscience that allows man to assimilate and appropriate the truth of God's law in formulating proximate norms for human action. These fundamental anthropological tenets comprise the foundation of an integral vision of man, in the light of which the

Magisterium has explicitly developed its understanding of the conjugal act. Thus, the Church's understanding of the conjugal act has progressed within the framework of developments in the field of theological anthropology, where the doctrines implicitly present in previous teachings are explicitly formulated. A true theology of the conjugal act emerges during the period following *Humanae vitae* precisely because of the organic relationship between the Church's theological anthropology and her concept of the conjugal act.

The anthropological vision that underlies the Church's concept of the conjugal act finds its greatest expression in the magisterial teachings of Pope John Paul II, for he has advanced our understanding of the person as a unified totality of body and soul, has clarified the relationship between freedom and God's law, and has confirmed conscience as the sacred place where man encounters and appropriates the truth of God's law. Consequently, the anthropological framework developed during his Pontificate has enabled John Paul II to make a singular analysis and description of the conjugal relationship of man and woman. By developing the anthropological basis for the Church's teaching of marriage and sexuality, John Paul II has made an unparalleled contribution to the study of marriage and the family while also solidifying the place of this field of study within an integral vision of man.

In the present chapter I focus on the theology of the conjugal act that has emerged since the promulgation of *Humanae vitae*, identifying both the central components of this theology of the conjugal act and the principal anthropological tenets upon which it depends. I begin with a consideration of *Humanae vitae* in which I concentrate on its formulation of the doctrine of the indissoluble connection between procreation and union. This doctrine, formulated in article 12 of the encyclical, represents the foundations of a renewed consideration of the conjugal act and becomes the central reference point of all subsequent teachings of the Church on the conjugal act. Next I summarize the teachings of John Paul II, focusing (though not exclusively) on his theology of the body developed in his general audiences, his understanding of the conjugal relationship in his apostolic exhortation *Familiaris consortio*, and his description of the relationship between human freedom, God's law, and the function of conscience as found in *Veritatis splendor*. I also include here a review of the documents *Persona humana* and *Donum vitae*, two documents from the Congregation for the Doctrine of the Faith that reiterate the relationship between man's sexual identity inscribed in human nature and the free exercise of the sexual faculty. Each of these various texts contributes to a theology of the conjugal act as a specific act of conjugal love in which husband and wife unite and procreate according to laws inscribed in their very being, loving each other according to the truth of their identities as sexual persons.

1. THE ENCYCLICAL *HUMANAE VITAE*

Scarcely any other magisterial document has generated as much energy or interest, both positive and negative, as that generated by this encyclical. At the time of its pronouncement, *Humanae vitae* was the controversial conclusion to an intense debate over contraception. More than thirty years later it continues to be the center of much debate. However, now it stands at the center of debate on matters far more extensive than contraception. The encyclical has fueled discussions on such matters as: the Magisterium's competency in matters of morality, objective moral norms, intrinsically evil acts, personal conscience versus the teachings of the Church, the nature of definitive doctrine, procreation's place within marriage, natural law, the relationship between nature and person, and finally the entire Christian moral teaching on human sexuality.[1] For some, the encyclical demonstrates the inadequacy of the "traditional" Catholic teaching on sexuality for the modern world. Yet, for others the encyclical represents a confirmation of the unchanging nature of the truth and teachings concerning human sexuality. Undoubtedly, the encyclical has transcended the issue of contraception and has become the focal point of the clash of entirely different moral systems.

Theologians have attacked and defended various aspects of the encyclical. Some have argued for and against the infallible nature of its condemnation of contraception. Others have examined its specific formulation for condemning contraception. Still others have argued for the persuasiveness and validity of the encyclical's internal arguments against contraception. Here, I am concerned only with its fundamental points and the manner in which the text contributes to the Catholic understanding of the conjugal act. The

[1] For an account of the various issues surrounding *Humanae vitae* and the immorality of contraception, consult: Pope John Paul II, General Audience of July 11, 1984–November 28, 1984, in *The Theology of the Body* (Boston: Pauline Books and Media, 1997); *"Humanae vitae": 20 anni dopo. Atti del II Congresso Internazionale di Teologia Morale* (Milan: Edizione Ares, 1989); Janet Smith, ed., *Why "Humanae Vitae" Was Right* (San Francisco: Ignatius Press, 1993); Janet Smith, *"Humanae Vitae", a Generation Later* (Washington, D.C.: Catholic University of America Press, 1991); Alfonso López Trujillo and Elio Sgreccia, eds., *"Humanae Vitae": Prophetic Service for Humanity* (Rome: Editrice Ave, 1995); Ramón García de Haro, *Marriage and the Family in the Documents of the Magisterium* (San Francisco: Ignatius Press, 1993); Alain Mattheeuws, *Union et procréation* (Paris: Les Éditions du Cerf, 1989).

foundational doctrines upon which Pope Paul VI articulated the immorality of contraception are of as much value and interest as his actual condemnation of contraception. HV makes a significant contribution to the Church's understanding of the conjugal act precisely because the Pope was led to focus on the conjugal act itself due to the proposals involving "the so-called principle of totality".[2] The encyclical explicitly answers the question of whether "the finality of procreation pertains to the ensemble of conjugal life, rather than to single acts".[3] Those who espouse the "totality" approach, while accepting the ordination of marriage and conjugal love to procreation, argue that each conjugal act need not express such an ordination. Instead, they suggest focusing on the "totality" of the conjugal acts over the course of a couple's entire life together. Thus, in order to respond to this line of argumentation, Paul VI approached the issue of contraception from the perspective of the conjugal act considered in its essence and meaning. He concluded that any act of sexual intercourse between husband and wife "must remain open to the transmission of life" in order to be an authentic *conjugal act* precisely because procreation is an essential aspect of the act itself.[4]

Pope Paul VI's teaching on the conjugal act centers upon the so-called "principle of inseparability", articulated in HV 12, a doctrine that has since become an integral part of the Church's teaching on human sexuality. Indeed, the doctrine contained in HV 12 is widely recognized as the fundamental idea upon which the Church's ethical discussion of the con-

[2] HV 3.

[3] Ibid.

[4] HV 11.

jugal act hinges.[5] The concept of an indissoluble connection between the procreative and unitive meanings of the conjugal act remains the most prominent dimension of the doctrine of HV 12. Though this concept was innovative in 1968, it constitutes an integral part of a larger theological tradition that entails a specific concept of marriage, conjugal love, the human body, and an "integral vision of man".[6] The various components of this theological tradition converge in HV to produce a concept of the conjugal act that intrinsically excludes the possibility of contraception. In other words, according to HV, the immorality of contraception derives from its incompatibility with the nature of marriage, of conjugal love, of the human person, and of the conjugal act.

The Conjugal Act according to HV 12

In HV 12, Pope Paul VI states,

> That teaching, often set forth by the Magisterium, is founded upon the indissoluble connection, willed by God and unable to be broken by man on his own initiative, between the two meanings of the conjugal act: the unitive meaning and the procreative meaning. Indeed, by its intimate structure, the conjugal act, while most closely uniting husband and wife,

[5] Both those who accept Catholic sexual teaching and those who reject it recognize the fundamental importance of this doctrine. For example, see: K. Wojtyla, "La visione antropologica della *Humanae vitae*", *Lateranum* 44 (1978): 125–45; B. Ashley, "The Use of Moral Theory in the Church", in *Human Sexuality and Personhood* (St. Louis, Pope John Center, 1981), p. 223; B. Häring, "The Inseparability of the Unitive-Procreative Functions of the Marital Act", in *Contraception, Authority, and Dissent*, ed. C. Curran (New York: Paulist Press, 1971), p. 176; R. McCormick, "Notes on Moral Theology", *Theological Studies*, vol. 29, no. 4 (December 1968), p. 728.

[6] HV 7.

> capacitates them for the generation of new lives, according to laws inscribed in the very being of man and woman. By safeguarding both these essential aspects, the unitive and procreative, the conjugal act preserves in its fullness the sense of true mutual love and its ordination towards man's most high calling to parenthood. We believe that the men of our day are particularly capable of seizing the deeply reasonable and human character of this fundamental principle.

Principally HV 12 comprises a set of affirmations concerning the conjugal act that express a "fundamental principle" described as "reasonable and human". The teaching of HV 12 is a statement or affirmation and is not an argument. The Pope does not construct HV 12 as a syllogism whose parts follow one upon the other leading to a conclusion. Nor is HV 12 the conclusion to some previous or unstated argument. Because the teaching of HV 12 expresses a fundamental principle, the truth of these affirmations must be grasped on the basis of other known truths, but it cannot be deductively proven or demonstrated. The veracity of the doctrine of HV 12 derives from the definitions of the terms employed (procreation, union, conjugal act, and so on) and from the nature of the human person. Thus, the truth of the principle of inseparability "has to be shown rather than demonstrated".[7] Therefore, those who expect the Pope (or others) to provide arguments to *demonstrate* the affirmations contained in HV 12 misunderstand the character of the doctrine itself.

What, then, does Pope Paul VI state or affirm in this paragraph? Though not necessarily in this order, the Pope affirms:

[7] Cf. Martin Rhonheimer, "Contraception, Sexual Behavior, and Natural Law: Philosophical Foundations of the Norm of *Humanae Vitae*", in *"Humanae vitae": 20 anni dopo* (Edizione Ares, 1989), pp. 87–88.

- There are two essential aspects (procreation and union) of the conjugal act.
- These two aspects are the "meanings" (the procreative and unitive) of the conjugal act.
- There is an unbreakable connection (*nexu indissolubili*) between these two meanings/aspects of the conjugal act.
- This connection is willed by God.
- The conjugal act has an intrinsic "structure" that safeguards the two essential aspects and preserves the sense of true mutual love and its ordination to parenthood.
- These statements comprise a fundamental principle.
- The unbreakable connection between the two meanings of the conjugal act is the foundation for the statement "each and every conjugal act must remain open to life" (HV 11).

These affirmations focus on the essence of the conjugal act and describe it both objectively (ontologically) and from the perspective of the subjects. The essence and intimate structure of the conjugal act originate from the two essential aspects of procreation and union, the goods to which the act is ordered. The definition of the conjugal act includes procreation and union inasmuch as these two goods enter into the essence of the conjugal act as a human act (*actus humanus*). Every conjugal act is both procreative and unitive because these two characteristics pertain to its essence as the ends intended in the act. The "intimate structure" of the conjugal act both unites husband and wife and capacitates them for the generation of new life. In safeguarding these essential aspects, the conjugal act preserves the mutual love of husband and wife and the ordination of this love to the calling to parenthood.

In addition to describing the essence of the conjugal act in objective terms (that is, the essential aspects, intrinsic structure), HV 12 also describes the conjugal act from the perspective of the subjects of the act by its emphasis on the *meanings* of the act and the indissoluble connection between them. Procreation and union are both *essential aspects* and *meanings* of the conjugal act, and the difference in terminology corresponds to diverse perspectives for viewing the realities. The term "meaning" implies the perspective of the subject of the act and corresponds to the level of human awareness.[8] Procreation and union belong to the nature of the conjugal act as essential aspects or parts of the act's intimate structure. However, by virtue of human awareness or consciousness, these essential aspects become the meanings of the act. Inasmuch as the meanings are the essential aspects seen from the perspective of human awareness, the meanings belong to the essence of the act. Thus, the *essential aspects* of the act and the *meanings* of the act cannot be separated, but the distinct terms indicate diverse approaches to the same realities. According to Pope John Paul II, HV 12 describes the conjugal act in terms of two distinct yet related "dimensions": the "ontological dimension" (essential aspects) and "the subjective and psychological dimension" (meanings).[9] Because of the intrinsic link between these two dimensions, the meaning of the act is objective; it pertains to conscious

[8] Cf. K. Wojtyla, "The Teaching of *Humanae Vitae* on Love", in *Person and Community* (New York: Peter Lang, 1993), p. 308: "By appealing to the meaning of the conjugal act, the Pope places the whole discussion not only and not so much in the context of the nature of the act, but also and even more in the context of human awareness, in the context of the awareness that should correspond to this act on the part of both the man and the woman—the persons performing the act."

[9] General Audience of July 11, 1984, pp. 387–88.

intention but is not entirely dependent on the conscious intention of the subjects. Principally, then, Pope Paul VI affirms the connection between procreation and union in the conscious intention of the subjects of the conjugal act (in the subjective dimension). According to Paul VI, this connection results from the Divine Will, and as such it is independent of the conscious intention of the subjects even while pertaining to this order. Thus, in both the ontological and the subjective dimension, the conjugal act is necessarily unitive and procreative.[10] And because the definition of the conjugal act entails the perspective of the agents, the *definition* of the act implies these two *meanings* as well as the essential aspects.[11]

Pope Paul VI's statements in HV 12 fundamentally regard the definition of the conjugal act from various perspectives and are not *directly* normative statements, though they do have considerable ethical or normative value. The doctrine of HV 12 is descriptive in the sense that it states what the case is and not what the case ought to be. Paul VI states that there *is* an indissoluble connection between the meanings of the conjugal act, not that there *ought to be* such a connection. However, the task of accurately grasping the sense of this paragraph on this point is somewhat complicated by the various available translations of the text.

Most available translations of the encyclical are based on the Italian version, and some suggest that the encyclical was originally written in Italian and French.[12] While on the whole

[10] I consider in more detail the presence of procreation and union in the "ontological" and "subjective" dimensions of the conjugal act in section 3 of the current chapter and in section 3 of chapter 3.

[11] Cf. Mattheeuws, *Union*, p. 113.

[12] Cf. Smith, appendix, *Why "Humanae Vitae" Was Right*, pp. 533–34.

the Italian differs only slightly from the official Latin text, the respective accounts of HV 12 suggest diverse senses of the doctrine on initial consideration. Although both the Italian and the Latin texts refer to the connection as "unbreakable" or "indissoluble",[13] the Italian text can be read as stating that man *cannot* break the connection, while the Latin text seems to state that man is *not permitted* to break the connection.[14] The Italian text seems to state what the case is: The connection is unbreakable and therefore man cannot break it. The Latin version seems to state what the case is and what man ought to do, thus giving a normative tint to the sentence: The connection is unbreakable and man is not permitted to break it, or man ought not to break it. Therefore, the descriptive character of the principle of inseparability is more apparent in the Italian text.

Depending upon one's reading of the Latin text, it could suggest that the principle of inseparability is directly normative rather than descriptive with ethical value. A thoughtful reading of the text, however, reveals a fundamental coherence between the Latin and the Italian texts. In the Italian text the principle is one of a descriptive character. It describes what the case is regarding the nature of the connection between two realities. According to one reading of the

---

[13] The term *inscindibile* appears in the Italian and the term *indissolubili* appears in the Latin. Both mean essentially the same thing. They are adjectives qualifying the connection as indissoluble, unbreakable, or inseparable. Neither the Latin or the Italian text contains any conditional or normative quality in this sentence; both are a statement of fact.

[14] The Italian text reads "che l'uomo non può rompere di sua iniziativa", and the Latin text reads "quem homini sua sponte infringere non licet". The Italian phrase "non può rompere" could carry the same meaning as "non deve rompere", which means "should not or ought not break", but "non può rompere" most likely means "cannot break".

Latin text, however, this principle describes the nature of the connection and also proscribes activity for man in regard to this connection. Within this understanding of the text, the principle of inseparability is *directly* normative. The apparent conflict between the two respective texts vanishes if one considers the logical inconsistency that this reading inserts into the Latin text. If the text states that man is not morally permitted to break the connection between the two meanings of the conjugal act, then it implicitly denies the indissoluble character of the connection between union and procreation. It is not logical to prohibit man from doing that which is intrinsically impossible. Man cannot dissolve indissoluble connections, or else they are not indissoluble connections by the very fact of his being able to dissolve them. How is it possible to prohibit or allow man to do that which he cannot do? This is tantamount to saying to someone, "you are not permitted to draw a square circle." The definitions of square and circle make it impossible for man to draw a square circle and therefore remove from any logical thought the ethical considerations of drawing square circles. It is not logical to discuss the licitness of drawing square circles. Similarly, it is not logical to discuss the licitness of dissolving indissoluble bonds or breaking unbreakable connections.

Due to the logical inconsistencies of this reading, a more reasonable understanding of the text presents itself. The text clearly describes the relationship between the two meanings of the conjugal act as an "indissoluble connection" (*nexu indissolubili*), thus establishing the fact that the bond between these meanings cannot be broken. When the text states that man is not permitted to break it through his own volition, it does not necessarily imply a case where one or both of the meanings remains intact apart from the other. Instead, the text most likely refers to the *destruction* of the bond between the two meanings, which in turn entails the destruction of the two meanings themselves. Procreation cannot be separated from union, because their relationship is intrinsic and not extrinsic, but it is possible to empty a sexual act of these two meanings. In such a case, the bond between these two meanings disappears from the act precisely because the meanings themselves disappear from the act. Understood from this perspective, the Latin text is directly normative in terms of prohibiting the destruction of the meanings of the conjugal act. It does not, however, prohibit the dissolution of an indissoluble connection, something which would be pointless. Regarding the connection between union and procreation, all versions of HV 12 are descriptive in the sense that each states a fact, on its most profound level an anthropological fact. In turn, this fact has ethical value because it bears directly on human action.[15]

The full significance of HV 12 emerges in light of its relationship to HV 11, which states that each and every conjugal act must be open to the transmission of life. According to Paul VI, HV 12 is the foundation for the conclusion expressed in HV 11. The phrase, "that teaching", in the first sentence of HV 12 refers to the last sentence of HV 11. The importance of this relationship should not be underestimated because this reference demonstrates the existential character of the principle of inseparability; that is, it explains the manner in which the fact of the indissoluble connection relates to human action. The relationship of HV 12 to HV 11 brings the principle from the realm of theoretical considerations into the realm of real acts. The existential character of

[15] Pope John Paul II, General Audience of July 11, 1984, p. 388: "The text of the encyclical stresses that in the case in question we are dealing with a norm of the natural law."

the indissoluble connection between procreation and spousal union runs counter to positions that see only a conceptual relationship between procreation and union. Some claim that while it is possible to see the conceptual relationship between the procreative meaning and the unitive meaning, human experience and scientific investigation suggest that in the concrete order the two can exist independently of each other.[16] According to this view, the concept of procreation is related to the concept of union, but not intrinsically so. The supposed proof of this claim is the fact that *conception* does not occur with every act of marital intercourse and that *conception* can occur in non-unitive acts such as rape.

Invariably, those who claim an existential denial of the principle of inseparability do so on the basis of a limited, usually biologistic, understanding of procreation. For most of these authors, procreation equals conception. Such a view reduces procreation to its physiological aspects and to the possible biological side effect of a couple's sexual union.[17] By all honest accounts, the Church rejects such a notion of procreation, for such a notion denies the personal nature of the act. At this point in my study it is premature for a defense of the existential nature of the principle of inseparability, for

[16] Some examples of this line of thinking can be found in McCormick, "Notes", p 728; Häring, "Inseparability," pp. 176–92; J. Hanigan, *What Are They Saying about Sexual Morality?* (New York: Paulist Press, 1982), pp. 33–34.

[17] Cormac Burke provides a concise summary and critique of this misguided notion of procreation. According to Burke, this position mistakenly holds that, "The marital act expresses love; it unites. It has, indeed, a possible procreative 'side-effect' which can result in children. But since this side-effect depends on biological factors, which science today permits us to control, the procreative aspect of marital intercourse can be nullified, while leaving its unitive function intact" ("Marriage and Contraception", in Smith, *Why "Humanae Vitae" Was Right*, p. 154). See the following pages for his analysis of this position.

this properly belongs to the next chapter. However, it is important to note here that Pope Paul VI gives every indication that he intends this principle to apply to a real concrete human act: the conjugal act. The text itself suggests the existential character of the principle. Moreover, in the context of HV 11 and 13, the Pope's teaching clearly refers to the conjugal act as it is executed and experienced by man in the existential order. The teaching of HV 12 regards the reality of the conjugal act, not simply its components on the conceptual level.

The suspicion that surrounds the existential nature of the principle has led some to ask of it, "Is it, perhaps, an ideal that cannot always be realized? Is it, perhaps, an ideal to be achieved in a total relationship and not in every specific act of sexual intercourse?"[18] Yet, the text itself provides an answer to this line of questioning. The procreative and unitive aspects of the act are *essential* to the act. Pope Paul VI is not describing an ideal, but rather the bare essentials of the conjugal act. The procreative aspect and the unitive aspect belong to the very essence of the conjugal act. Herein lies the key to understanding accurately the final phrase of HV 11, a normative implication of the doctrine of HV 12. By its very definition, every conjugal act must remain open to the transmission of life. Read in light of the doctrine of HV 12, this phrase could be reformulated as: In order to be the conjugal act, a sexual act must remain open to the transmission of life. Any sexual act devoid of the procreative or unitive aspect is, therefore, not a conjugal act. The relationship of the two meanings of the conjugal act outlined by HV 12 is not an ideal, but rather the minimum requirement for the conjugal act.

[18] Hanigan, *What Are They Saying*, p. 34.

HV 12 in Humanae Vitae

The concept of the conjugal act expressed by HV 12 derives from the theological principles of the encyclical and represents the relevance of these theological principles for the life of a married couple. The doctrine of HV 12 stands at the center of a vision of marriage and a vision of man that reiterates many of the teachings on marriage and sexuality reviewed in chapter 1 of my study. Pope Paul VI recalls the proper role of man in respect to the use of his generative faculty: man and woman collaborate with God in an institution of love according to the creative intention of God and according to laws inscribed in the very being of man and woman.

In the first sentence of the encyclical Paul VI reminds husband and wife that they have a "duty" (*munus*)[19] or a mission to be the "free and responsible collaborators of God the Creator" in the transmission of human life.[20] Because man and woman are only collaborators in the transmission of life, "they are not free to proceed completely at will, as if they could determine in a wholly autonomous way the honest path to follow; but they must conform their activity to the creative intention of God expressed in the very nature of marriage and of its acts."[21] Paul VI describes marriage as a "wise institution of the Creator to realize in mankind his design of love", not "the effect of chance or the product of the evolution of unconscious natural forces".[22] Marriage is

[19] For a discussion of the significance of this Latin term, see J. Smith, "The Importance of the Concept of '*Munus*' to Understanding *Humanae Vitae*", in *Why "Humanae Vitae" Was Right*, pp. 305–24.

[20] HV 1.

[21] HV 10.

[22] HV 8.

an institution of conjugal love, entailing a "personal gift of self" whose finality is the "mutual personal perfection" of the spouses and their collaboration "with God in the generation and education of new lives".[23] Paul VI formulates the doctrine of the encyclical on the basis of a proper understanding of conjugal love, responsible parenthood, and man's dominion over the human body.

Conjugal Love

In accord with the teaching of the Second Vatican Council, HV recalls the importance of conjugal love in marriage and its ordination to procreation. According to Paul VI, conjugal love is "fully human, that is to say, of the senses and of the spirit at the same time".[24] Conjugal love involves feelings and sentiment, but it also requires a free act of the will and, in this sense, entails all that is genuinely human. Conjugal love is both a bodily and a spiritual love. In this very special form of friendship, "husband and wife generously share everything, without undue reservation or selfish calculation."[25] Thus, according to Paul VI, conjugal love is a "total" love, or, in the words of *Gaudium et spes*, a love that embraces "the good of the whole person".[26] In the reciprocal gift of self at the heart of conjugal love, no aspect of either spouse is reserved or excluded; the spouses share everything "until death".[27] Because of its human and total character, conjugal love is necessarily ordered to procreation. The

[23] Ibid.
[24] HV 9.
[25] Ibid.
[26] GS 49.
[27] HV 9.

potential for parenthood constitutes an essential aspect of every human personality. Thus, excluding the potential for parenthood from the conjugal friendship would contradict the (human and total) nature of conjugal love. Indeed, marriage and conjugal love are ordered by their very nature to procreation. Conjugal love "is fecund, for it is not exhausted by the communion between husband and wife, but is destined to continue, raising up new lives".[28]

Responsible Parenthood

By its very nature conjugal love "requires in husband and wife an awareness of their mission of 'responsible parenthood'".[29] The very nature of conjugal love includes the task of responsible parenthood. Therefore, in order to live the conjugal friendship properly, spouses must properly understand and embrace the various elements of responsible parenthood. In HV 10, Paul VI discusses the notion of responsible parenthood under its various interrelated aspects. Fundamentally, responsible parenthood signifies an awareness and an acceptance of the spouses' role as collaborators with God in the transmission of life and a recognition of the manner in which God has chosen to accomplish this sacred task. As the Pope explains, "The responsible exercise of parenthood implies, therefore, that husband and wife recognize fully their own duties towards God, towards themselves, towards the family, and towards society, in a correct hierarchy of values."[30] In order to fulfill the requirements of responsible parenthood, spouses must recognize the personal nature of

[28] Ibid.

[29] HV 10.

[30] Ibid.

the body and proceed on the basis of a freedom that is not *wholly* autonomous.

In his discussion of responsible parenthood, Paul VI writes, "In relation to the biological processes, responsible parenthood means the knowledge and respect of their functions; human intellect discovers in the power of giving life *biological laws which are part of the human person*" (emphasis added).[31] These biological laws belong to the body and its organs, yet they are part of the human person. Since the body is a constitutive part of the person, the various organs and functions of the body are part of the person. As a constitutive part of the person, the body and its functions possess a certain dignity that man must respect in the exercise of his freedom. Mere biology does not demand this respect, but *human* biology does. In accord with the personal nature of the body, "man does not have unlimited dominion over his body in general, so also, with particular reason, he has no such dominion over his generative faculties."[32] Here, Pope Paul VI reiterates the understanding of man's dominion over the human body explicitly stated in the teachings of Pius XI and Pius XII.[33] Man is not the absolute master of his body because the body possesses a personal nature that requires its structure and finalities to be respected. In order to fulfill the mission of responsible parenthood, spouses "must necessarily recognize the insurmountable limits to the possibility of man's dominion over his own body and its functions; limits

[31] Ibid.

[32] HV 13.

[33] Cf. Pius XI, *Casti connubii*; Pius XII, "Address to the Micro-biological Union of San Luca, November 12, 1943", and "Address to the First International Congress on the Histopathology of the Nervous System, September 14, 1952".

which no man, whether a private individual or one invested with authority, may licitly surpass".[34] In the use of his sexual faculty, an inherently bodily/spiritual faculty, man does not have free reign because certain finalities and laws are inscribed in the very organs by which this faculty is exercised. Inscribed in the body, these finalities and laws are inscribed "in the very being of man and woman".[35] Here, Pope Paul VI cannot be accused of "biologism", only "personalism". Man's freedom is not limited by mere biology, but by his own person. As R. García de Haro summarizes:

> [Paul VI expounds] a very coherent and thoroughgoing personalism, which never considers the human body as a thing but as a reality inseparable from the substantial wholeness—body and soul—constitutive of the person. He in no way confuses moral laws with biological laws, but rather has the wisdom to judge what are the limits imposed upon man in his dominion over physical laws when his own body is concerned, precisely because the body is an integral part of the person and is not the body of an animal.[36]

This understanding of man's relationship to his own body corresponds to a specific understanding of freedom in general, an understanding in which man is free but not "wholly autonomous". Husband and wife must necessarily be free, for without freedom there is no love, but "they are not free to proceed completely at will, as if they could determine in a wholly autonomous way the honest path to follow."[37] Thus, man and woman are *free* without being *wholly autonomous*. Instead of possessing absolute autonomy, man and woman

---

[34] HV 17.

[35] HV 12.

[36] García de Haro, *Marriage*, p. 312.

[37] HV 10.

are collaborators with God, whose creative intention stands as a norm for their activity. God's creative intention is expressed in the "very nature of marriage and of its acts", "inscribed in the being of man and woman", and manifest in "His design for love".[38] Therefore, regarding the sexual faculty, the human intellect discovers this creative intention, but it does not determine the finalities of the sexual faculty or the form of its use.

Paul VI's teaching concerning love, the personal nature of the body, and human freedom are the foundations upon which the doctrine of HV 12 rests. These same ideas are integral elements of what Paul VI describes as "an integral vision of man and his vocation".[39] Principally a magisterial pronouncement on human life in its transmission, HV's most fundamental ideas belong to the field of anthropology. Paul VI states that the issues of the encyclical must be considered "in the light of an integral vision of man and his vocation", and this anthropological vision permeates practically every section of the encyclical. HV 12 represents a particularly clear emergence of the anthropological foundations of the encyclical. Consequently, though HV 12 explicitly regards the essence and meaning of the conjugal act and its proper performance, M. Rhonheimer describes the principle of inseparability as "an anthropological principle expressing the fundamental unity of human persons as compound beings of body and spirit".[40] The text explicitly affirms an indissoluble connection between the meanings of the conjugal act, yet it can and should be read as an affirmation of the unity of the human person. According to Pope John Paul II, HV 12

---

[38] HV 10, 12, and 8 respectively.

[39] HV 7.

[40] Rhonheimer, "Contraception", p. 87.

affirms that the body is a constitutive part of the human person, that it belongs to his *being* and not his *having*.[41] Because of the anthropological nature of its doctrine, HV 12 should be read as an integral component of the anthropology of the encyclical. On its most profound level, the doctrine of HV 12 constitutes an element of the integral vision of man in the light of which the issues of birth regulation (and other issues of sexual ethics) are resolved.

While the doctrine of HV 12 is essentially an element of the greater anthropological vision of the encyclical, it holds a unique place among the other ideas expressed in the encyclical.[42] Ultimately, the doctrine of HV 12 stands at the focal point of the encyclical because its analysis of the conjugal act implicitly rejects the "totality" approach, the most prominent justification for acts of contraception. In one sense HV 12 is simply one among thirty-one other paragraphs in the encyclical. HV 12 does not stand out in terms of its language or placement within the encyclical. However, its significance within the encyclical derives from its place within the anthropological vision upon which the other teachings of the encyclical rest. The encyclical contains several specific teachings in the area of sexual morality, such as those

---

[41] Cf. John Paul II, *Discourse to Priests Participating in a Seminar on "Responsible Parenthood"*, September 17, 1983, in *Insegnamenti di Giovanni Paolo II*, 6, 2 (1983).

[42] Carlo Caffarra writes, "Everyone knows that one of the main points of H.V. is the affirming of an inseparable connection between the procreative and unitive meanings" ("Who Is Like the Lord, Our God?", in Smith, *Why "Humanae Vitae" Was Right*, p. 258). K. Wojtyla described the principle as "essenziale dal punto di vista della dottrina morale contentuta nel documento" (see "Visione", p. 135). Even some who doubt the veracity of the principle of inseparability acknowledge its importance for the encyclical: "The crucial point of the papal discussion . . . always returns to the 'inseparable connection' (Hanigan, *What Are They Saying*, p. 38). Cf. also Häring, "Inseparability" pp. 176–92.

concerning the immorality of contraception, man's freedom regarding his body, and the licitness of periodic continence. Fundamentally, each of these teachings depends upon the underlying anthropological vision of the encyclical. Therefore, inasmuch as HV 12 stands at the heart of the encyclical's anthropological vision, the doctrine of HV 12 implicitly relates to each of the encyclical's other teachings. Thus, the doctrine of HV 12 possesses great significance by virtue of its central place within the anthropology of the encyclical.

HV 12 as Doctrinal Development

The doctrine of HV 12 exemplifies doctrinal development insofar as it is innovative while also being grounded in ideas traditionally expressed by the Magisterium. Paul VI firmly grounds the theology of HV in ideas expressed by Pius XI, Pius XII, and the Second Vatican Council as well as more traditional sources. On the basis of these ideas, the Pope considers the issue of contraception and develops a theology of the conjugal act that advances the Church's understanding of these respective questions. While relying upon previously articulated dimensions of the Church's teaching on marriage and sexuality, HV gives these foundational ideas renewed significance by applying them specifically to the conjugal act considered as a human act of love. The doctrine of HV 12 presents a theology of the conjugal act that reflects the Church's effort to harmonize the intimate expression of conjugal love with moral requirements derived from the nature of the human person and the nature of marriage. As such, HV 12 continues the Church's effort to harmonize the juridical dimension of conjugal life with the personal dimensions of conjugal love. However, in addition to this renewed application of foundational concepts, HV 12 introduces an entirely new perspective to the Church's theology of the conjugal act through the notion of *meaning*. Yet, because the new perspective represented by "meaning" builds upon and intrinsically relates to elements of the Church's traditional description of the conjugal act, even in its novelty HV 12 recalls and depends upon traditional doctrines.

In considering the relation of HV 12 to the past magisterial pronouncements, it is interesting to note that the author refers to no source, either magisterial or non-magisterial, as a basis for the doctrine of HV 12. The encyclical contains forty-one footnotes, spanning documents from the Catechism of the Council of Trent to the documents of the Second Vatican Council, but no references appear in HV 12. Judging from the notes of the encyclical, the Pope does make an effort to recall the past magisterial teachings, but he refers to no past teaching in articulating the principle of inseparability in HV 12. Yet, the innovative character of HV 12 does not derive simply from the absence of references. Instead, HV 12 is innovative in that it describes the conjugal act from a new perspective relative to previous magisterial pronouncements. The lack of references bears witness to the novelty of the perspective taken by the author. However, insofar as the content of HV 12 depends upon and implicitly recalls traditional descriptions of the conjugal act, the novelty of HV 12 consists in a deeper penetration of the tradition rather than a move away from the tradition.

As indicated in HV 3, Pope Paul VI is concerned with the question of whether "the finality of procreation pertains to the ensemble of the conjugal life, rather than to single acts". In responding to this line of questioning in HV 12, Paul VI focuses on the essence and meaning of the conjugal act, relying upon principles of the Christian married life present in the works reviewed in chapter 1. For example, Paul VI recalls the fundamental principle of Pius XI's *Casti connubii* regarding the divine authorship of marriage. According to Pius XI, marriage did not emerge in the human community by chance or accident, as though through some unconscious evolution of natural forces. Nor is marriage merely a human institution created by the forces of human culture and society. Instead, marriage belongs to God's original plan for creation. Though marriage pertains to the intimate relationship between man and woman, the nature, ends, and laws of marriage are established by divine decree independently of the human will. Man cannot expand or limit the content of marriage because it is willed by God ontologically prior to man's participation in marriage as an institution. Paul VI explicitly recalls the divine authorship of marriage in HV 8,[43] and this doctrine also finds expression in HV 12 when Paul VI describes the indissoluble connection between the meanings of the conjugal act as *willed by God*. The indissoluble connection between the two meanings of the conjugal act arises neither from unconscious natural forces nor from the will of man. Instead, God wills the connection independently of (ontologically prior to) the intentions of man, and thus, it is "unable to be broken by man on his own initiative".[44]

While confirming marriage as a natural institution arising by divine decree, Pius XII promoted recognition of the relationship between conjugal love and procreation because some had denied the importance of procreation in a misguided attempt to promote the loving friendship involved in marriage. Indeed, a fundamental principle of the discourses

---

[43] HV 8: "Marriage is not, then, the effect of chance or the product of evolution of unconscious natural forces; it is the wise institution of the Creator to realize in mankind his design of love."

[44] HV 12.

of Pius XII concerned the inseparability of procreation and conjugal relations. This principle finds an obvious expression in HV 12. Pius XII affirmed that the proper place for procreation is in the conjugal relation of man and woman and condemned the practice of artificial fecundation. He also condemned genital acts intentionally devoid of their procreative potential. Pius XII promoted both the so-called "personal values" of the conjugal act and the good of procreation and sought to highlight the mutual relation between them. According to Pius XII, it is "never permissible to separate these different aspects so as to exclude positively either the aim of procreation or the conjugal relation".[45] However, his comments on this issue were primarily normative in nature, manifest in his condemnation of contraception and artificial fecundation. In contrast, HV 12 refers to the connection of procreation and the union of the spouses in descriptive rather than normative terms. Moreover, the descriptive character of HV 12 refers not only to its analysis of the conjugal act but also to the anthropological tenets to which it implicitly refers. On its most profound level, HV 12 affirms the personal nature of the body and the substantial unity of the human person. Thus, the doctrine of HV 12 approaches the connection between conjugal love and procreation from a different perspective from the teachings of Pius XII. Yet, the two cases are very much related because HV 12 articulates the anthropological principle that serves as the foundation for the normative statements of Pius XII.

HV 12 advances the teaching of Pius XI and Pius XII inasmuch as it reaffirms previously articulated principles in the context of an analysis of the conjugal act while also

[45] Pius XII, "Address to the Second World Congress on Fertility and Sterility, May 19, 1956", *AAS* (1956), p. 470.

referring to the anthropological foundations of these principles. Consequently, a concept of the conjugal act emerges in which God directs man to a specific expression of conjugal love, just as God determines the nature of marriage by inscribing it in the very being of man and woman. Since marriage and the marital act are inscribed by the Creator in human nature, man cannot reduce or expand either marriage or the intrinsic structure of the marital act, and this is why he cannot extract either of the two essential aspects of the act. For this reason man cannot break a connection that God has established. Though guided by the creative intentions of God, husband and wife remain the agents of the marital act, inasmuch as it is a human act that they freely choose to execute. Husband and wife are the subjects of the conjugal act, and its meaning regards their awareness as acting persons, but just as they cannot bring a marriage into being unless their intention is in conformity with the nature of marriage, neither do they perform the conjugal act unless their intention conforms to the nature of the conjugal act, which contains two indissolubly connected essential aspects.

The application of these principles, which had formerly been applied to marriage or married love in general, to the marital act advances the Church's teaching on the conjugal act because it positions the conjugal act within the requirements of conjugal love itself. Such a move not only precludes the so-called totality approach, to which the encyclical explicitly responds, but also signals the emergence of a theology of the conjugal act. Practically all Catholic theologians would admit that God has authored marriage in such a way that the union of the spouses is linked or connected to their procreative potential. Many would concede that conjugal love is ordered to procreation and thereby connected to it. Nevertheless, some dissenting theologians would argue that these truths need not be manifest in every sexual encounter of a couple in order for each of these encounters to be a *conjugal act*. This is the thrust of the argument that prefers to consider only the "totality" of the conjugal life. The totality argument acknowledges that every marriage must be open to procreation, but does not apply the same standard to each conjugal act. The doctrine of HV 12 rejects such an argument by teaching that each conjugal act is necessarily procreative and unitive in its very essence (ontological dimension) and its meaning (subjective dimension). Thus, the encyclical holds spouses' individual acts of conjugal love to the same standards that govern the conjugal life of the couple.

The value of HV 12 derives from its clarification that the conjugal act by its very definition must correspond to those same standards and principles that apply to marriage and conjugal love in general. As such, the conjugal act entails a complete union of persons, and it is ordered to procreation. Moreover, according to HV 12, the intrinsic relationship between procreation and spousal union in the conjugal act results from God's creative intention (is *willed by God*). Just as man must submit to God in accepting the structure, content, meaning, and complete reality of marriage, he must also accept from God the structure, content, meaning, and the whole reality of the marital act. If one considers the conjugal act as the corporal expression of marital consent, then it is not surprising that this act must express a complete, unreserved donation of each spouse to the other and a willingness on their part to collaborate with God in the transmission of human life. The clarification provided by HV 12 points to a specific theology of the conjugal act within the Church's theology of marriage.

In addition to containing a renewed application of previously articulated principles, HV 12 advances the Church's theology of the conjugal act by describing procreation and union as the meanings of the conjugal act, thus adding a relatively new perspective to the Church's analysis of the act. Prior to HV, the Magisterium and the theological tradition viewed and described marriage and the conjugal act in terms of the *goods* and the *ends* to which they naturally tend. In the context of a discussion of the conjugal act, the notions of good and end refer to the essence and fundamental structure of the act, identifying the sources of the goodness and intrinsic structure of the act. Among the goods and ends of marriage we find ideas that fundamentally correspond to procreation and union, and, thus, HV 12 describes procreation and union as the essential aspects of the act. The fundamental structure and essential content of the conjugal act derive from laws inscribed in the very being of man and woman. Viewing the conjugal act in terms of its essential aspects and fundamental structure leads to a description of the act in its ontological dimension. Prior to HV, descriptions of the conjugal act primarily referred to this ontological dimension in articulating its objective structure and value.

While recalling the ontological dimension (the intimate structure) of the conjugal act, HV 12 includes an additional perspective for viewing the conjugal act represented by the term "meaning". The term "meaning" refers to what Pope John Paul II has described as the subjective dimension of the conjugal act in contrast to the ontological dimension.[46] Inasmuch as procreation and union are both the meanings and the essential aspects of the act, the subjective and ontological dimensions of the act are directly related; however, they represent diverse modes of describing the act. Whereas procre-

[46] Cf. John Paul II, General Audience of July 11, 1984.

ation and union are the ends and goods of the conjugal act with regard to volition, these two essential aspects become the meanings of the conjugal act with regard to the awareness or experience of the spouses. By virtue of human awareness or consciousness, the essential aspects of the ontological dimension enter into the subjective dimension, consequently acquiring the character of meaning. Thus, by describing the conjugal act in terms of its meanings, HV 12 adds the perspective of human awareness to the notion of human volition. However, procreation and union are the meanings of the conjugal act to the extent that the spouses intend them as ends because spouses can have an authentic experience only of that which is really taking place. Moreover, due to the interdependence of these diverse modes of describing the conjugal act, an emphasis on the subjective dimension never displaces or discounts the importance of the ontological dimension of the act. Though describing the conjugal act in innovative terms, HV 12 grounds itself in the traditional description of the conjugal act and relies upon that tradition for its coherency.

2. *PERSONA HUMANA*

The Congregation for the Doctrine of the Faith promulgated *Persona humana* in 1975, a time when the full effects of the so-called sexual revolution were being manifested in society. Concerned with certain questions of sexual ethics, PH aims to articulate the moral principles of sexual behavior found in the nature of the human person. The value of the document for the present study derives from the emphasis that it places on the role of the truth regarding sexuality inscribed in human nature as the objective criterion for action in the sexual sphere. Additionally, the document clarifies the relationship between human nature and the intentions of the person. Within the framework of PH, human nature is not simply available as a possible criterion upon which to judge and order our actions; instead, it places demands on us. Thus, the document refers to the "true moral exigencies of the human person" and "the authentic moral exigencies of human nature".[47] Because these requirements are grounded in human nature, they are universal and immutable. In the sexual sphere these exigencies are manifested in the finality of human sexuality, which directs man to marriage as the only adequate context for the exercise of the sexual faculty.

As the opening paragraphs indicate, PH was issued in response to the rapidly declining societal standards of sexual conduct. This decline in moral standards centered upon a denial of universally valid criteria upon which moral judgments could be made. Hence, in its response to this situation, PH directs the reader to the values innate in human nature,[48] so as to promote true human dignity. According to PH, "there can be no true promotion of man's dignity unless the essential order of his nature is respected."[49] Human intelligence discovers moral principles within man himself. Thus, while man can gain greater insight into the moral life, any evolution of morals "must be kept within the limits imposed by the immutable principles based upon every human person's constitutive elements and essential relations—elements and relations which transcend historical contin-

[47] Congregation for the Doctrine of the Faith, *Persona humana* (January 22, 1976), 2 and 4 (hereafter abbreviated as PH).

[48] PH 3.

[49] PH 4.

gency".[50] These fundamental principles are contained in the eternal, objective, and universal law "whereby God directs and governs the entire universe and all the ways of the human community, by a plan conceived in wisdom and love".[51] Man discovers the divine law inscribed within his own person (written on his heart). Thus, the principles and norms that govern man's sexual activity "in no way owe their origin to a certain type of culture, but rather to knowledge of the divine law and human nature".[52]

Because these principles are found in human nature itself and are part of the divine law, they are objective and universal. PH affirms "the existence of immutable laws inscribed in the constitutive elements of human nature and which are revealed to be identical for all beings endowed with reason".[53] The laws that govern human sexual activity do not change, because they are "inscribed" in humanity itself. A person would have to cease to be human in order no longer to be bound under these norms. Likewise, no human person exists (or could exist) outside the jurisdiction of this law, because it is not the product of culture or historical circumstances. Instead, the norms of sexual behavior inscribed in the constitutive elements of human nature are identical for everyone endowed with human nature. The immutability and universality of the principles of sexual ethics derive from their being rooted in human nature (itself essentially unchanging) and the divine eternal law that governs the entire universe.

---

[50] Ibid.

[51] Second Vatican Council, *Dignitatis humanae*, 3.

[52] PH 5.

[53] PH 4.

In the area of sexual ethics the laws inscribed into human nature are the finalities of the sexual faculty itself. PH 5 contains an interesting exposition of the conjugal morality of *Gaudium et spes* that indicates the Church's understanding of the nature of the human person as moral criterion for conjugal morality. GS 51 referred to the need to evaluate questions of conjugal morality on the basis of objective criteria, "criteria drawn from the nature of the human person and human action, criteria which respect the total meaning of mutual self-giving and human procreation in the context of true love". According to PH, in the doctrine of the Council the criteria that concern human sexuality in marriage "are based upon the finality of the specific function of sexuality".[54] The sexual faculty is inherently ordered to self-donation and human procreation in the context of true love, and this finality serves as the principle criterion upon which to judge the moral goodness of sexual acts. The moral goodness of "the acts proper to conjugal life, acts which are ordered according to true human dignity", is determined in light of the finality of the sexual faculty, for "it is respect for its finality that ensures the moral goodness of this act."[55] Thus, according to this section of PH, in the order of sexual ethics there is a correspondence between "true human dignity", "the nature of the human person and his acts", and "the finality of the specific function of sexuality". The true dignity of the human person is promoted by acts that respect the essential order of the nature of the person, and this essential order of nature is manifested in the finalities of sexuality itself. "Respect for its finality" ensures the moral goodness of the conjugal act because respect for this finality

[54] PH 5.

[55] Ibid.

is a respect for the essential order of man's nature, which in turn was created in wisdom and love. The normative value of human nature and the finality of the sexual faculty lie in their divine origin.

What is the finality of the sexual faculty? In one sense mutual self-giving and human procreation in the context of true love constitute the finality of the sexual faculty. Yet, as PH concludes, more concisely the finality of the sexual faculty is *marriage*. Thus, "the use of the sexual function has its true meaning and moral rectitude only in true marriage."[56] From the outset of the document, PH indicates the significance sexuality possesses in the view of the Church: it is a fundamental aspect of the person that gives to each person characteristics "on the biological, psychological and spiritual levels".[57] Sexuality makes each person either a man or a woman and fundamentally refers to the masculine or feminine personality of the individual. Therefore, in referring to the finality of sexuality, PH refers to the complementary finality of masculinity and femininity as well as the finality of the sexual organs themselves. The presence of sexuality in the human person relates inherently to marriage, as evidenced by the creation accounts. In turning to the finality of sexuality, PH necessarily arrives at marriage itself. This methodology produces the conclusion that "every genital act must be within the framework of marriage."[58] Only in marriage can the genital encounter of man and woman "preserve the full sense of mutual self-giving and human procreation in the context of true love".[59]

[56] Ibid.

[57] PH 1.

[58] PH 7.

[59] GS 51.

3. MAGISTERIAL TEACHING OF POPE JOHN PAUL II

Pope John Paul II has made an unparalleled contribution to the Church's (and the world's) understanding and appreciation of marriage and the family. Certainly, in the context of this study I can provide only a limited summary of the main ideas expressed by the Pope. John Paul II's most significant contributions to the study of marriage and sexuality result from the manner in which he has clarified many of the anthropological concepts underlying the Church's previous teachings while also examining these concepts and their implications with unequaled insight and penetration.[60] In particular, the Holy Father has developed and deepened our understanding of the anthropological principles underlying Catholic sexual ethics and the Catholic concept of the con-

[60] For a good overview of John Paul II's contribution to anthropology, consult: Kenneth Schmitz, *At the Center of the Human Drama* (Washington, D.C.: Catholic University of America Press, 1993); John Saward, *Christ Is the Answer: The Christ-Centered Teaching of Pope John Paul II* (New York: Alba House, 1995); Ronald Lawler, *The Christian Personalism of John Paul II* (Chicago: Franciscan Herald Press, 1982); María José Franquet Casas, *Persona, Acción y Libertad: Las Clavas de la Antropología de Karol Wojtyla* (Pamplona: Ediciones Universidad de Navarra, 1996); and R. Buttiglione, *Il pensiero di Karol Wojtyla* (Milan: Jaca Books, 1982). For a review of the manner in which the Pope's anthropological positions enter into discussions of marriage and sexuality, consult: Mary Shivanandan, *Crossing the Threshold of Love* (Washington, D.C.: Catholic University of America Press, 1999); William May, "The Sanctity of Human Life, Marriage and the Family in the Thought of Pope John Paul II", *Annales Theologici* 2:1 (1988); Smith, *"Humanae Vitae"*, pp. 230–65; Francisco Gil Hellín and Angel Rodríguez Luño, "Il Fondamento Antropologico della *Humanae Vitae* nel Magistero di Giovanni Paolo II", in *"Humanae vitae": 20 anni dopo*; Ronald Modras, "Pope John Paul II's Theology of the Body", in *John Paul II and Moral Theology*, eds. Charles Curran and Richard McCormick (New York: Paulist Press, 1998); John Crosby, "The Personalism of John Paul II as the Basis of His Approach to *Humanae Vitae*", *Anthropotes*, vol. 5, no. 1 (May 1989); and Richard Hogan, "A Theology of the Body", *Fidelity* 1 (December 1981).

jugal act. The timing of this development is significant because contemporary man often experiences a philosophical "allergic reaction" to ethical systems that even appear to guide human choice on the basis of principles extrinsic to the person. By developing his anthropological vision and by grounding Catholic sexual ethics in the identity and vocation of the human person (understood in the light of Christ), John Paul II eliminates many of the false dichotomies (such as that between nature/person, law/freedom, and truth/conscience) that many contemporary authors attempt to insert into sexual ethics.

Many of the most profound and significant aspects of John Paul II's theological anthropology result from his reflection on the creation accounts in the book of Genesis.[61] However, while John Paul II is able to discover much about man and his vocation through a reflection on the creation account of man and woman, he never loses sight of the fact that a full understanding of man and his vocation is possible only in the light of the Person of Jesus Christ.[62] In fact, even the Pope's turning to Genesis is christological inasmuch as it follows from the example of Christ in the Gospel.[63] Yet, from John Paul II's perspective it is not enough for man to see the example of Christ and to hear his words; man understands himself by *entering* the mystery of Christ. According to the Pope,

[61] John Paul II, General Audience of September 5, 1979–April 2, 1980.

[62] Cf. John Paul II, encyclical letter *Redemptor hominis*, 10 (hereafter abbreviated as RH).

[63] Cf. John Paul II, General Audience of September 5, 1979. On the basis of Christ's words in the Gospel of Matthew (19:3–9) and the Gospel of Mark (10:1–6) the Holy Father turns his attention to "the beginning", to the creation accounts of Genesis as a means of understanding marriage in terms of the nature of the human person.

> The man who wishes to understand himself thoroughly—and not just in accordance with immediate, partial, often superficial, and even illusory standards and measures of his being—he must with his unrest, uncertainty and even his weakness and sinfulness, with his life and death, draw near to Christ. He must, so to speak, enter into Him with all of his own self, he must "appropriate" and assimilate the whole reality of the Incarnation and Redemption in order to find himself.[64]

This interpretation of *Gaudium et spes* 22, in which the Council affirms that "only in the mystery of the Word does the mystery of man take on light", helps us to understand that Christ's revelation of man and his most high calling takes place by *participation* in the mystery. Man receives a fuller understanding of himself when he "assimilates" the reality of the Incarnation and Redemption in himself. Christ fully reveals man to himself and brings to light his most high calling by opening a mystery into which man can enter and be "newly created".[65] According to the mystery of Christ, the basis of personal communion is self-sacrificial love, a pouring out of oneself for the sake of others.

John Paul II's complex and profound anthropological vision seems to center on the idea of self-actualization through action in conformity with the nature, identity, and vocation of the human person. In a sense, then, John Paul II's anthropology calls man to *become* what or who he is by accepting and living out the identity and vocation that God has inscribed in his very being. The development of this central idea hinges upon certain fundamental anthropological principles that provide the rationale for the development of man's

[64] RH 10.

[65] Ibid.

identity through freedom. These fundamental principles revolve around the idea that man possesses a God-given identity that can be appropriated (through conscience) and developed (through free choice). For John Paul II, man's identity is inscribed into his very being and reveals itself in the "nuptial meaning of the body" when the body is understood as a constitutive part of the person. In addition to revealing the "fundamental characteristic of personal existence" (man's identity), the body possesses a sacramentality that manifests in the world the mystery of God and his plan for creation. These ideas converge to create an image of human life in which God and man are co-subjects in both the perfection of man as a person and in the manifestation of God's love in creation. In the context of and in the light of this anthropological vision a profound theology of the conjugal act emerges, in which the act itself is seen as a specific moment for man and woman to become who they are. In my review of John Paul II's teachings, I focus principally upon the relationship between freedom and conscience in the development of man's identity and the relevance of these fundamental principles for a theology of the conjugal act.

John Paul II's Vision of Man

Pope John Paul II explicitly addresses the call "become what you are" to the family in his apostolic exhortation *Familiaris consortio*.[66] According to John Paul II, "The family finds in the plan of God the Creator and Redeemer not only its *identity*, what it *is*, but also its *mission*, what it can and should

[66] Cf. *Familiaris consortio*, November 22, 1981, 17 (hereafter abbreviated as FC).

do."[67] Thus, the Holy Father identifies two distinct yet related dimensions of the family: what the family is and what the family can and should do. Both of these dimensions are found in the plan of God, that is, they represent the creative intentions of God for family life. In this plan, the family "finds within itself a summons that cannot be ignored" or a call to act and undertake a "dynamic and existential development of what it is".[68] In turn this dynamic and existential development is derived from the nature of the family itself. Therefore, both the identity and the mission of the family are interrelated because the mission is derived from the identity (within the identity of the family there is a call or summons to the mission) and because the fulfillment of its mission develops and perfects the family's identity. The dynamic and existential development of the family proceeds according to the nature of the family, but only inasmuch as the family responds to its mission in action.

The call "become what you are" also applies to each human person. Each human person has a certain identity or essence that also entails a mission, or more properly a "vocation".[69] As in the case of the identity and mission of the family, the essence of the human person and the vocation of man are distinct yet interrelated concepts. The very concept of the human person entails reference to "man's proper and primordial nature".[70] Each human person shares in this common nature by his very creation. Yet, through free action man is also able to "create" himself and determine the type

[67] Ibid.

[68] Ibid.

[69] John Paul II distinguishes "who man is" from "who he should be" through action. See, for example, his General Audience of February 13, 1980.

[70] VS 50.

of person he will be. In other words, human acts "do not produce merely a change outside of man but, to the extent that they are deliberate choices, they give moral definition to the very person who performs them, determining his profound spiritual traits."[71] Self-determination is a hallmark of the person and allows for the development of character over and above the performance of good and evil acts. However, in the light of John Paul II's doctrine on freedom, law, and conscience in *Veritatis splendor*, it is apparent that man's self-determination does not mean the ability to determine himself in a wholly autonomous way (that is, apart from the law).[72] Instead, self-determination consists in the dynamic and existential development of human nature, which entails a final end and a vocation (indicated by the law written on man's heart) that direct man to God himself.[73]

Self-determination properly understood signifies the ability to choose for the sake of an end or the possession of free will. Essentially, self-determination is the ability to be the source of the "dynamic and existential development" of the person. It does not require the person to determine the course or form of this development; that is, the person does not

[71] VS 71.

[72] I consider the relationship between freedom, law, and conscience in greater detail in section 2 of chapter 4. For further reading on the teachings of John Paul II in *Veritatis splendor*, consult: Ramón Lucas Lucas, ed., *"Veritatis splendor": Testo Integrale e Commento Filosofico-Teologico* (Milan: Edizione San Paolo, 1994); J. A. DiNoia and Romanus Cessario, eds., *"Veritatis Splendor" and the Renewal of Moral Theology* (Chicago: Midwest Theological Forum, 1999); Giovanni Russo, ed., *"Veritatis Splendor": Genesi, elaborazione, significato*, 2d ed. (Rome: Edizioni Dehoniane, 1995); and Curran and McCormick, *John Paul II*. Cf. also William May, *An Introduction to Moral Theology*, rev. ed. (Huntington, Ind.: Our Sunday Visitor, 1994).

[73] Cf. VS 35.

have to be the source of the end to which the development is ordered. Instead, another can determine the end, and, so long as the choice of whether or not to order each act to the end is left to each individual person, self-determination remains intact. In such a case, the person, in accepting the end determined by the other, makes the end his own. Such is the case with the human person. God determines the final end of man (in his very creation of man), as well as the path to be followed in its attainment (the natural moral law), but man freely chooses to direct himself to this end in each action deliberately performed. God directs man's "dynamic and existential development" through the answer he has given to the question of goodness: the natural moral law.[74]

While God directs man's existential development, the human person still remains the source of that development and, in doing so, remains *free* without being *wholly autonomous*. Indeed, God rules or governs man as he rules every creature, but he gives man a participation in this rule through the human powers of intellect and will. Thus, we can speak of "*theonomy*, or *participated theonomy*, since man's free obedience to God's law effectively implies that human reason and human will participate in God's wisdom and providence".[75] Between the extremes of *heteronomy* and *absolute autonomy* (or absolute sovereignty) rests the idea of *participated theonomy*, in which God rules man while preserving a genuine moral autonomy of the human person. God's rule over man is not a heteronomy, because God accomplishes this rule

[74] "Only God can answer the question about the good, because he is the Good. But God has already given an answer to this question: he did so *by creating man and ordering him* with his wisdom and love to his final end, through the law which he inscribed in his heart, the natural law" (VS 12).

[75] VS 41.

through the natural moral law that is inscribed in man himself by the Creator. According to John Paul II, "The rightful autonomy of the practical reason means that man possesses in himself his own law, received from the Creator." [76] In this case, the law must be considered "an expression of divine wisdom: by submitting to the law, freedom submits to the truth of creation".[77] Freedom and self-determination properly conceived view God and man as cooperators in the perfection of each person.

Participated theonomy is possible because God and man meet in the heart of the person, in his moral conscience. Conscience plays an indispensable role in the authentic existential development of each person because in the moral conscience "the relationship between man's freedom and God's law is most deeply lived out." [78] God orders man to his final end through the natural moral law inscribed in man. Conscience brings this law to bear on the actions of the person in his particular situation. As the Pope explains, "whereas the natural law discloses the objective and universal demands of the moral good, conscience is the application of the law to a particular case; this application of the law thus becomes an inner dictate for the individual, a summons to do what is good in this particular situation." [79] In formulating "the proximate norm of personal morality",[80] conscience does not determine what is good, but instead it bears witness to the truth and is "the witness of God himself, whose voice and

[76] VS 40.
[77] VS 41.
[78] VS 54.
[79] VS 59.
[80] VS 60.

judgement penetrate the depths of man's soul".[81] By speaking to man in his conscience, God

> cares for man not "from without", through the laws of physical nature, but "from within" through reason, which, by its natural knowledge of God's eternal law, is consequently able to show man the right direction to take in his free actions. In this way God calls man to participate in his own providence, since he desires to guide the world—not only the world of nature but also the world of human persons—through man himself, through man's reasonable and responsible care.[82]

The human person possesses the ability to recognize the truth of creation (the eternal law) and the truth about himself and also the ability to make this truth his own in the sense of conforming his actions to this truth. Through conscience the universal truth about man becomes the personal truth for the individual. In the words of John Paul II, "The acting subject personally assimilates the truth contained in the law. He appropriates this truth of his being and makes it his own by his acts and the corresponding virtues."[83] By this act of appropriation or assimilation, the identity of man (who man is) encounters and influences the mission or vocation of man (what man can and should do). And because the mission/vocation is derived from the identity, it is possible to read the one through the other. Thus, in a sense the vocation of man reveals his identity.

It is interesting to note that for Pope John Paul II the vocation of man and the mission of the family revolve around

---

[81] VS 58.

[82] VS 43.

[83] VS 52. Note that the Pope also uses the terms "appropriation" and "assimilation" in reference to the mystery of Christ in the Incarnation and Redemption in RH 10.

the same profound reality: love. In order to discover its mission the family must turn to God's creative intentions so as "to attain self-knowledge and self-realization in accordance with the inner truth not only of what it is but also of what it does in history".[84] When John Paul II reflects on the creative intentions of God, he sees the family as a community of life and love, and so the mission of the family is "to become more and more what it is, that is to say, a community of life and love".[85] Thus, the Pope concludes, "we must say that the essence and role of the family are in the final analysis specified by love." [86] The family finds in love its "inner principle", "permanent power", and "final goal".[87] The specific mission of the family is "to guard, reveal, and communicate love", and in doing so it reflects and sacramentally represents the love of God for humanity and Christ for the Church.[88]

Man, too, finds his essence and vocation in love. How important is love for the human person? In his first encyclical, John Paul II reminded the world, "Man cannot live without love. He remains a being that is incomprehensible for himself, his life is senseless, if love is not revealed to him, if he does not encounter love, if he does not experience it and make it his own, if he does not participate intimately in it." [89] Man is incomprehensible apart from love because both his origin and his end are love. According to John Paul II, God, who is love, calls man into existence "through love" and "for love" and, by creating man in his image, has

[84] FC 17.

[85] Ibid. See also, Vatican Council II, GS 48.

[86] FC 17.

[87] FC 18.

[88] FC 17.

[89] RH 10.

"inscribed in the humanity of man and woman the vocation, and thus the capacity and responsibility, of love and communion".[90] "Love is therefore the fundamental and innate vocation of every human person."[91] The vocation to love necessarily entails the sincere gift of self, for to "love means to give and receive something which can neither be bought nor sold, but only given freely and mutually."[92] Thus, the vocation of man and the mission of the family are inherently linked because they both revolve around the call to love and communion. Both entail a communion achieved by the gift of self, inclusive of all that is human.

Man's vocation is inscribed in his very nature and manifests itself especially in human sexuality, the existence of masculinity and femininity. As is well known, a central component of John Paul II's anthropology is his reflection on the creation account and the "theology of the body" that he developed on the basis of this reflection. In the anthropology of John Paul II the body "belongs to the structure of the personal subject"[93] because man is "an incarnate spirit, that is a soul which expresses itself in a body and a body informed by an immortal spirit".[94] The body expresses "the person in his ontological and existential concreteness" or "the human personal 'self'".[95] As a constitutive element of the person, the structure or design of the body tells us something about the nature of personhood. Sexuality is an outstanding feature of the human body and reveals, especially in light of the cre-

---

[90] FC 11.

[91] Ibid.

[92] John Paul II, *Letter to Families*, 11 (hereafter abbreviated as LF).

[93] General Audience of October 31, 1979.

[94] FC 11.

[95] General Audience of December 19, 1979.

ation account, an "other-directedness" or an ordination to communion. According to John Paul II, "The body, which expresses femininity and masculinity, manifests the reciprocity and communion of persons."[96] The body tells us that "human beings, created as man and woman, were created for unity."[97] In creating a helper for Adam, God gave him Eve, in whom Adam recognized one like himself through her body. In many ways the female body is unlike the male body, but, just like the male body, its sexuality manifests an other-directedness (the ordination to a complementary other); that is, it possesses a "nuptial meaning". For John Paul II this part of the creation account reveals "the very essence of personhood": the need to exist *with* and *for* someone.[98] The nuptial meaning of the body expresses the ordination of the person to love and communion through self-donation (for the Pope self-donation necessitates self-mastery or self-possession because one cannot give that which he does not possess).[99] Ultimately, this is the need for love described by the Pope in *Redemptor hominis* 10. Thus, the "very essence of personhood" and the vocation of man are bound to love and communion.

Human sexuality is inextricably linked to the essence of personhood and the vocation of man, both as the revelation and manifestation of the ordination to love and communion and as the means by which this ordination is fulfilled. The complementarity of masculinity and femininity expresses the other-directedness of the human person and points to

[96] General Audience of January 9, 1980.

[97] General Audience of November 21, 1979.

[98] General Audience of January 9, 1980.

[99] General Audience of January 9, 1980. As he commonly does, here the Pope is building upon the Second Vatican Council, GS 24.

the need for each person to make a sincere gift of self. Moreover, sexuality is also the means by which "man and woman give themselves to one another through the acts which are proper and exclusive to spouses."[100] The communion to which man and woman are ordered relies upon the complementarity between masculinity and femininity or "sinks its roots in the natural complementarity that exists between man and woman"[101] (this is why God gave Adam a woman rather than another man as a "helpmate"). Sexual complementarity is most visible in the manner in which the male body and the female literally "fit together" and physically complement each other precisely with respect to the sexual organs. The complementarity of man and woman, however, extends beyond the physical level, because sexuality is "by no means something purely biological, but concerns the innermost being of the human person as such".[102] In other words, the complementarity of masculinity and femininity exists "on the biological, psychological and spiritual levels".[103] Because the male and female bodies complement each other, a physical union between them is possible. However, because "the body expresses the person" and because sexual complementarity extends beyond the physical level, the physical union of man and woman can and should be "the sign and fruit of a total personal self-giving" in which the whole person is present.[104] Yet, "the only 'place' where this self-giving in its whole truth is made possible is marriage, the covenant of conjugal love freely and consciously chosen,

---

[100] FC 11.
[101] FC 19.
[102] FC 11.
[103] PH 1.
[104] FC 11.

whereby man and woman accept the intimate community of life and love willed by God himself."[105] In other words, the physical, sexual union of man and woman is the fruit and sign of a total personal gift only when it is the conjugal act (that act proper and exclusive to spouses). Thus, by beginning from John Paul II's anthropological perspective concerning the meaning of personhood we have arrived at the conjugal act and are able to view it in its proper relation to the essence and vocation of the human person.

The Conjugal Act

In the theology of John Paul II the conjugal act takes on a greater anthropological significance than had been previously articulated by the Church. Previous magisterial pronouncements primarily described the conjugal act in terms of its relationship to the institution of marriage and to the conjugal love of husband and wife. In such a context, the conjugal act represents the consummation of matrimonial consent and the embodiment of the love of husband and wife. Certainly, this remains true within John Paul II's doctrine on marriage and sexuality. He goes farther, however, by linking these ideas to the essence and vocation of the human person. The essence of personhood centers on the sincere gift of self in love, the capacity and responsibility to exist with and for another. The vocation of man refers to the dynamic and existential development of this essence. Man's identity as the image and likeness of God calls him to love and communion, self-gift to a complementary other. As John Paul II indicates, the gift of self is uniquely (though not

[105] Ibid.

exclusively) possible in the conjugal act because sexuality is the means by which the gift is made in its whole truth.[106] While every man and woman fully realizes himself or herself through the sincere gift of self, "the moment of conjugal union constitutes a very particular expression of this" because "it is then that man and woman, in the truth of their masculinity and femininity, become a mutual gift to each other." [107] However, the physical union in the conjugal act is the sign and fruit of a total personal self-giving when its essence and meaning are preserved "in conformity with the objective truth of the man and woman who give themselves".[108] Properly undertaken, the conjugal act allows man to live his innate vocation in a truly profound and comprehensive way.

Read in this light, the doctrine of the indissoluble connection between procreation and union, as articulated by Paul VI in HV 12, has a twofold anthropological significance. The indissoluble connection between procreation and union relates to the essence and vocation of man inasmuch as its preservation allows man to achieve a sincere gift of self in love. However, it is also anthropological in that the connection itself results from and affirms the nature of the human person as a unity of body and soul. According to John Paul II, the indissoluble connection between the unitive and procreative meanings of the conjugal act affirms that the body is a constitutive part of the person, that it belongs to the *being* of the person, not to his *having*.[109]

---

[106] Cf. LF 12.

[107] Ibid.

[108] Ibid.

[109] John Paul II, *Discourse to Priests*, 2: "La connessione inscindibile, di cui parla l'enciclica, fra il significato unitivo e il significato procreativo, inscritti nell'atto coniugale, ci fa capire che il corpo è parte costitutiva dell'uomo, che esso appartiene all'essere della persona e non al suo avere."

Pope John Paul II has repeatedly affirmed the personal nature of the body (that is, that it is a constitutive part of the person), and his doctrine in this regard represents one of his most important contributions to the Church's teaching on marriage and sexuality. Throughout this century the teachings of the Church have referred to man's limited dominion with regard to the human body, but the reasoning behind this doctrine was not fully expressed. However, John Paul II clarifies the source of the respect due to the human body and its finalities. The human body is not merely a material possession of the person but rather a constitutive part of the person. The human person exists as a unity of body and soul, and the human body enters into man's very subjectivity.[110] Because of this unity, the body expresses the person; that is, "in the body and through the body, one touches the person himself in his concrete reality." [111] For this reason, the Pope rejects a view of the body that reduces it to a "raw datum" or something extrinsic to the person.[112] By virtue of its substantial union with the soul, the body and its finalities must be respected.[113]

John Paul II's theology of the body has direct implications for a theology of the conjugal act and for an understanding of the indissoluble connection between the two meanings of the act. While the conjugal act is the act in which man and woman give themselves to one another by virtue of their sexuality, it is a sign and fruit of a total personal self-giving

---

[110] Cf. General Audience of October 31, 1979.

[111] "Discourse to the Members of the 35th General Assembly of the World Medical Association", October 29, 1983, *AAS* 76 (1984), p. 393.

[112] Cf. VS 48.

[113] This theology of the body is related to, and in some sense derived from, fundamental doctrines of the Christian faith such as the resurrection of the body after death or the principles of sacramentology.

only when "the whole person, including the temporal dimension, is present".[114] If either the man or woman "were to withhold something or reserve the possibility of deciding otherwise in the future, by this very fact he or she would not be giving totally".[115] Nothing that constitutes the being of the spouses can be excluded from the conjugal act if the total character of the donation is to be preserved.[116] Because the body is a constitutive part of the person (that is, "belongs to the being of the person, not his having"), total personal union cannot take place without incorporating the body and its finalities into the gift of self. In other words, the bodily dimension of sexuality must be not only the *context* (or means) of the gift of self but also part of the *content* of the gift. The gift of self does not take place through the body as if the body were not also the self, as if it were some independent medium at the disposal of the man and woman. Instead, the gift of self is "communicated" through the body and includes the body. An inherent and central aspect of bodily sexuality is its potential for fertility. Therefore, personal union is possible only when the fertility of the body (with its limitations and according to its intrinsic structure) is incorporated into the gift of self. This is the basis for the indissoluble connection between procreation and union in the conjugal act; personal union is impossible without an openness to fertility.

---

[114] FC 11.

[115] Ibid.

[116] Cf. John Paul II, "Message to the Centre for Research and Study on the Natural Regulation of Fertility", *L'Osservatore Romano* (English ed.), March 11, 1998, p. 2: "The truth of this act [the conjugal act] stems from its being an expression of the spouses' reciprocal personal giving, a giving that can only be total since the person is one and indivisible. In the act that expresses their love, spouses are called to make a reciprocal gift of themselves to each other in the totality of their person: nothing that is part of their being can be excluded from the act."

The Pope's approach to the conjugal act via the theology of the body allows him to make a profound and innovative analysis of contraception. Because conjugal union requires an openness to fertility, contraception "leads not only to a refusal to be open to life but also to a falsification of the inner truth of conjugal love, which is called to give itself in personal totality".[117] Contraception expresses an objective refusal to give oneself to the other. Since conjugal union is not possible except through a sincere gift of self, the refusal to procreate (which is the refusal to give oneself) precludes any possibility for conjugal union between man and woman. However, in light of John Paul II's theology of the body this loss of union takes on new moral significance. Even in the case of contracepted intercourse, "the innate language [of the body] that expresses the total and reciprocal self-giving of husband and wife" remains, but it is "overlaid, through contraception, by an objectively contradictory language, namely that of not giving oneself totally to the other".[118] In genital intercourse, the body expresses a total personal gift of self in the name of the person; it speaks for the person "in his name and with his personal authority".[119] In contracepted intercourse, the person "states" something, in and through the language of the body, that in fact is not true. The body bespeaks gift and union when in fact the person has negated both of these in the choice to contracept. Therefore, on the basis of John Paul II's theological anthropology, the withholding of one's capacity to procreate negates the gift of self, precludes personal union, and amounts to a sexual "lie" in the language of the body.

[117] FC 32.

[118] Ibid.

[119] General Audience of January 26, 1983.

On the other hand, the practice of periodic continence preserves both the gift of self and the personal union characteristic of the conjugal act because the couple acts according to the plan of God and without manipulation or alteration.[120] Thus, we come to understand that "the positive will of avoiding children"[121] does not negate the gift of self or preclude personal union. Instead, the manipulation and alteration of the body (and hence the self) entailed in contraception makes union impossible. Contraception amounts to a withholding of one's procreative potential, or a destruction of the body's inherent fertility, whereas periodic continence amounts to a giving of one's procreative potential on its own terms and an acceptance of the body's natural (that is, inherent) periods of infertility (at least in the case of the woman). Only from the perspective of "an integral vision of man" is the difference between natural, inherent infertility and unnatural, coerced infertility visible and comprehensible. When the human body is seen as a constitutive part of the person, the destruction or manipulation of the body's fertility results in a destruction of conjugal union between man and woman. Another view of the body, one that reduces the human body to a raw datum, devoid of any inherent meaning and moral value,[122] yields a different conclusion. Thus, within John Paul II's theological perspective, the difference between contraception and periodic continence "involves in the final analysis two irreconcilable concepts of the human person and human sexuality".[123]

[120] Cf. FC 32.
[121] HV 16.
[122] Cf. VS 48.
[123] FC 32.

In addition to lending itself to this type of analysis of contraception, John Paul II's theological anthropology yields a specific theology of the conjugal act. Many of the main tenets of John Paul II's anthropology are directly applicable to the conjugal act because the conjugal act represents a unique moment in the "dynamic and existential development" of man's identity as a person. As with any human act (*actus humanus*), the very possibility of the conjugal act is dependent on man's freedom and conscience, the ability to be the source of a free, conscious act. In light of the doctrine of theonomy, a true conjugal act must represent an acceptance of and obedience to the law of God inscribed in the very nature of the human person. The freedom implied by the conjugal act entails a submission to "the truth of creation" on the part of man and woman in such a way that they participate in Gods law by making this truth their own. Such a freedom is possible only to the extent that the person "assimilates the truth contained in the law" and "appropriates this truth of his being and makes it his own by his acts and corresponding virtues".[124] Authentic freedom requires man to participate with God in his own rule and necessitates the appropriation of God's law on the part of the acting person. Herein lies the indispensable role of conscience. Only through conscience can the universal, objective law become the "inner dictate for the individual"[125] or the "proximate norm of personal morality".[126] Regarding the conjugal act, man and woman must appropriate that aspect of God's law which is inscribed in human sexuality (expressed in the nuptial meaning of the body) and thus the ontological dimension of the conjugal act itself.

[124] VS 52.
[125] VS 59.
[126] VS 60.

In analyzing the act itself, John Paul II considers the conjugal act in terms of two distinct yet related dimensions: the *ontological dimension* and the *subjective and psychological dimension*.[127] The ontological dimension of the act corresponds to what HV 12 describes as the "fundamental structure" of the act manifest in laws written into the nature of man and woman as sexual persons. The ontological dimension of the act, then, refers to the essence or "the nature" of the act.[128] God is the original author of this dimension of the conjugal act inasmuch as it pertains to the law "that man possesses in himself"[129] or the "laws inscribed in the very being of man and woman".[130] In other words, the intrinsic structure of the act pertains to the natural moral law and is "an expression of divine wisdom".[131] The nature of the act in a certain sense precedes the moment of human choice because it is inscribed in the very being of man and woman; it is the finality of human sexuality. The structure of the act is best understood in terms of the two essential aspects, the unitive and procreative, that the act "safeguards" or in terms of the fact that the structure unites husband and wife and capacitates them for the generation of new lives.[132] Just as the objective universal law becomes the proximate norm of personal morality through the conscience, so too the ontological dimension (the nature or essential aspects) of the conjugal act enters the subjective dimension and becomes the meaning of the

[127] Cf. General Audience of July 11, 1984.

[128] Ibid.

[129] VS 40.

[130] HV 12.

[131] VS 41.

[132] Cf. HV 12.

act when it is "carried over into the conscience and decisions of the acting parties".[133]

John Paul II identifies the "subjective and psychological dimension" of the conjugal act with what HV 12 refers to as the procreative and unitive "meanings" or "significances" of the conjugal act.[134] These two "meanings" of the act are intrinsically linked to the ontological dimension of the act because "the fundamental structure (that is, the nature) of the marriage act constitutes the necessary basis for an adequate reading of the two significances."[135] The ontological dimension of the act serves as the "basis" of the subjective dimension and, in a sense, "becomes" the subjective dimension when it is "carried over into the conscience and the decisions of the acting parties".[136] The "essential aspects" of the act become the "meanings" of the act when "the (ontological) truth enters, so to speak, into the cognitive dimension—the subjective and psychological."[137] In formulating the proximate norm of personal morality, conscience *appropriates* the truth contained in the law, but it does not *create* the truth. With respect to the conjugal act, the "meanings" of the act result from an act of appropriation of the part of conscience by which the ontological truth (the essential aspects) enters the subjective psychological dimension. Neither the conscience nor human consciousness creates the "meanings" of the conjugal act, because the meanings exist first in the ontological dimension, whose original author is God himself. As the Pope states, "It is a question here

[133] General Audience of July 11, 1984.

[134] Ibid.

[135] Ibid.

[136] Ibid.

[137] General Audience of July 18, 1984.

of the truth first in the ontological dimension ('fundamental structure') and then—as a result—in the subjective and psychological dimension ('significances')."[138]

When describing the ontological and subjective dimensions of the conjugal act, John Paul II maintains a clear order between the two dimensions. The truth exists "first" in the ontological dimension "and then as a result" in the subjective and psychological dimension. In this sense, if the subjective dimension is to contain the "truth" it must be the same truth found in the ontological dimension. However, it is not simply a matter of a "correspondence" between the two dimensions. Instead, it is a matter of the ontological dimension being appropriated or assimilated by the acting subject, so that the content of the subjective dimension is the same as the truth of the ontological dimension (that is, it is "the correct understanding of the intimate structure of the marital act").[139] The "meanings" of the conjugal act are not products of the human conscience or consciousness that happen to correspond to the truth of the ontological dimension but rather are that ontological truth "carried over into the conscience" of the person[140] and experienced in the very decision to execute this particular act. The value of the meanings of the act derives from their ability to bear witness to an objective truth in the act of the personal subject. The conjugal act is "objective", then, in both the ontological dimension and the subjective dimension.

Where does the conscience first encounter the ontological dimension? The truth of the ontological dimension of the conjugal act is "inscribed in the very being of man and

[138] General Audience of July 11, 1984.
[139] General Audience of July 18, 1984.
[140] General Audience of July 11, 1984.

woman".[141] This brings us full circle to John Paul II's theological anthropology, and in particular to the theology of the body. In speaking of the appropriation of the truth of the ontological dimension by the conscience, "we are dealing with nothing other than reading the language of the body in truth."[142] One perceives the intrinsic structure of the conjugal act in the nature of the human person, provided that one perceives the human body as a constitutive part of the person expressive of ontological truth and not as a raw datum expressive of biological truth. In light of a "specifically human meaning of the body",[143] man's natural inclinations take on moral relevance because they pertain to the nature of the person, and they reveal an ordination to both personal union and fertility. The body possesses a "nuptial meaning" that reveals man's ordination to love and communion based upon the sexual complementarity of man and woman, and in particular the complementarity of the generative potential of each. In the human sexual faculty the ordination to union is intrinsically linked to the potential to procreate. The two essential aspects (the ontological dimension) of the conjugal act correspond to the finality of the sexual faculty itself, indeed to the nuptial meaning of the body expressed in masculinity and femininity, which directs man to a total gift of self.

The nuptial meaning of the body and the finalities of the sexual faculty, in which the ontological dimension is first perceived, belong to the nature of the human person. Therefore, when the ontological truth of the conjugal act "enters into the cognitive dimension" it enters not from *without* but

[141] HV 12. Cf. also FC 32.

[142] General Audience of July 11, 1984.

[143] VS 50.

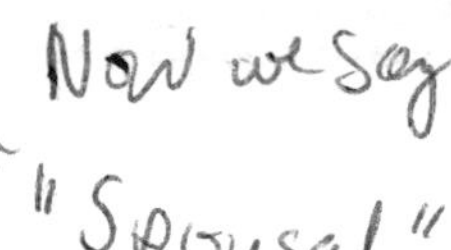

from *within* the person himself. The ontological dimension is not extrinsic to the person but rather pertains to the truth of his being. In a certain sense, the ontological dimension is nothing other than the nuptial meaning of the body understood in light of an integral vision of the human person, that is, one that recognizes the body as a constitutive part of the person. Since God has given the body its nuptial meaning in the very creation of man and woman, the ontological dimension of the conjugal act derived from the nuptial meaning of the body belongs to the eternal law or "the truth of creation". In this sense, the conjugal act possesses an objective structure and content that are discernable from the very nature of man and woman as sexual persons.

An Interpretation of HV 12

John Paul II's theology of the conjugal act, because it considers the act in its two dimensions and in the context of natural law, provides the theoretical keys for an adequate interpretation of Pope Paul VI's teaching in HV 12. Inasmuch as it refers to the meanings of the conjugal act, the indissoluble connection pertains to the subjective dimension of the act. If the subjective dimension of the act were merely the product of the human intellect, any intrinsic connection between the meanings would rely on the human intellect and not on the will of God. However, since the subjective dimension of the act derives from an act of appropriation in which the truth of the ontological dimension enters the subjective dimension, God wills the indissoluble connection between the two meanings of the act inasmuch as he wills the intrinsic structure of the act and inscribes it into the very being of man and woman. The indissoluble connection, existing first on the ontological level, is unable to be broken by man in the subjective dimension because of the manner in which truth passes from the ontological to the subjective in an act of assimilation. God's creative intention for the conjugal act (the laws inscribed in the very being of man and woman) enters the conscious intention of the acting person when man accurately reads the language of the body and "appropriates this truth of his being and makes it his own by his acts and corresponding virtues".[144] Only in the light of such an interplay between the ontological and subjective dimensions is the doctrine of HV 12 rightly understood.

The Language of the Body

According to John Paul II, the body not only expresses the person but it does so through a "language" or symbolism all its own. The language of the body is essential to marriage and conjugal love because "spouses are called to form their life and their living together as a communion of persons on the basis of that language."[145] Indeed, "on the level of this language, man and woman reciprocally express themselves in the fullest and most profound way possible to them by the corporal dimension of masculinity and femininity. Man and woman express themselves in the measure of the whole truth of the person."[146] In *Familiaris consortio* the Pope describes the language of the body as "innate", not a construct of the human intellect like a spoken language.[147] Because it is inscribed in the nature of the body, the language of the body

---

[144] VS 52.

[145] General Audience of January 26, 1983.

[146] General Audience of August 22, 1984.

[147] Cf. FC 32.

belongs first to the ontological dimension of conjugal relations but can and does enter into the subjective dimension when it is read in truth. According to the Pope, there is an "organic bond" between "the integral significance of the language of the body and the consequent use of that language in conjugal life".[148]

The use of the language of the body should develop out of and in conformity with its integral meaning or fundamental truth. However, when expressing their love in the language of the body, spouses do not utilize the body as an instrument but instead allow the body to speak on their behalf with their personal authority.[149] In genital intercourse, the language of the body "expresses the total reciprocal self-giving of husband and wife" whether or not this innate meaning corresponds to the conscious intentions of the spouses.[150] If the intentions of the man and woman do not correspond to this innate expression of self-gift, the result is a falsification of the act or a sexual "lie".[151] On the other hand, when the man and woman "perceive, love and practice those meanings of the language of the body", they practice and live conjugal chastity.[152] The language of the body, belonging first to the ontological dimension of the conjugal act, should enter into the subjective intentions of the spouses, becoming a basis of their communion in the conjugal act.

[148] General Audience of January 26, 1983.

[149] Cf. ibid.: "In this sense man—male and female—does not merely speak with the language of the body. But in a certain sense he permits the body to speak 'for him' and 'on his behalf,' I would say, in his name and with his personal authority."

[150] FC 32.

[151] Cf. General Audience of January 26, 1983, and FC 32.

[152] General Audience of October 24, 1984.

The Institution of Marriage

John Paul II applies his doctrine on freedom and the relationship between the ontological order and the subjective order in a similar manner to the question of the relationship of the institution of marriage and the friendship between husband and wife. The institution of marriage corresponds to the ontological order inasmuch as it belongs to the eternal law and is inscribed in the very being of man and woman (that is, is the finality of masculinity and femininity). It is the only place where the gift of self can be made "in its whole truth".[153] According to John Paul II, the institution of marriage is an "interior requirement of the covenant of conjugal love" and is not "the extrinsic imposition of a form".[154] In accord with the nature of the natural law, the institution of marriage represents the assimilation of the truth about man into the love of husband and wife. Spouses, in and through matrimonial consent, appropriate the institution and make it their own. The institution of marriage, far from restricting human freedom, "protects and promotes that freedom".[155] Rather than hindering or restricting the love of husband and wife, the institution of marriage guards conjugal love and gives it an objectivity that corresponds to the demands of human dignity and freedom.

Become What You Are

Ultimately, John Paul II's theology of the conjugal act represents the application of the idea "become what you are" to the unique moment of the conjugal union of husband and

[153] FC 11.

[154] Ibid.

[155] VS 35; see also FC 11.

wife. The Pope's theology of the conjugal act incorporates many of the principal tenets of his theological anthropology and contains a summary of the integral vision of man in the light of which questions of conjugal morality must be answered. According to this anthropological vision, man possesses an identity as a person. This identity, inscribed by God into the very being of man and woman, manifests itself in the "nuptial meaning" of the body, which reveals what it means to be person. In the nuptial meaning of the body, the identity of the person is revealed to be self-gift in love (indeed, this is the essence of personhood) or, in biblical terms, "the image and likeness" of God, who is love. Man's identity can be known by man and assimilated or appropriated by the acting subject in and through the conscience. Through such an act of assimilation objective truth enters into the subjective dimension and becomes the truth also of the subjective dimension. The idea of objective truth entering into the subjective dimension hinges upon and expresses a concept of consciousness in which cognitive objects are constituted *in* consciousness but *not by* consciousness. As such, consciousness mirrors or reflects the object of cognition and in so doing interiorizes the object in its own specific manner (assimilates). Inasmuch as the assimilated identity serves as the basis for action (choice), man becomes his identity (who he is). Furthermore, because God is the author of the human person's identity (he has not only created man but also created him in the image and likeness of God), man becomes who God wills him to be and, thus, lives out his vocation.

Sacramentality

According to John Paul II, "Those who seek the accomplishment of their own humanity and Christian vocation in marriage are called, first of all, to make this 'theology of the body' ... the content of their life and behavior."[156] The "accomplishment" of one's own humanity is certainly reason enough to endeavor to make the truth of creation the content of one's life and behavior. However, Christian spouses encounter a further incentive to appropriate the nuptial meaning of the body into their lives, one that concerns the sacramentality of the body and of marriage. In his theology of the body, the Pope uses the terms "sacrament" and "primordial sacrament" as meaning "a sign that transmits effectively in the visible world the invisible mystery hidden in God from time immemorial".[157] Here sacrament essentially means the announcement and realization of the mystery or the manifestation of the mystery "in a sign which serves to not only proclaim the mystery, but also to accomplish it in man".[158] The human body possesses a sacramentality because it "was created to transfer into the visible reality of the world the mystery hidden since time immemorial in God, and thus be a sign of it".[159]

The fundamental function or role of a sacrament (the broad sense of the word) is the manifestation and realization of the mystery (God and his plan for creation, that is, man's election in the Son) in the world on the part of something visible (material). In order that the mystery not be misconstrued or blurred, it is essential that the material of the sacrament have a specific and perennial meaning. The body then possesses a sacramentality because it possesses a designated, perennial meaning: its nuptial meaning. In the action of the

[156] General Audience of April 2, 1980.
[157] General Audience of February 20, 1980.
[158] General Audience of September 8, 1982.
[159] General Audience of February 20, 1980.

acting person, the body is the external sign of the person's self-determination through self-donation. In the language of the body, through which the nuptial meaning of the body is spoken, both "the fundamental characteristic of personal existence" (self-gift in love) and the mystery of creation in love are announced.[160] In other words, on the basis of its nuptial meaning, the body is "a witness to creation as a fundamental gift, and so a witness to Love as the source from which the same giving springs".[161] However, the body witnesses to love only in its nuptial meaning; if this nuptial meaning is lost to the eyes of men or read in a mistaken way (though it is intrinsic to the body itself), the announcement of the mystery will be obscured. Therefore, the nuptial meaning of the body is "important and indispensable [not only] in order to know who man is and who he should be"[162] but also so that the body may bear witness to a truth which the world so desperately needs.

Just as man "by means of his corporeality, his masculinity and femininity, becomes a visible sign of the economy of the truth and love",[163] so too the conjugal union of man and woman, inasmuch as it is a communion of persons based on the language of the body, possesses a sacramentality in the primordial sense. Marriage is the primordial sacrament because it "expresses the salvific initiative of the Creator, corresponding to the eternal election of man"[164] inasmuch as it is the "place" (the context) in which man and woman live out the nuptial meaning of the body "in its whole

[160] Ibid.

[161] Ibid.

[162] General Audience of February 13, 1980.

[163] General Audience of February 20, 1980.

[164] General Audience of October 6, 1982.

truth".[165] For the same reason, the conjugal act, an integral part of marriage, possesses a sacramentality when the physical union of man and woman is the fruit and sign of a personal union based on self-donation. Marriage and the conjugal act itself have their sacramental value so long as they are based upon and represent an authentic assimilation of the nuptial meaning of the body into the life of the spouses. When spouses fail to make the nuptial meaning of the body "the content of their life and behavior",[166] the sacramental value of their life together is diminished, if not entirely lost.

The sacramentality of the conjugal union of husband and wife acquires greater significance in light of salvation history, becoming the symbol of God's love for his Chosen People and ultimately Christ's love for the Church. According to John Paul II, "The communion of love between God and his people, a fundamental part of the Revelation and faith experience of Israel, finds a meaningful expression in the marriage covenant which is established between a man and a woman." [167] By virtue of their baptism into the Christian mystery, the conjugal covenant of Christian spouses acquires a renewed, elevated sacramental symbolism.[168] Christian marriage sacramentally represents the love of Christ for the Church, the New Covenant sanctioned by the blood of Christ on the Cross. However, the renewed sacramental symbolism

[165] FC 11.

[166] General Audience of April 2, 1980.

[167] FC 12.

[168] Cf. ibid.: "Indeed, by means of baptism, man and woman are definitively placed within the new and eternal covenant, in the spousal covenant of Christ with the Church. And it is because of this indestructible insertion that the intimate community of conjugal life and love, founded by the Creator, is elevated and assumed into the spousal charity of Christ, sustained and enriched by His redeeming power."

of the conjugal covenant, like its original symbolism, is preserved to the extent that spouses preserve the integrity of their conjugal relationship. Thus, in the renewed sacramental symbolism of marriage, Christian spouses find an even greater responsibility and incentive to preserve the integrity of their love and to form their conjugal life on the basis of the truth of the nuptial meaning of the body.

4. *DONUM VITAE*

The Congregation for the Doctrine of the Faith promulgated *Donum vitae* in February of 1987, almost a decade into the Pontificate of Pope John Paul II. Properly in the field of bioethics, DV focuses on the specific question of medical interventions into the generation of human life. The general principles formulated by the document are: (1) the child has a right to be the fruit of the specific act of the conjugal love of his parents and has the right to be respected as a person from the moment of his conception,[169] and (2) the only acts of medical intervention that are morally acceptable are those that facilitate the performance of the conjugal act or the completion of its natural objective without replacing the conjugal act itself.[170] Thus, the conclusion, "the gift of human life must be actualized in marriage through the specific and exclusive acts of husband and wife, in accordance with the laws inscribed in their persons and their union."[171]

The value of DV for the current study rests in the manner in which it develops these general principles from the per-

[169] CDF, *Donum vitae*, February 27, 1987, II, 8 (hereafter abbreviated DV).
[170] DV, II, 7.
[171] DV, intro., 5.

spective of the anthropological vision found in *Humanae vitae* and the teachings of John Paul II and in the manner in which the document employs the doctrine of the indissoluble connection between the meanings of the conjugal act in responding to the issue of artificial fecundation. The content of DV results from the application of the Church's integral vision of man to certain bioethical questions. In the process of answering these questions of bioethics, the document clarifies the anthropological vision itself, the doctrine of the indissoluble connection, and the nature of the conjugal act. In my review of the document I prescind from the specific biomedical questions addressed and instead focus on these latter points.

DV's Anthropological Perspective

In responding to the bioethical questions at issue, the authors of DV operate with the notion that the "moral criteria" for medical intervention into the generation of human life "are deduced from the dignity of human persons, of their sexuality and their origin".[172] In other words, the conclusions of the document derive from moral criteria perceived in the nature of the human person and the nature of the sexual union of persons. Specifically, the document refers to "a proper idea of the nature of the human person in his bodily dimension" as a necessary presupposition for answering biomedical questions.[173] A proper theology of the body is crucial for questions of sexual morality or bioethics because the body is the sphere or medium in which acts of this nature are executed. The deciding factor in the document's concept

[172] DV, II, 7.

[173] DV, intro., 3.

of the body is its substantial union with the soul because this places it in the realm of the personal and, thus, morally significant. As the text states,

> For it is only in keeping with his true nature that the human person can achieve self-realization as a "unified totality": and this nature is at the same time corporal and spiritual. *By virtue of its substantial union with a spiritual soul*, the human body cannot be considered a mere complex of tissues, organs and functions, nor can it be evaluated in the same way as the body of animals; rather *it is a constitutive part of the person who manifests and expresses himself through it* [emphasis added].[174]

By virtue of its substantial union with a spiritual soul the body is personal, that is, a constitutive part of the person. Therefore, in the body (his person) man discovers laws that transcend the biological order and pertain to the personal order. This anthropological perspective implies that interventions on (and also acts in and through) the human body affect not only the tissues, the organs, and their functions but also the person on different levels.[175] According to DV, the body "involves, therefore, perhaps in an implicit but nonetheless real way, a moral significance and responsibility".[176] This moral significance, implicit in the body, is made explicit in the precepts of the natural law, "which are based upon the bodily and spiritual nature of the person"[177] and which serve to promote the good of the person as a unified totality. According to these precepts of the natural law, based upon the nature of the person, "man is called by the Creator

[174] Ibid.

[175] Ibid.

[176] Ibid.

[177] Ibid.

to direct and regulate his life and actions and in particular to make use of his body."[178]

DV puts forward a vision of man in which the substantial union of the human body and soul is significant not only for describing who man is but also in determining how man is "to direct and regulate his life and actions and in particular to make use of his body". Thus, the very nature of man serves as a reference point for his moral decision-making. Yet, it is not only his identity that possesses moral significance for man but also his vocation. In addition to the norms of the natural law, God "has inscribed in man and woman the vocation to share in a special way in His mystery of personal communion and in His work as Creator and Father".[179] According to DV, "marriage possesses specific goods and values in its union and in procreation which cannot be likened to those existing in lower forms of life."[180]

The Indissoluble Connection

Developed from an anthropological perspective that recognizes the "moral significance" of the corporal and spiritual nature of the human person, the conclusions of DV relate directly to the indissoluble connection between procreation and union (hereafter IC). The importance of the doctrine of the IC emerges most clearly in chapter 2 of DV, when the authors address the question of homologous artificial fertilization. The authors of DV appeal to the IC because "the doctrine concerning the link between the meanings of the conjugal act and the goods of marriage throws light on

---

[178] Ibid.

[179] Ibid.

[180] Ibid.

the moral problem of homologous artificial fertilization."[181] Finding evidence for the IC in both the teachings of Pius XII and *Humanae vitae*, DV explains that just as "contraception deliberately deprives the conjugal act of its openness to procreation and in this way brings about a voluntary disassociation of the ends of marriage . . . , seeking procreation which is not the fruit of a specific act of conjugal union, objectively effects an analogous separation between the goods and the meanings of marriage."[182] The fundamental notion of the IC is illustrated in the manner in which choices regarding one of the meanings or goods necessarily have implications and ramifications for the other good. According to DV, not only does artificial fertilization disassociate the ends of marriage, but "from the moral point of view procreation is deprived of its proper perfection when it is not desired as the fruit of the conjugal act, that is to say of the specific act of the spouses' union."[183] Thus, the IC possesses a moral significance inasmuch as its violation deprives the realities of union and procreation of their proper moral perfection.

The text then enters into an important and intricate explanation of the rationale or "source" of the moral significance of the IC, an explanation that clarifies the IC's proper anthropological nature:

> The moral value of the intimate link between the goods of marriage and the meanings of the conjugal act is based upon the unity of the human being, a unity involving body and spiritual soul. Spouses mutually express their personal love in the "language of the body," which clearly involves both "spousal meanings" and parental ones. The conjugal act by

[181] DV, II, 4, a.

[182] Ibid.

[183] Ibid.

> which the couple mutually express their self-gift at the same time expresses an openness to the gift of life. It is an act that is inseparably corporal and spiritual. It is in their bodies and through their bodies that spouses consummate their marriage and are able to become father and mother. In order to respect the language of their bodies and their natural generosity, the conjugal union must take place with respect for its openness to procreation; and the procreation of a person must be the fruit and result of married love. . . . Fertilization achieved outside the bodies of the couple remains by this very fact deprived of the meanings and the values which are expressed in the language of the body and in the union of human persons.[184]

This paragraph represents the most explicit statement of the anthropological nature of the doctrine of the IC found in the documents of the Magisterium. The argument of this paragraph, though subtle, is powerful. It begins by stating that the IC is based upon "the unity of the human being, a unity involving body and spiritual soul". Why? Because the body is a constitutive part of the person, and because the person expresses himself through the body, communion (or communication) between persons must take place in and through the body. This is particularly true of the communion between spouses, who "express their personal love in the language of the body". Spousal union is based upon more than simple communication; it is founded upon the gift of self. Moreover, since the person is composed of body and soul, the gift of self required by spousal union must be "an act which is inseparably corporal and spiritual". If anything proper to the body is excluded from this act, the act fails to effect a personal union, and so "conjugal union must take

[184] DV, II, 4, b.

place with respect to its [the body's] openness to procreation." Thus, if the act of donation excludes the procreative finality inscribed in the nature of the body itself and expressed in the language of the body, it is not a personal donation, and no personal, conjugal union is achieved. This explains why conjugal union must necessarily be procreative.

Likewise, the paragraph argues that procreation cannot take place outside of "an act that is inseparably corporal and spiritual" and ultimately unitive. The argument here presupposes that the human person must be the *fruit* of conjugal love, or else he is reduced to a *product* or an *object*, which is utterly incompatible with the dignity of the human person.[185] Thus, the dignity of the child generated outside the context of love is offended. According to the argument of DV, if a child is generated outside of the conjugal act, procreation loses it proper moral perfection (and in that sense ceases to be procreation). Why? Because the body is a constitutive part of the person and because the person expresses himself through the body, the conjugal love (inasmuch as it "embraces the good of the whole person")[186] between spouses must take place in and through the body. Moreover, conjugal love is based upon self-donation, and, because of the substantial unity of the person, conjugal self-donation must include the body (that is, it must be an act that is inseparably corporal and spiritual). In other words, without a bodily union there is no personal (conjugal) self-donation. Since it is not possible to make the conjugal gift of self without (outside) the body, and especially because it is in "the language of the body" that spousal love is expressed, conjugal love must be expressed in a bodily act.

---

[185] DV, II, 4, c.

[186] GS 49.

Thus, we can summarize: Without a bodily gift of self, there is no total self-donation. Without total self-donation, there is no conjugal love. Without conjugal love, there is no procreation, only the reproduction, of a child. Therefore, without the bodily gift of self, there is no procreation. With one further step the argument leads from a necessary connection between procreation and the bodily gift of self to the necessary connection between procreation and union. By virtue of the complementarity of man and woman inscribed in the human body, the bodily gift of self effects a union between man and woman. The bodily gift of self and spousal union are bound together in the nature of human sexuality, upon which each is inherently based. Therefore, inasmuch as procreation requires conjugal love, it necessarily requires the bodily gift of self and necessarily entails the union of spouses.

Though the various aspects of the doctrine of the IC are subtle and complex, the text clearly identifies the substantial unity of the person as the basis for this doctrine, because without this fundamental principle the doctrine loses its basic rationale. If the body is not a constitutive part of the person, then a love that embraces the good of the whole person need not necessarily be bodily. Once the body becomes an optional part of conjugal love, the whole face of love changes. We could now think of a love that is based solely upon the union of mind and will, that is, common desires and goals. These desires need not even include the transmission of life, because a love that is not bodily need not incorporate the inherent procreative generosity of the body. On the other hand, if conjugal love need not be bodily, then we could describe the transmission of life outside the body as the fruit of love, as the fruit of a common will and desire. Finally, the most popular option would be a love that is bodily in the sense that it utilizes the body, not as a constitutive part of the person, but as an instrument capable of producing shared experiences of the mind and heart. Therefore, the doctrine of the IC is "based upon the unity of the human being",[187] because once this substantial unity is lost, conjugal love is not necessarily procreative or unitive, and certainly not both intrinsically.

The Conjugal Act

In light of DV's anthropological vision, the significance of the conjugal act becomes more clear. The fundamental tenets of this anthropology "enable us to understand why the act of conjugal love is considered in the teachings of the Church as the only setting worthy of human procreation".[188] In this anthropological context the conjugal act, *the* act of conjugal love, emerges as the only place where a child can be "accepted as a gift and blessing from God" and at the same time "be the fruit and sign of the mutual self-giving of the spouses, of their love and their fidelity".[189] Thus, the conjugal act is the manner in which man and woman respond to their God-given "vocation to share in His mystery of personal communion and in His work as Creator and Father".[190] If man is a unity of body and soul, only the conjugal act, "an act inseparably corporal and spiritual",[191] expresses and perfects that love which embraces the good of the whole person. The value of DV, over and above the answers to the biomedical questions it addresses, derives from

[187] DV, II, 4, b.
[188] DV, II, 5.
[189] DV, II, 1.
[190] DV, intro., 3.
[191] DV, II, 4, b.

the fact that it reminds the world of this anthropological vision and the implicit but nonetheless real moral significance of viewing man as a unified totality when considering questions of human sexuality.

CONCLUSION

Faced with an approach to sexual intercourse and contraception that restricted the finality of procreation to the whole ensemble of the conjugal life, beginning with *Humanae vitae* the Church has responded to this challenge with a profound and intricate theology of the conjugal act that centers on the doctrine of an indissoluble connection between the procreative and unitive meanings of the conjugal act. Ultimately, the Church's theology of the conjugal act reflects her approach to the conjugal life in general, where man freely cooperates with God but does not proceed in a wholly autonomous way. As a natural institution, as a specific form of friendship, and as a vocation, the conjugal life possesses a determined content (that is, structure, purposes, laws) insofar as it is inscribed by God in the very being of man and woman. Thus, we can speak of the objective, universal concept of marriage. In living the conjugal life, husband and wife must make the universal content of marriage the content of their own particular relationship. The idea of the universal becoming the particular applies equally to the conjugal act, a specific act that relates to marriage as an institution, friendship, and vocation. The conjugal act possesses a determined content (that is, structure, purposes, laws) and presents itself to the married couple as a specific and unique way of expressing their conjugal relationship according to the truth of masculinity and femininity. Yet, this "prescribed" form of conjugal love becomes for a married couple their own personal expression of love when they exercise their freedom in accord with the truth. Like the Church's theology of marriage, the Church's theology of the conjugal act harmonizes the objective moral requirements of human nature with the level of the personal expression of intimate love.

However, as this review of the magisterial teachings since the time of HV has demonstrated, this theology of the conjugal act depends greatly upon a precise vision of man, because only a specific concept of the person provides the rationale for the idea of a prescribed act becoming the intimate, personal expression of love. While this vision of man, because of its complexity, cannot be reduced to a few basic elements, three main tenets of this anthropology appear especially significant for the Catholic concept of the conjugal act: (1) human freedom understood as *theonomy*, (2) a conscience that assimilates the truth rather than creating it, and (3) the substantial unity of the body and soul that places the body in the realm of the personal. These three fundamental components not only provide the basis for a theology of the conjugal act but also strengthen the Church's previous teachings on marriage and family because they explain the manner in which man can freely cooperate in God's plan of fruitful love while making that plan the content of his life. Freedom allows man to love and to cooperate with God, while conscience allows man to exercise his freedom authentically and in accord with the truth of his own being. For its part, the body helps to reveal the truth of man's being because as a constitutive part of the person it expresses the person.[192]

[192] I consider the relevance of these anthropological principles for the theology of the conjugal act in greater detail in section 2 of chapter 4.

While these fundamental anthropological principles provide the framework for the Church's theology of the conjugal act, this concept of the conjugal act centers on the doctrine of the indissoluble connection between the procreative and unitive meanings of the act. A complex doctrine, possessing "great importance on the anthropological and moral planes",[193] the doctrine of the IC confirms the inherent link between procreation and union and also the personal nature of the body.[194] As a fundamental principle that must be demonstrated rather than proven, the truth of the doctrine of the IC is bound up in the definitions of the terms of the doctrine. These definitions, complex and profound themselves, provide an understanding of how procreation and union are the indissolubly bound meanings of the conjugal act. Therefore, in order to consider further the Church's concept of the conjugal act, in chapter 3 I examine the significance of the four core terms of the doctrine of the IC: *procreation*, *union*, *meaning*, and the *indissoluble connection*.

[193] DV, II, 4, c.

[194] Cf. John Paul II, *Discourse to Priests*, 2.

Chapter Three

What God Has Joined

A Consideration of Procreation and Union as the Indissolubly Connected Meanings of the Conjugal Act

The teachings of the Church on marriage and sexuality contain a profound theology of the conjugal act that emerges from the framework of authentic Christian anthropology. According to this theology of the conjugal act, husband and wife express and perfect their conjugal love on the basis of the language of the body while cooperating with God in the procreation of new life when they unite in and through the masculinity and femininity manifest in their bodies. The conjugal act, then, constitutes a particular act of conjugal love by which husband and wife procreate and unite according to laws inscribed in their very being as man and woman. At the center of this concept of the conjugal act we find the doctrine of HV 12, which recognizes "the indissoluble connection, willed by God and unable to be broken by man on his own initiative, between the two meanings of the conjugal act: the unitive meaning and the procreative meaning". Considered by many as one of the central doctrines of *Humanae vitae*,[1] the doctrine of HV 12 possesses great significance for

[1] Cf. for example, Carlo Caffarra, "Who Is Like the Lord, Our God?" in *Why "Humanae Vitae" Was Right*, ed. Janet E. Smith (San Francisco: Ignatius Press, 1993), p. 258.

the Catholic theology of the conjugal act. Yet, much of this significance remains implicit within *Humanae vitae* because Paul VI does not elaborate on the fundamental terms of the doctrine. The full significance of the doctrine of HV 12, and consequently the Church's theology of the conjugal act, becomes clear only in light of the definitions of the doctrine's fundamental terms: *procreation*, *union*, *meaning*, and *indissoluble connection*.

This chapter contains a reflection on the significance of each of these four fundamental terms of the Church's theology of the conjugal act. The Church describes the conjugal act as inherently procreative and unitive, and rests her theology of the conjugal act on the notion of an indissoluble connection between procreation and union. Consequently, in order to grasp/explain this theology of the conjugal act we are compelled to consider these fundamental terms: What is procreation? What is spousal union? How do these realities enter into the conjugal act? What is a meaning of an act? What is the indissoluble connection? These are the questions I address in the present chapter.

I begin with a consideration of procreation, identifying its essential characteristics. Specifically, I focus on the manner in which procreation differs from mere reproduction because it requires spouses to cooperate with God in the transmission of life in an act of love. The procreated child is the fruit and sign of his parents' love precisely because procreation requires spouses to give themselves to each other through their sexuality in order fulfill their role in God's plan of fruitful love. The character of love that distinguishes procreation provides for the intrinsic link between procreation and union. Spousal union always accompanies procreation insofar as procreation entails the gift of self and the pursuit of a common good. Spousal union, the oneness effected by conjugal love, intrinsically relates to procreation, the common good around which the conjugal friendship forms. I follow my analysis of procreation and spousal union with an examination of the concept of *meaning* by comparing and contrasting it with the more fundamental notions of *good* and *end*. This examination of meaning produces an understanding of meaning as a component of human action pertaining to the level of human awareness. Finally I discuss the nature of the indissoluble connection as an anthropological fact. Here I consider the exceptionless character of the connection by virtue of the intrinsic relationship of procreation and union, the connection's existential significance, and the manner in which the connection is self-evident in the light of the definitions of procreation and union.

1. PROCREATION

The origin of every human person is a creative act of God.[2] A child is the fruit and the completion of the conjugal union of man and woman.[3] These two statements, both affirmed by the Magisterium, reveal the complexity and profundity of the transmission of human life. The child to whom life is transmitted results from a creative act of God and is the fruit of the encounter of man and woman. Thus, the human

---

[2] Cf. John Paul II, *Discourse to Priests Participating in a Seminar on "Responsible Parenthood"*, September 17, 1983, in *Insegnamenti di Giovanni Paolo II*, 6, 2 (1983): "All'origine di ogni persona umana v'è un atto creativo di Dio: nessun uomo viene all'esistenza per caso; egli è sempre il termine dell'amore creativo di Dio."

[3] Cf. DV, II, 1: "The parents find in their child a confirmation and completion of their reciprocal self-giving: the child is the living image of their love, the permanent sign of their conjugal union."

person finds his source ultimately in God but also in a very significant way in human sexuality. God creates each and every human person inasmuch as "every spiritual soul is created immediately by God—it is not 'produced' by the parents."[4] However, God creates each human person within the context of human sexuality, and man and woman, as the subjects of human sexuality, play a unique and irreplaceable role in the transmission of life. For this reason, the child is said to be the fruit of their union. The activity of man and woman in fulfilling their role in the transmission of life is properly termed *procreation.* While God *creates* each human person, man and woman *procreate* when they cooperate with God in the transmission of life. Procreation is fundamentally the human role in the transmission of life, a role that remains inseparable from God's loving act of creation of a new life. For this reason, an adequate description of procreation must account for the manner in which man and woman are able to cooperate with God's act of creation as well as the essential characteristics of this human role in the transmission of life. As an analysis of procreation reveals, the "specific characteristics" of procreation are determined by and correspond to "the personal dignity of the parents and the children".[5]

The Transmission of Human Life: Procreation vs. Reproduction

"At the origin of every human person there is a creative act of God: no man comes into being by chance. He is always the result of God's creative love."[6] This statement of John

[4] *Catechism of the Catholic Church,* 366 (hereafter abbreviated as CCC).
[5] DV, II, 1.
[6] John Paul II, *Discourse to Priests.*

Paul II should begin every discussion of procreation, for it immediately brings to light the truly sacred and profound nature of the coming to be of the human person. Man's coming to be is the result of a creative act of God, which at the same time is linked to a human act. As José Miguel Ibáñez Langlios states, "Each human being is begotten at the same time, in an indissoluble way, in the motherly womb and in the heart of God. God is the Owner and Lord of all life. Only He can give it, only He can create it."[7] In some sense all life comes from God, indeed God is the ultimate source of the entire created universe. However, there is something unique about God's role in the transmission of human life as compared to other animal life because, as John Paul II states, "God himself is present in human fatherhood and motherhood quite differently than he is present in all other instances of begetting."[8] God is the *Father* of all men while he is simply the *Creator* of the animals.[9] The uniqueness of God's role in the transmission of human life manifests the uniqueness of the human person, expressed in the now famous statement of *Gaudium et spes* that man is the only visible creature willed for his own sake.[10] Unlike the other animals, man is a

---

[7] "The Theological Argument at the Basis of *Humanae Vitae*", in *"Humanae vitae": 20 anni dopo. Atti del II Congresso Internazionale di Teologia Morale* (Milan: Edizione Ares, 1989), p. 116.

[8] John Paul II, LF, 9.

[9] Damian Fedoryka explains, "Fatherhood is a distinct moment from creatorhood as such because fatherhood implies a self-giving and a transmission of one's own life to the son. This cannot occur with the creation of non-personal beings" ("Man: The Creature of God", in *Creative Love: The Ethics of Human Reproduction*, ed. John Boyle [Front Royal, Va.: Christendom Press, 1989], p. 82).

[10] GS 24. Regarding this idea, José Miguel Ibáñez Langlios writes, "The direct divine origin is a privilege of the human person, held as something unique in the wholeness of the cosmos" ("The Theological Argument at the Basis of *Humanae Vitae*", in *"Humanae vitae": 20 anni dopo*, p. 118).

person; he is made in the image and likeness of God. Man differs ontologically from the other animals; he possesses a unique finality, and the transmission of human life reflects this uniqueness.

From a physiological point of view, the transmission of human life resembles the reproduction of other living creatures, but upon further analysis it proves quite different. As *Donum vitae* reminds us, "By comparison with the other forms of life in the universe, the transmission of human life has a special character of its own, which derives from the special nature of the human person."[11] Due to the personal nature of human beings, the coming to be of a new human person is radically different from the generation of any other living creature.[12] As a person there is something profoundly unique about each human being. The human person is not simply an example or instance of the species as a whole.[13] Instead, each person is an unrepeatable and irreplaceable self. Furthermore, each human person is created in the image and likeness of God and possesses a supernatural ordination to communion with God that is made possible by the spiritual

---

[11] DV, intro., 4.

[12] Cf. David Q. Liptak, *The Gift of Life* (Lakeforth: Liturgical Press, 1988), p. 21: "Since the human person cannot be reduced simply to a complex of tissue but must be seen as a composite of body and soul—spirit expressed by body—human sexuality cannot be equated with that found in the animal world."

[13] Karol Wojtyla writes, "We speak of individual animals, looking upon them as single specimens of a particular species. And this definition suffices. But it is not enough to define a man as an individual of the species Homo. . . . The term 'person' has been coined to signify that a man cannot be wholly contained within the concept of 'individual member of the species', but that there is something more to him, a particular richness and perfection in the manner of his being, which can only be brought out by the use of the word 'person'" (K. Wojtyla, *Love and Responsibility*, trans. H. Willets [San Francisco: Ignatius Press, 1993], pp. 21–22).

nature of the human person. Therefore, the conception of each human person effects more than a biological replication of the parents or the numerical increase of the human species. For the same reason, Wojtyla writes, "the simple natural fact of becoming a father or mother has a deeper significance, not merely a biological but also a personal significance."[14] Each human person possesses an interiority or a spiritual dimension that does not and cannot result from biological forces. Man's interiority lies beyond even the spiritual powers of the human parents. Because the human soul cannot be produced by the powers of the human person, the coming to be of a human person can only result from the creative act of God. According to Janet Smith, this special act of creation on the part of God represents the "chief and inestimable difference between the bringing forth of animal life and the bringing forth of human life".[15]

We properly speak of animal reproduction because animals do not possess an interiority that establishes in them a radical uniqueness with respect to the other members of their species. Each animal is essentially a reproduction of the other members of its species, with, of course, slight accidental variations and even particular traits. In contrast, the human person is not a reproduction of his species. Each human person shares the same human nature with other men, yet each is a unique personal self who is the result of a creative act of God. Reproduction is acceptable only with regard to biochemical organisms that do not possess the uniqueness and dignity proper to persons. The "reproduction"[16] of a human

[14] Ibid., p. 135.

[15] Janet Smith, "The Vocation of Marriage", in Boyle, *Creative Love*, p. 126.

[16] In reference to the human child, I use the term "reproduction" in a qualified sense throughout this section, since the child could never be produced by

person necessarily offends the dignity of the child produced, violating one of his fundamental rights: to be the fruit of love.[17] The child's right to be the fruit of love derives from his being a human person, a "someone" and not "a something".

Procreation and reproduction differ, then, by virtue of the love found at the heart of procreation. The human person originates in love because the very gift of life that results from God's creation of the soul is an act of love. God calls each soul into existence in love. Nothing compels God to create the soul, rather his creation is entirely gratuitous, entirely a gift. The gift of life, then, is bestowed entirely out of God's love and generosity. Reproductive acts reduce the child to the product of a physiological or technical process, thus failing to acknowledge that as a gift given in love the child is meant to be received in love. Procreation, on the other hand, provides the appropriate context for the reception of a child precisely because it is an act of love. Rather than producing a child, the couple that procreates lovingly receives the child as a gift. Procreation preserves the very context, namely love, in which God calls the child into existence. The context of love prevents the reduction of the child to a product and corresponds to the dignity of the child, a creature willed for his own sake. Thus, procreation reflects the uniqueness of the human person both from the perspective of God's cre-

---

the powers of the human parents the way animals are produced from biological forces. The term "reproduction" when applied to the child, then, refers to the case in which the child is treated as a product of a physiological or technical process (i.e., when a child comes to be outside the context of an act of conjugal love).

[17] Cf. DV, II, 8.

ation of the soul and from the human perspective because the child is loved into existence.

Procreation: The Human Role in the Transmission of Life

Clearly procreation is not simply an act of God, as was the creation of the first man, and neither is the gift of life solely an act of God, as was the first gift of life. Rather, the creative act of divine donation takes place in the context of human sexuality and is a work of both God and man.[18] In accordance with the personal nature and the dignity of the human person, God does not use man's sexuality in a passive manner. As Janet Smith states, "Although God is the true creator of each and every human life, the role of the parents is neither unimportant nor simply mechanical."[19] The Creator has destined man and woman to participate in the transmission of life as *persons*, as "human beings made of flesh and blood, endowed with minds and hearts".[20] Therefore, the human couple fulfills an active and significant role in the transmission of life in conformity with their dignity and freedom as human persons. The sacred and profound character of this moment cannot be exaggerated. Carlo Caffarra states that this divine donation and human reception "constitutes the mysterious tangential point between the created universe of being *and* God's creative love; it is even the point at

[18] "La creazione del primo uomo e della donna è esclusiva opera di Dio; la generazione dei discendenti è opera dell'uomo e della donna in collaborazione con Dio" (Gino Concetti, *Sessualità, amore, procreazione* [Milan: Edizione Ares, 1990], p. 115).

[19] Smith, "Vocation", p. 126.

[20] Pius XII, "Address to Midwives", in *Major Addresses of Pius XII* (St Paul: North Central Publishing, 1961), p. 172.

which this creative love comes *within* the created universe of being, with a view to the *new* term of its potency."[21]

While they fulfill an active and significant role in the transmission of life, the role of the human parents remains secondary and collaborative. Man is not the master over the transmission of life but a "servant"[22] or a "minister"[23] who carries out God's plan. For that reason, the procreative power, inscribed in human sexuality, is in its deepest truth a *cooperation* with God's creative power.[24] Man's power to procreate is fundamentally the power to cooperate with God in the transmission of human life. This fundamental truth about procreation implies three principal ideas: (1) man and woman alone cannot generate a child, (2) man and woman must be co-subjects with God in the transmission of life (that is, they must actively do something *with* God), and (3) as cooperators, the behavior of man and woman is modeled upon and corresponds to that of the principal agent, namely, God.

Man and woman cannot of themselves create a child. This fundamental truth was recognized by humanity's first mother[25] and remains true for all human parents. While we can speak of the human generative power or faculty, it never functions independently of God's immediate creation of the human soul. Thus, man possesses the capacity to cooperate in the transmission of life without being the ultimate source of life. However, as a "cooperator" in the transmission of life, the human person becomes a co-subject with God. This coop-

---

[21] Caffarra, "Who Is Like the Lord", p. 257.

[22] DV, II, 4c.

[23] John Paul II, *Discourse to Priests.*

[24] Cf. ibid.

[25] "Adam knew Eve his wife, and she conceived and bore Cain, saying, 'I have gotten a man with the help of the LORD'" (Gen 4:1).

eration or co-subjectivity means that man and woman not only play an active role in the generation of life but also do so together with God's creative activity. In procreating, man and woman do something *with* God, not something of their own, not something prior to God, or even alongside God. Man and woman cooperate with God in the transmission of life by virtue of a *formal cooperation*, signifying an actual intentional concurrence between the cooperator (the human parents) and the principal agent (God). In other words, in order to avoid a mere material cooperation, "the will of the parents should be in harmony with the will of God." [26] Thus, the human couple shares a certain co-agency with God insofar as they and God both will the same goal: namely, that children be loved into existence in a due and honorable way. Moreover, as cooperators, their behavior is guided by and corresponds to the activity of God, the principal agent. For this reason, in the transmission of life man and woman "are not free to proceed completely at will, as if they could determine in a wholly autonomous way the honest path to follow; but they must conform their activity to the creative intention of God." [27]

All of this serves to point out that man and woman are the ministers of God's plan for the transmission of life, not its arbiters.[28] The procreative faculty amounts to a potential that must be guarded and cultivated, yet it always remains a potential because man is not the deciding factor in the coming to be of a new human person. No act of the human will can ensure the conception of a child. No power of the human person can generate the spiritual, immortal soul present in

[26] John Paul II, LF 9.

[27] HV 10.

[28] John Paul II, *Discourse to Priests*.

each human person. Instead, "Marital relations between two persons 'may' give life to a new person."[29] In other words, man does not possess an absolute power to generate life, or even the right to a child.[30] He cannot demand from God a child, since such a demand would negate the gift that is at the heart of the transmission of life, for nothing that can be demanded is a gift freely given. Moreover, if man negates the conjugal act's potential for generating new life by altering the sexual faculty, he likewise destroys the gift that is at the heart of the transmission of life. In doing this, man in effect wishes to manipulate God's gift, and such manipulation stands in direct contradiction to the nature of donation. God's gift cannot be freely given to the man who takes it upon himself to mitigate the potential of the conjugal act to give life to a new person or to the man who produces a child by manipulating the biological dimension of the sexual faculty. Only the man who cooperates with God's act of loving donation by conforming his will to God's can procreate.

The Subject(s) of Procreation

The nature of procreation is greatly determined by the nature of the subjects who procreate (as every philosophy student knows, *action follows being*). According to the nature of human sexuality, procreation entails a union of man and woman in and through their sexuality, for it is only in this context that humans can cooperate with God in the transmission of life. No single human person can execute an act that has the potential to be a cooperation with God in giving life to a new person. Each human person is sexual; each

[29] Wojtyla, *Love and Responsibility*, p. 227.
[30] Cf. DV, II, 8.

has a sexual faculty. Yet, no one human person possesses the potential to procreate. Neither man nor woman alone can turn to God and offer to cooperate in the transmission of life. Instead, every conception of a child, whether it is procreative or reproductive, requires at some point the encounter of a female element and a male element.[31] The potential to cooperate with God in the transmission of life exists in the encounter or union of masculinity and femininity.

An act of reproduction necessitates only a meeting of the genetic material from a male with that of a female. Reproduction requires only an essentially biochemical encounter because there is no necessary cooperation between man and woman.[32] The quality and efficacy of a reproductive act depends entirely on biological or technical factors. Whereas reproduction is simply the biochemical encounter of genetic elements, procreation requires an encounter of a different type. Due to the cooperation entailed in procreation, the encounter at the center of procreation must be an encounter of persons who complement each other precisely with regard to the generative faculty. In order to be able to cooperate with God in the transmission of life, each person must

[31] Cormac Burke writes, "Human life has its origins in sex. . . . The generation of each child, which marks the renewal and perpetuation of creation, is always and necessarily the result of the union of sexual differences" ("Marriage and Contraception", in Smith, *Why "Humanae Vitae" Was Right*, p. 167.

[32] William May distinguishes laboratory generation from procreation: "Laboratory generation of new human life, whether this involves artificial insemination, in vitro fertilization, or cloning, *is not an act in which male and female cooperate to unite their persons* [emphasis added] and in doing so give life to a new human person. Such modes of generating life *are not acts of procreation* [emphasis added], nor are they acts of the sexual persons who provide the 'material' that is used by others. They are by no means *marital* acts. They are rather acts of human art and technology, of laboratory production" (*Sex, Marriage and Chastity* [Chicago: Franciscan Herald Press, 1981], p. 30).

encounter someone of the opposite sex. The procreative potential of a single person amounts to the ability to unite and cooperate with a complementary other.

In a procreative context, there must be a co-agency or a complex agency that is established by a choice of each person to enter into this co-agency. Reproduction does not require this co-agency because the encounter of the female and male elements can take place through the act of one agent.[33] In contrast to reproduction, procreation requires man and woman to choose to encounter each other in such a way that they become co-subjects of the act. Moreover, the encounter that each must choose to participate in is very specific in nature, for if their encounter is to enable them to cooperate with God in the transmission of life, it must possess the potential to give life to a new person. A non-sexual encounter does not constitute a meeting of masculinity and femininity that possesses the potential for cooperation with God in the transmission of human life. A handshake simply will not do. Instead, the encounter must take place through their sexuality, through their being male and female. However, not just any sexual act is sufficient. An act of oral sex or manual sex simply will not do. Only the genital encounter of man and woman possesses a procreative potential.[34]

While some view the genital encounter of man and woman principally from the biological perspective, this encounter

---

[33] An example of this would be an act of rape that results in pregnancy. The woman who is raped is not a co-agent with her assailant, rather she is being acted upon, treated as an object.

[34] Concerning the genital act, William May writes, "This way of touching is unique ... because it is the only sort of touch that makes it possible for the male and female to exercise their procreative powers and to give life to a new person" (*Sex*, p. 13). *Humanae vitae* 12 states that the marital act "capacitates" man and woman for the generation of new lives.

necessarily transcends the biological order because of the substantial union between body and soul. Certainly, the genital encounter of man and woman and the transmission of life are dependent upon and pertain to certain biological factors, but they are not limited to this dimension. Because the body expresses the person and is a constitutive part of the person, the genital encounter of man and woman tends to something greater, a personal unity among the two. From this perspective, the genital encounter is not merely a biological prerequisite for procreation but also a moment in which man and woman encounter each other as persons. Inasmuch as it is a personal encounter, genital intercourse puts man and woman in a position to cooperate with each other, to become co-subjects in the act of procreating. Because of the personal nature of the body, the genital encounter of man and woman becomes an opportunity for a personal encounter; however, in light of the complementarity inherent in human sexuality, genital intercourse becomes not only the moment of *personal encounter* but also the moment of *personal union*. In other words, by virtue of the complementarity inherent in human sexuality, the physical self-giving of man and woman in the genital encounter can be "the fruit and sign of a total personal self-giving" that creates a bond between the two so long as all the values intrinsic to sexuality are preserved and protected.[35]

Human sexuality pertains to and expresses a "difference" that exists between persons. Yet, this sexual difference is not a simple difference, one that divides the human race into two categories. Rather, sexual differentiation manifests a complementarity that is the principle of and ordered to union.

[35] FC 11.

F.C.

Sexual complementarity has a priority over sexual distinction.[36] That is, masculinity and femininity, visibly present in the body, express the human person's ordination to gift and communion.[37] The sexual "differences" between man and woman are not obstacles to their union but rather constitute the possibility for union and even the means by which they can give themselves to each other.[38] Apart from sexual complementarity total self-gift and total personal union remain impossible. Furthermore, while sexual complementarity may appear to exist primarily on the level of physical structures, the bodily manifestation of sexual complementarity points to something greater, something that pertains to "the person in his ontological and existential concreteness".[39] The physical, sexual complementarity of man and woman reveals their ordination to each other as persons because sexuality is "by no means something purely biological, but concerns the innermost being of the human person as such".[40]

Because the complementarity of masculinity and femininity is an inherent and fundamental aspect of human sexuality, each authentic use of the sexual faculty must incorporate and respect this complementarity and the union to which it is ordered. In other words, each authentic use of the sexual faculty possesses a unitive aspect that corresponds to this complementarity. Certainly, the sexual organs can be used and even manipulated in non-unitive circumstances, but

---

[36] Regarding the complementarity of man and woman, consult: William May, "Marriage and the Complementarity of Male and Female", *Anthropotes*, vol. 7, no. 1 (June 1992), pp. 41–60, and *Sex;* Paul Quay, *The Christian Meaning of Human Sexuality* (San Francisco: Ignatius Press, 1985), pp. 24–31.

[37] John Paul II, General Audience of January 9, 1980.

[38] FC 11.

[39] John Paul II, General Audience of December 19, 1979.

[40] FC 11.

in this case the intrinsic purpose and symbolism of the sexual faculty is contradicted. When genital intercourse is not the fruit and sign of a total personal self-giving that results in an intimate union between man and woman, such intercourse contradicts the innate language of the body "that expresses the total reciprocal self-giving of husband and wife".[41] If we follow John Paul II's definition of chastity, in the genital encounter man and woman are called to perceive, love, and practice the meanings of the language of the body.[42] For this reason, genital intercourse is "chaste" only if it is the sign and fruit of a total personal self-giving of man and woman to each other in accordance with the language of the body. Therefore, inasmuch as it necessarily requires man and woman to encounter each other through an act of genital intercourse, procreation requires man and woman to enter into a personal union, a union based upon the complementarity inherent in human sexuality.

While the chaste exercise of the sexual faculty requires personal union, personal union is also necessitated by the cooperation of man and woman with God in the transmission of human life. Neither one person acting alone nor two persons acting separately can offer themselves to God as cooperators in his work of creation. Rather, cooperation in this case requires of man and woman a certain co-agency. In order to cooperate with God in the transmission of life, man and woman must become "one common subject, as it were, of the sexual life".[43] Man and woman are able to become "one common subject" in the act of sexual intercourse for

[41] FC 32.

[42] John Paul II, General Audience of October 24, 1984.

[43] Wojtyla, *Love and Responsibility*, p. 30.

two parallel reasons, both of which are related to man's capacity to love.

Genital intercourse presents an opportunity for man and woman to become "one flesh", or one common subject, inasmuch as it is a unique moment in which man and woman can become a mutual gift to each other through their masculinity and femininity.[44] However, sexual complementarity does not act as an irresistible force that unites the couple, because this would be contrary to the nature of human freedom. Instead, sexuality is the means by which man and woman can unite, on the basis of sexual complementarity, when genital intercourse expresses a total personal self-gift. Thus, while sexual complementarity is the principle of union and sexual intercourse is the context of union, the free choice of self-donation on the part of each person effects personal union. The choice of self-donation brings us directly into the realm of love, because to "love means to give and receive something which can neither be bought or sold, but only given freely and mutually."[45] In order to cooperate with God in the transmission of life, man and woman must become co-subjects of an act that possesses a procreative potential and offers the opportunity for a personal union between them. While genital intercourse inherently possesses a procreative potential, it effects a personal union only when it is an act of love, the fruit and sign of a total personal gift of self. Therefore, man and woman become co-subjects of the sexual life only when they love each other.

But what does it mean for man and woman to become co-subjects of the sexual life? Most fundamentally, man and woman become co-subjects in their sexual acts when they

---

[44] LF 12.

[45] LF 11.

pursue a common good together, which in turns implies that they have identified some common aim to which they subordinate and direct the sexual faculty. The goal is a common good inasmuch as they pursue it *together*. In turn, the pursuit of a common good creates a bond among persons that "unites the persons involved internally".[46] The pursuit of a common good again brings us into the realm of love, for man's "capacity to love depends upon his willingness consciously to seek a good together with others, and to subordinate himself to that good for the sake of others, or to others for the sake of that good".[47] Thus, man and woman become co-subjects of the sexual life when they love each other, when they share a common end to which they direct the sexual faculty and to which they subordinate themselves.

By the very nature of man and woman, each must go outside of himself and encounter a complementary other in order to generate new life (that is, the human person is not biologically capable of self-replication). Moreover, the encounter sought must be a genital encounter, for these faculties alone possess the ability to generate new life. When this encounter is viewed from an adequate anthropological perspective, it not only presents itself as a unique opportunity for man and woman to enter into a personal union but even demands such a union in the order of chastity. Personal union is possible in genital intercourse because the body is a constitutive part of the person and because the complementarity of masculinity and femininity is a principle of union. However, personal union is achieved in genital intercourse when it is "the fruit and sign of a total personal self-giving, in which the whole person, including the temporal dimension, is

[46] Wojtyla, *Love and Responsibility*, p. 28.
[47] Ibid., p. 29.

present".[48] Such a total personal gift of self is possible only in the context of conjugal love. Thus, for biological reasons man must seek a complementary other in order to generate new life, and for moral reasons man must be united with that complementary other in a personal union that results from love.

From this perspective we see that in order to cooperate with God in the transmission of life, man and woman must be a couple, or better yet they must be "coupled" in an act of love. The possibility for such a loving union resides in human sexuality, the means by which man and woman give themselves to each other. Therefore, ontologically (not chronologically) prior to cooperating with God in the transmission of life, man and woman must choose to couple sexually or unite themselves to each other through a sincere gift of self. In and through this sincere gift of self, man and woman form a specific communion of persons born of their love and expressed in the language of the body. The communion formed is marriage, the only place where this gift of self is accomplished in its whole truth.[49] Thus, we have arrived at a crucial point in the identification of the subjects of procreation. In order to procreate, each human person must encounter a complementary other in and through their sexuality in a genital act. According to the nature of human sexuality and its chaste exercise, the genital encounter must entail a personal gift of self, a gift that is possible only in the context of conjugal love and marriage. Therefore, procreation is possible only in marriage, and the only possible subjects of procreation are spouses. This is precisely the conclusion arrived at in the teaching of *Donum vitae*, which states, "the gift of

[48] FC 11.

[49] Ibid.

life must be actualized in marriage through the specific and exclusive acts of husband and wife."[50]

Can we really say that only spouses united in the conjugal act cooperate with God in the transmission of life? Human life is generated in many other circumstances, and perhaps the people in these circumstances are also cooperating with God. After all, he still creates the soul, and they still perform some action that makes the generation of life possible. How can we be sure that God and man are not cooperating in these circumstances but only in the conjugal act? In the light of moral criteria "deduced from the dignity of human persons, of their sexuality and their origin",[51] we can conclude that every use of the sexual faculty and every generation of life outside the conjugal act necessarily entails some injustice or immorality. In other words, we can conclude with Pope John Paul II that "to eliminate the corporeal mediation of the conjugal act as the place where a new human life can originate means at the same time to degrade procreation from a cooperation with God the Creator to the technically controlled 'reproduction' of an exemplar of the species, and thus to lose the unique dignity of the child."[52] Thus, the transmission of human life outside the conjugal act necessarily offends the dignity of the child by reducing him to a product and an exemplar of the species. If we were then to suggest that God is cooperating with the people in such circumstances, we would make him a party to injustice and moral evil, something outside the bounds of possibility. Instead, when a child is conceived outside the conjugal act, we must

[50] DV, intro, 5.

[51] DV, II, 7.

[52] John Paul II, "Human Life Must Originate in the Conjugal Act", *L'Osservatore Romano* (English ed.), September, 1, 1999.

conclude that God and man are acting separately or perhaps in a parallel manner, but never together in a formal cooperation. God creates every human soul, and "every human being is always to be accepted as a gift and blessing of God." [53] God's creation of the soul does not, however, signify that every human person is the result of a cooperation between man and God, for many times a child is begotten in an immoral or unjust way. While all children possess the same dignity and rights, those conceived outside the conjugal act have had their dignity and rights violated or ignored. We cannot describe such conceptions as *procreation*, for this would make God a cooperator in affronts to human dignity, again, something outside the bounds of possibility. Thus, we can comfortably conclude that "from a moral point of view a truly responsible procreation *vis-à-vis* the unborn child must be the fruit of marriage." [54] Consequently, only spouses truly procreate; only a married couple is the "subject" of procreation; and this only when they are the subjects of the conjugal act.

Procreation as Active Receptivity

By starting from the Church's definition of procreation as the human cooperation with God in the transmission of life, we have concluded that the only persons capable of procreation are spouses engaging in the conjugal act. How is it that man and woman so coupled cooperate with God? What form does their procreative cooperation take? The nature of the role played by man and woman in the transmission of life corresponds to and complements the creative activity of God

---

[53] DV, II, 1.
[54] Ibid.

himself in the transmission of human life. In the generation of a new human person, each child is "a gift and blessing" from God to the parents.[55] Man and woman adequately fulfill their role by establishing the proper context in which this gift of life may be received worthily (that is, in accord with their own human dignity and the dignity of the child). As with any act of giving, God's gift of a child must be received. Thus, the primary quality of the couple's cooperation in the transmission of human life is receptivity. God's creative act is the origin of human life. The human child comes from God as a gift. The role of the couple (in addition to simultaneously "coupling" themselves and thus capacitating themselves for this role), then, is to receive the gift of life from God. In other words, as a form of cooperation with God, procreation is essentially an *active receptivity* on the part of a married couple. The reception of a child is *active* precisely because God does not make use of the couple as though they were passive receptacles. Instead, he gives them a role to fulfill on the basis of their dignity and freedom as persons. The couple's activity is *receptive* because, strictly speaking, they do not generate the new human person, but rather actively receive him from God as a gift freely given.

The Christian tradition possesses in Sacred Scripture a wonderful model for the active receptivity practiced by married couples in the procreation of new life. The account of the Incarnation in the Gospel of Luke provides an exemplar for the role of human couples in the transmission of life.[56] Though there are undoubtedly miraculous circumstances involved in the Incarnation, this event centers on the gift of a child on the part of God and the human response to God's gift. The

---

[55] Ibid.

[56] Cf. Lk 1:26–36.

angel of God announces to the Blessed Virgin Mary that she will conceive and bear a son in a truly miraculous and supernatural manner. The angel announces God's gift of a child to her. God makes this gift of a child gratuitously; the Blessed Virgin has not merited the gift.

Mary responds to God's gift of a child by simply saying, "Behold I am the handmaid of the Lord; let it be done unto me according to your word." Mary's response is a simultaneous acceptance of God's will and the child that he has willed to give to her. The essence of her response is an unconditional and complete acceptance of the gift of the child that God gives her, the unconditional acceptance of divine donation. Moreover, Mary's acceptance of this gift extends not simply to the content (the child) but also, and more importantly, to the manner in which the gift is given (God's design for making this donation). In addition to accepting God's gift and his design for bestowing it, Mary inserts into her response the gift of herself in service to God, saying, "I am the handmaid of the Lord." Unconditional acceptance of both the content of divine donation and the manner in which this donation takes place, as well as a simultaneous placing of oneself in service to God, is the essence of the active receptivity entailed in man's response to God's gift of a child. Mary's *fiat* is the form that a couple's cooperation in the transmission of life should take. The role of Mary in the Incarnation represents the most profound and dramatic human cooperation with God, and as such it is the model for all human cooperation with God.

Because God's gift of a child does not normally take place in a miraculous manner, the manner in which a couple makes their *fiat* differs from that of Mary. In procreating, married couples cooperate with God in a way that, while imaging Mary's *fiat*, is entirely their own, a way that is proper and exclusive to spouses. As the cooperation of persons, procreation involves both the spiritual and bodily aspects of each spouse. Thus, the married couple's *fiat* cannot simply be an interior act of the will; it must be a bodily act. Indeed, more than simply a bodily act, cooperation in procreation must necessarily take the form of a genital act. Therefore, the human cooperation in the transmission of life consists in a genital act that manifests an acceptance of God's gift of life and the design that God wills for bestowing this gift. In other words, it consists in a genital act that manifests an acceptance of the manner in which God wills children to come into the world. The procreative act manifests an acceptance of the full significance of human sexuality and the integration of sexuality into the person of the man and the woman. As a human act, procreation essentially consists in the personal encounter of man and woman, in and through their sexuality, which manifests both an acceptance of their potential to become parents of a new person and an acceptance of God's design for human sexuality.

Accepting a child from God requires the couple to regard the child as a gift and to respect the child from the moment of conception as a fully human person. Any actions that involve the manipulation of the potential for conception that is inherent in the sexual encounter of masculinity and femininity (that is, acts of contraception or artificial fecundation) negate the donational character of God's gift of a child. Manipulations of the human potential for fertility amount to demanding God's gift of a child or to rejecting God's gift of the child. Rather than being a cooperation with God, such acts are a manipulation of God. Any action that involves the violation of the dignity of either of the spouses cannot be a cooperation with God because this would make God an accomplice to injustice. For the same reason, any action that does not respect and express the dignity of the child as a human person cannot be an act of cooperation with God in the transmission of life. In order to accept God's gift of a child in a worthy manner, married couples "must conform their activity to the creative intentions of God, expressed in the very nature of marriage and of its acts, and manifested by the constant teaching of the Church".[57] Authentic procreative acts respect the human dignity of the parents and child and the values of conjugal life.

In order to "conform their activity to the creative intentions of God" concerning the transmission of life, married couples must accept the potential and the limitations of human sexuality, as well as its intrinsic structure and finalities. God has chosen to bestow the gift of new life through human sexuality. Human sexuality has great potential, both toward parenthood and toward the union of persons. The acceptance of human sexuality's inherent design entails the acknowledgment, in action, of both of these potentials, for one cannot say that he accepts sexuality if he does not accept its powers. However, there are also limitations to human sexuality. For example, one person's sexuality does not enable that person to actualize the potentials of human sexuality, for it is only in an encounter with a complementary other that this actualization can take place. In this sense, the use of the sexual faculty is always an other-directed activity. Other limitations arise from the bodily nature of sexuality. For example, the woman's menstrual cycle is part of the bodily dimension of her sexuality. This cycle limits the time in which the physical conception of a child is possible. The potential and the various limitations of human sexuality represent God's

[57] HV 10.

design for human sexuality, and the acceptance of human sexuality entails the acceptance of its potential and these limitations. In turn, the acceptance of human sexuality's inherent design is a necessary element of procreation, for it is precisely in and through human sexuality that God chooses to bestow the gift of a child.

Only the conjugal act fulfills all of the above-mentioned criteria. Only the conjugal act manifests an acceptance of the child as the gift of God in accord with the child's dignity, while simultaneously manifesting an acceptance of the potential and the limitations of human sexuality. All other human acts can be shown to lack, in some manner, one or more of these elements that are essential to cooperation with God in the transmission of human life. Therefore, the essence of procreation, viewed from the perspective of the married couple, is a choice to engage in the conjugal act as the appropriate context for the coming to be of a child in a due and honorable way; the actual *conception* of a child is not necessary in order for the married couple to fulfill their role as cooperators or ministers in the divine plan. Procreation (understood as establishing the proper [that is, just] context for the transmission of life) is present in every conjugal act inasmuch as this act embraces all the potential and all the limitations of human sexuality in conformity with God's creative intentions, thereby satisfying the requirements of justice both toward the potential child and among the man and woman. Therefore, in order to "procreate" (cooperate with God in the transmission of life according to his creative intention), a married couple need only engage in the conjugal act in a manner suitable to and worthy of human nature and the nature of human sexuality.

Those who equate procreation with the conception of a child often miss this last point. The Church, however, has consistently expounded an understanding of procreation as "something more than the union of two seeds".[58] For example, the 1944 Roman Rota statement on the ends of marriage, their proper meaning, and the hierarchy among them described procreation from the perspective of the married couple as the conjugal act performed according to its natural structure, for this act by its very nature contains "all that is requested and suffices on the part of human activity for the generation of offspring".[59] Furthermore, the procreative aspect of the conjugal act, "which exists through its natural structure in the naturally completed conjugal act, is observed and is verified even in the wedded union of sterile persons or of others who for causes extrinsic to the act cannot generate offspring with the natural use of marriage".[60]

Thus, while sterile couples cannot *conceive*, they most certainly "procreate" each time they engage in the conjugal act in a manner suitable to and worthy of human nature because in doing so they cooperate with God in the transmission of life and accept his design for human sexuality (including the biological possibility of sterility), thereby establishing the proper context for the coming to be of a child. Married couples who practice periodic continence also "procreate" inasmuch as they engage in the conjugal act in conformity with God's creative intention for the sexual faculty, which itself limits the time in which conception can occur. Procreation, understood as the human role in the transmission of life, transcends the notion of conception and is present in every conjugal act, whether or not the act bears its full fruit.

[58] Pius XII, "Address to Midwives".

[59] Sacra Romana Rota, *AAS* 36 (1944):184–86.

[60] Ibid., p. 186.

The Fruit and Sign of Love

When procreation is viewed against the background of an integral vision of man, the profound significance of children for the married life becomes clear. Because procreation is more than the conception of a child and because procreation requires a communion between the parents, each child procreated is truly the fruit and sign of his parents' love and union. Indeed, when they procreate, "parents find in their child a confirmation and completion of their reciprocal self-giving: the child is the living image of their love, the permanent sign of their conjugal union, the living and indissoluble concrete expression of their paternity and maternity."[61] As my analysis and description of procreation has revealed, the essence of procreation is the cooperation of man and woman with God in the transmission of life, a cooperation that is possible only when the man and woman are united in an act of conjugal love. The child who is "produced" does not signify conjugal union or express conjugal love, but the child who is procreated necessarily is the fruit of an act of conjugal love and remains forever a sign and living testimony to the generosity and fecundity of that love.

Most fundamentally procreation entails the cooperation of man and God in the coming to be of a new human person. However, such human and divine cooperation is possible only to the extent that man and woman become co-subjects of their sexual life and direct their sexual faculties to a common good. Man and woman are able to procreate (cooperate with God) when they encounter each other as sexual persons, each as a self-determining subject. The order of justice requires them to act *with* each other as common subjects, seeking

[61] DV, II, 1.

together a common good.[62] The pursuit of a common good creates a bond between the persons involved because the common good by its very nature unites individuals; its commonality intrinsically possesses this unitive effect.[63] Therefore, the common good itself signifies and reflects the communion formed in and by its pursuit. Like other common goods, the procreation of a child signifies and manifests a bond and a communion between the subjects who participate in procreation, the parents (and in some sense God himself). However, by virtue of its sexual nature, procreation signifies love and union on a much deeper level than other common goods.

In procreating, man and woman are biologically dependent upon each other by the very nature of the sexual faculty. The sexual faculty of each becomes fertile only in relation to the sexual faculty of the other. Therefore, in order to procreate the man and woman must not only share a common aim but must also literally *share* their sexual faculties in an act of genital intercourse. Genital intercourse, by virtue of the complementarity of masculinity and femininity and the language of the body, is inherently unitive when it takes place according to the creative intentions of God inscribed in the very being of man and woman. The chaste exercise of the sexual faculty requires man and woman to practice the meanings of the language of the body and to make these meanings the content of their behavior.[64] Chastity requires the physical intercourse and physical union achieved in the genital

---

[62] This is one of the fundamental points of K. Wojtyla's classic *Love and Responsibility*. See in particular pp. 22–69.

[63] LF 10: "The common good, by its very nature, both unites individuals and ensures the good of each."

[64] Cf. John Paul II, General Audience of October 24, 1984.

act to be "the fruit and sign of a total personal self-giving"[65] or "a sign and pledge of spiritual communion".[66] Therefore, in addition to testifying to a physical and biological union between two persons, the procreated child is "a confirmation and completion of their reciprocal self-giving",[67] the "fruit and fulfillment"[68] of their mutual donation. For this reason, the procreation of a child signifies a union that exceeds the bond established in the pursuit of other common goods, a union by which man and woman become "one flesh" as an expression of unity on the most profound personal level.

Unlike most common goods, the procreation of a child requires a unity of the flesh that effects a personal union by virtue of the personal nature of the body, so long as this unity of flesh is the fruit and sign of a total personal self-giving. Inasmuch as the procreated child is a confirmation and completion of this mutual self-donation, he is the fruit and fulfillment of love, for the gift of self is an act of love.[69] Therefore, the procreated child signifies not only co-agency and mutual self-donation but also *love* itself. Moreover, because procreation entails the *sexual* gift of self, the love signified in procreation is *conjugal* love, the love of husband and wife, for "the only 'place' in which this self-giving in its whole truth is made possible is marriage, the covenant of conjugal love freely and consciously chosen."[70] Only spouses, in an act of love proper and exclusive to them, can procreate,

---

[65] FC 11.
[66] CCC 2360.
[67] DV, II, 1.
[68] CCC 2366.
[69] LF 11.
[70] FC 11.

and the child, once procreated, remains in the world as a "living image" of their spousal love and a "permanent sign of their conjugal union".[71]

According to the nature of the human person and the inherent design of human sexuality, procreation proceeds only from an act of love and personal union, and the child who results from this act becomes a living testimony to this love and personal union. In a very real sense conjugal love and conjugal union "capacitate" man and woman to collaborate with God in the transmission of life. However, love is not merely a prerequisite for procreation, nor is procreation a possible (that is, optional) fruit of conjugal love. Instead, conjugal love is ordered to procreation by its very nature[72] in such a way that a "child does not come from the outside as something added on to the mutual love of the spouses, but springs from the very heart of that mutual giving, as its fruit and fulfillment."[73] In other words, procreation and conjugal union are intrinsically linked not only from the perspective of responsible procreation but also from the perspective of authentic conjugal union. This intimate relationship becomes clearer in an analysis of conjugal union, the subject of the following section.

2. SPOUSAL UNION

All love and every form of friendship tends toward union because love and friendship require the sincere gift of self and the pursuit of a common good, both of which create a

[71] DV, II, 1.

[72] Cf. GS 48 and 50.

[73] CCC 2366.

bond between the lover and the beloved. While love cannot be reduced to the pursuit of a common aim, "love between two people is quite unthinkable without some common good to bind them together."[74] For this reason, any love or friendship creates a bond or unity between the friends or lovers. Likewise, any union between persons results from love as an effect of the shared love or friendship. As an effect of love, union is appropriate to or corresponds to the type of love shared. In other words, the quality and level of union depends upon the quality and level of friendship, which itself is determined by the character of the common good upon and around which the friendship forms. Thus, we have friendships of varying levels and quality due to the various types of goods we seek with others.[75] From this perspective we see that conjugal union is an effect of conjugal love that expresses the nature of the conjugal friendship itself. While the idea of conjugal union is best represented by the biblical notion of two in "one flesh", its full significance derives from a proper understanding of conjugal love, the love of which it is an effect. Therefore, I begin my definition or description of conjugal union with a discussion of conjugal love, its defining characteristics, and the common good upon which it is based.

Conjugal Love

The very notion of conjugal love is inseparable from self-donation in marriage because "love between man and woman is achieved when they give themselves totally, each in turn

[74] Wojtyla, *Love and Responsibility*, p. 28.

[75] Cf. Wojtyla, *Love and Responsibility*, pp. 84–88.

according to their own masculinity and femininity".[76] The conjugal friendship begins through the mutual generous surrender of man and woman to each other in marital consent.[77] Prior to this moment, prior to this sacred act, they share a different kind of friendship. While engaged couples and other young couples may love each other truly and intensely, *conjugal love* only exists between spouses. Only spouses love "conjugally" because the mutual gift of self that begins and informs the conjugal friendship is possible only in marriage, "the covenant of conjugal love freely and consciously chosen".[78] Moreover, conjugal love cannot be separated from the institution of marriage because the institution of marriage is "an interior requirement of the covenant of conjugal love".[79] The very act (marital consent) that brings the conjugal friendship into existence also establishes the juridical institution of marriage.

The gift of self at the basis of conjugal love must conform to the same standards as marital consent. Thus, the mutual surrender of man and woman in conjugal love is a human act or "a firm and deliberate act of the will".[80] Conjugal love results from a choice that each person (the man and the woman) must make freely and consciously. Therefore, the gift of self that joins man and woman in marriage and begins the conjugal friendship "is a far cry from mere erotic attraction"[81] and from animal unions, which do not involve the exercise of reason and will. Moreover, inasmuch as the gift

[76] Pontifical Council for the Family, *The Truth and Meaning of Human Sexuality*, 14.

[77] *Casti connubii, AAS* 22 (1930):548.

[78] FC 11.

[79] Ibid.

[80] Pius XI, *Casti connubii*, p. 542. Cf. GS 48 and CCC 1627.

[81] GS 48.

of self must be free and conscious, those same impediments that invalidate marital consent also obstruct conjugal love. The gift of self cannot occur in the context of coercion, fear, or deception. Fundamentally, then, any reason based in natural or ecclesiastical law that would invalidate marital consent also renders conjugal love between two persons impossible because the ability to love conjugally is inseparable from the ability to enter into marriage.

What, then, are the fundamental and defining characteristics of this unique friendship that begins with mutual self-donation in the act of marital consent? Conjugal love is best described as "an eminently human love" that "embraces the good of the whole person"[82] because its essential qualities derive from these two fundamental ideas. Conjugal love is *human* in the sense that it concerns all that is fully human. Man and woman are called by God to love each other as human beings made of flesh and blood and endowed with minds and hearts,[83] and so conjugal love pertains to both the senses and the spirit at the same time.[84] Conjugal love is human because it depends upon an act of free will, proceeds from knowledge grasped by the intellect, and is energized by the emotions. All the human powers converge to make conjugal love possible. As a "human" love, conjugal love cannot be relegated to one or another dimension of the person but rather is spiritual, psychological, and physical because the human person exists on all of these various dimensions.

Conjugal love is *total* because in this "very special form of friendship" husband and wife "generously share everything,

[82] Ibid.
[83] Cf. Pius XII, "Address to Midwives".
[84] HV 9.

without undue reservations or selfish calculations".[85] Conjugal love embraces the good of the whole person in the sense that man and woman exclude nothing of themselves from the mutual self-donation at the heart of conjugal love. Every aspect and quality of each spouse must be included in the gift of self and in turn received and accepted by the other. In order to preserve the fundamental character of conjugal love, no aspect of the person can be excluded from this mutual donation of the spouses to one another.[86] Moreover, every aspect of the person is given to the highest possible degree without undue reservation or calculation. This totality includes the characteristic of unity and exclusivity, which in turn include a permanence not found in other friendships. You can only make the total gift of self to one person, and "by its very nature the gift of the person must be lasting and irrevocable".[87] Thus, the conjugal friendship cannot end the way other friendships do because the totality of spousal donation embraces the whole of the person for the whole of one's life.

Conjugal love is necessarily *sexual*. The sexual nature of conjugal love follows both from its human and total character and from the self-donation required by conjugal love, a form of donation made possible by human sexuality. Because conjugal love involves every aspect of the person it

[85] Ibid.

[86] Cf. Antonio Miralles, *Il Matrimonio* (Cinisello Balsamo, Milan: Edizione San Paolo, 1996), p. 45: "L'amore, perché sia specifico dei coniugi, deve essere intimo e totale, comprendente cioè la persona amata in tutta la sua integrità spirituale e corporale che include la mascolinità/femminità." Pope John Paul II clarifies that nothing can be excluded from the spousal gift of self precisely because "the person is one and indivisible" ("Message to the Centre for Research and Study on the Natural Regulation of Fertility", *L'Osservatore Romano* (English ed.), March 11, 1998).

[87] LF 11.

necessarily extends to and includes the sexuality of husband and wife. If no aspect of the person can be excluded from the spousal donation at the heart of the conjugal friendship, then certainly the sexuality of the persons involved cannot be excluded. However, in conjugal friendship human sexuality is not only part of the *content* of spousal donation but also the *context* of spousal donation, the means by which "man and woman give themselves to one another through the acts which are proper to and exclusive to spouses."[88] Sexuality itself is "ordered to the conjugal love of man and woman".[89] The very finality of human sexuality includes the idea of conjugal love precisely because masculinity and femininity, the distinction upon which sexuality is based, express an ordination to love and communion in marriage.

Spousal donation takes place in and through human sexuality inasmuch as the complementarity of masculinity and femininity provides the possibility for such a gift of self. Indeed, the basis for conjugal friendship is the complementarity of masculinity and femininity, so this "very special form of personal friendship"[90] cannot exist between members of the same sex. Sexuality is able to serve as the basis of a personal friendship precisely because it extends to "the biological, psychological and spiritual levels"[91] and "concerns the innermost being of the human person as such".[92] By virtue of human sexuality, man and woman complement each other not only in their *bodies* but also, and perhaps more so, in their *persons*. Man and woman are able to give themselves

[88] FC 11.

[89] CCC 2360.

[90] HV 9.

[91] PH 1.

[92] FC 11.

to each other because each is able and prepared to receive the other in a way that complements or "completes" the potential of the other. Masculinity finds its full actualization in relation to femininity, just as femininity finds its full actualization in relation to masculinity, especially with respect to the generative faculty. Isolated from each other, neither the male generative power nor the female generative power can of itself generate life, instead, the potential for life resides in the union of the two. The sexual nature of spousal donation (and hence conjugal love) specifies the conjugal friendship and distinguishes it as a unique friendship among the various others that persons may share, particularly because of the bodily nature of sexuality and conjugal love and because of the inherent procreative potential of human sexuality.

Conjugal love is a *bodily* love. While all friendships are bodily inasmuch as the communication essential to friendship takes place through the body because the body expresses the person, conjugal love is bodily in a much more radical way, captured in the biblical notion of the two becoming "one flesh". Since conjugal love is human, total, and sexual, it must necessarily be bodily because the body is a constitutive part of the person. However, in addition to being a necessary part of the content of spousal donation, the body plays a vital role in conjugal love as the "substratum" of love on the basis of the innate language of the body. The language of the body is essential to conjugal love and marriage because "spouses are called to form their life and their living together as a communion of persons on the basis of that language."[93] The language of the body enables spouses

[93] John Paul II, General Audience of January 6, 1983.

to express and communicate the total gift of self in the conjugal act in a unique way, one that surpasses words or other gestures. According to John Paul II, through the language of the body "man and woman reciprocally express themselves in the fullest and most profound way possible to them by the corporeal dimension of masculinity and femininity. Man and woman express themselves in the measure of the whole truth of the human person."[94] Because this bodily or physical gift of self is absolutely essential to conjugal love, the impotent person cannot enter the conjugal covenant; there is no substitute for this unique, physical expression. As *Donum vitae* reminds us, "it is in their bodies and through their bodies that spouses consummate their marriage."[95] Because the body is a constitutive part of the person and according to the language of the body, "the *physical* intimacy of the spouses becomes a sign and pledge of *spiritual* communion" (emphasis added).[96]

Conjugal love is necessarily *procreative*. Conjugal love is ordered by its nature to the procreation of children.[97] Inasmuch as conjugal love is human, total, sexual, and bodily it must be procreative, because the power to procreate is fundamental to every person and is an inherent aspect of sexuality that cannot be excluded from the gift of self in conjugal love. Sexuality, the means by which man and woman give themselves to one another, is inherently procreative. As a sexual love that embraces the good of the whole person, conjugal love must accept, promote, and incorporate

[94] John Paul II, General Audience of August 22, 1984.
[95] DV, II, 4a.
[96] CCC 2360.
[97] Cf. GS 48 and 50.

the procreative potential of man and woman.[98] The unwillingness to procreate contradicts the very meaning of conjugal love because it expresses an objective refusal to give oneself.[99] The love between husband and wife is ordered to the procreation of new life as its fruit and fulfillment. Rather than something added on to the love of husband and wife, the child springs from the heart of spousal donation[100] and becomes a living image of their love.[101]

All love is expressed in action and proved by deeds, and conjugal love is expressed in acts that are proper and exclusive to spouses.[102] Marital consent, which brings the conjugal friendship into being, consists in the gift of self through words, but it includes the commitment to the gift of self in a bodily act. Thus, conjugal love begins with a promise, but it is consummated in "an act that is inseparably corporal and spiritual"[103] in accord with the nature of the spouses. In accord with the nature of conjugal love, consummation occurs in a sexual act that expresses the total and reciprocal gift of self while at the same time capacitating them to cooperate with God in the transmission of life. This sexual, giving, and procreative act embodies conjugal love to the extent that it can be designated *the conjugal act.* Among all the other

---

[98] K. Wojtyla writes, "Neither in the man nor in the woman can the affirmation of the value of the person be divorced from an awareness and willing acceptance that he may become a father and she may become a mother." Elsewhere he restates this thought: "Unwillingness for parenthood in a man and a woman deprives sexual relations of the value of love, which is a union on the truly personal level, and all that remains is the sexual act itself, or rather reciprocal sexual exploitation"(*Love and Responsibility*, pp. 228 and 249).

[99] Cf. John Paul II, *Discourse to Priests.*

[100] Cf. CCC 2366.

[101] DV, II, 1.

[102] FC 11.

[103] DV II, 4a.

actions a couple may perform together, only the conjugal act "incarnates" the conjugal love of man and woman, becoming a singular and irreplaceable moment of conjugal love and union. However, the conjugal act not only expresses conjugal love but also perfects the love of husband and wife inasmuch as it fosters the self-giving it signifies.[104] The conjugal act confirms the bond established by the gift of self in the words of marital consent, and from that moment the marriage bond acquires a heightened degree of indissolubility. In a very real sense, the conjugal love of man and woman cannot be separated from the actions to which they commit themselves in marital consent, principal among these being the conjugal act itself.

A description of conjugal love remains incomplete without mention of its sacramentality, both in the order of creation and in the order of redemption. Based on the language and sacramentality of the body, the conjugal love of man and woman is a sacrament in the sense that it announces and realizes in history the plan of God's love for humanity. Marriage is the primordial sacrament because it "expresses the salvific initiative of the Creator, corresponding to the eternal election of man" [105] inasmuch as it is the context in which man and woman live out the nuptial meaning of the body. The sacramentality of conjugal love is elevated to a new and supernatural level when the spouses are baptized Christians. As a sacrament of the New Law, marriage "perfects the human love of the spouses" because it "gives spouses the grace to love each other with the love with which Christ has loved his Church".[106] By virtue of sacramental grace, the love of

[104] Cf. GS 49.
[105] John Paul II, General Audience of October 6, 1982.
[106] CCC 1661.

man and woman becomes "a symbol of that new and eternal covenant sanctioned in the blood of Christ" and a "permanent reminder to the Church of what happened on the Cross".[107] By considering what conjugal love symbolizes we gain a greater insight into the very nature of conjugal love itself, that is, we see in the Cross a model for the relationship of husband and wife.

Spousal Union as the Effect of Conjugal Love

As an effect of conjugal love, conjugal union is only possible in an act of conjugal love, and it manifests the essential attributes of conjugal love. While all love unites the friends to a certain degree, the extent of the union effected by conjugal love surpasses that of other friendships. The biblical idea of the two becoming "one flesh" recalls both the uniqueness and the bodily nature of conjugal union. In no other friendship do the lover and beloved become "one flesh", because in no other friendship do the lover and beloved unite in such a physical and comprehensive manner. No matter the degree of union achieved in other forms of human friendships, even those based on close family ties, only the conjugal friendship produces a oneness as comprehensive and as firmly established as the two in one flesh terminology suggests. Conjugal love produces such a unique and secure bond by virtue of its sexual, bodily nature, which allows for a unique mutual self-donation among the spouses. In other words, conjugal union surpasses the union effected by other friendships because conjugal love provides for a type of self-donation that is unique in both its quality and degree. In turn, this

[107] FC 13.

self-donation entails the pursuit of a unique common good that establishes a union found in no other relationship, the union of being mother and father to the same child.

Union among persons results both from the gift of self and by virtue of the pursuit of a common good. The bodily and sexual nature of the gift of self in conjugal union fundamentally distinguishes conjugal union from other types of union. While other friendships may incorporate physical signs of affection such as a hug or a kiss, conjugal love entails a physical unity not found in other friendships. Because the body is a constitutive part of the person, "that unity which is realized through the body indicates, right from the beginning, not only the 'body' but also the 'incarnate' communion of persons." [108] Viewed from the proper anthropological perspective, the physical intimacy of man and woman reveals itself as "a sign and pledge of spiritual communion".[109] In other words, as an act of conjugal love bodily union expresses and realizes a personal affective union. The physical unity proper and exclusive to spouses not only signifies but also effects and perfects a communion between man and woman precisely because the body is a constitutive part of the person that "expresses" the person.

The physical union of husband and wife effects a personal union not only because the body expresses the person but also because it takes place through the sexual complementarity of the body, its being masculine and feminine.[110] Sexuality refers to the complementarity of masculinity and

---

[108] John Paul II, General Audience of November 14, 1979.

[109] CCC 2360.

[110] "L'unità coniugale è fondata sulla complementarità" (Miralles, *Matrimonio*, p. 30). Cf. also Emiliano Jimenez Hernández, *Uomo e donna, immagine di Dio* (Naples: Editrice Grafite, 1998), pp. 8–9.

femininity, a complementarity that is a principle of union. The bodies of husband and wife not only fit together physically but complement (or complete) each other in every respect. The sexual faculties of the male body remain unintelligible without reference to the female body as does the female body without reference to the male body. The structure and purpose of each helps to explain the structure and purpose of the other. More importantly, the structure and purpose of each helps to *fulfill* the structure and purpose of the other. The male sexual faculty unleashes the power of the female sexual faculty as the female faculty does for the male. Together man and woman are able to become what neither could possibly be alone or with another of the same sex: together they are able to become parents. Thus, because they give themselves sexually, spouses are able to give to each other their respective procreative powers, something that cannot be given outside the conjugal covenant.

Like conjugal love, conjugal union is necessarily procreative. Inasmuch as man and woman form a communion of persons on the basis of a sexual gift of self, their union must embrace the capacity of each to procreate because this power is a fundamental, inherent aspect of human sexuality, and thus of the human person. As K. Wojtyla states, "Acceptance of the possibility of procreation in the marital relationship safeguards love and is an indispensable condition of a truly personal union."[111] Sexual intercourse effects and signifies union between man and woman only when it is accompanied by the conscious acceptance of the procreative finality of human sexuality. Thus, Wojtyla concludes,

[111] Wojtyla, *Love and Responsibility*, p. 230.

> [Since] willingness for parenthood is an indispensable condition of love . . . it follows that sexual intercourse between husband and wife has the value of love, that is to say of a true union of persons, only when neither of them deliberately excludes the possibility of procreation, only when in the mind and will of husband and wife respectively it is accompanied by the acceptance of the possibility of paternity or maternity.[112]

Because it includes the possibility of procreation, conjugal union possesses a "totality" not found in other types of personal union precisely because they do not incorporate this fundamental power of the person. Whatever else may be said of non-conjugal unions, this procreative dimension is universally absent. However, the value of the procreative character of conjugal union derives not only from the totality that it lends to conjugal union but also from the fact that it presents to man and woman a unique common good around which a unique bond forms. Inasmuch it is procreative, conjugal love gives to man and woman the possibility to be bound together as parents, linked inseparably by the life of a child who is *theirs*. A child is the "permanent sign of conjugal union"[113] precisely because procreation requires of man and woman a unifying co-agency that extends to a whole series of acts, indeed to a lifetime of commitments (here it is important to recall the intrinsic link between the procreation and education of a child). Conjugal union surpasses the union achieved in other friendships because conjugal love unites man and woman in a unique and profound way through the life of a child who is the fruit of their love and a common good that binds them together. Conjugal love effects a

[112] Ibid., pp. 236–37.
[113] DV, II, 1.

radical union of persons by providing man and woman the opportunity to become the fount, as it were, of a family. As a common good the child creates a living bond between man and woman, contributing greatly to their good as husband and wife.[114]

In its essence, then, union refers to a "oneness" that is brought about by the mutual self-donation and the pursuit of a common good that are intrinsic to love. All love tends to union, and union between persons is possible only in the context of love. Union is indeed an effect of love, but more specifically union is the fruit and sign of self-donation and the pursuit of a common good, and thus the fruit of a choice.[115] Self-donation and co-subjectivity effect union, not as a *product* separate from these realities, but as an interior requirement, as their *fruit*. In other words, union springs from the very heart of self-donation and co-agency as a sign of the health and proper functioning of these movements. Therefore, describing the conjugal act as a "unitive" act principally designates it as an act of love and more particularly as an act that entails self-donation and co-subjectivity. The conjugal act is unitive insofar as it proceeds from a specific choice that entails a particular mode of self-donation and co-subjectivity.

The conjugal act possesses a unitive aspect/meaning precisely as an act of love, and not just any love, but *conjugal* love. However, more specifically the conjugal act unites husband and wife because it presents them with the opportunity for mutual self-donation and the pursuit of a common good. As an act that effects conjugal union, the conjugal act entails the sexual, bodily self-donation proper and exclusive

[114] Cf. GS 50.

[115] Cf. John Paul II, General Audience of November 21, 1979.

to spouses and the pursuit of procreation, the common good proper to conjugal love. The conjugal act entails genital intercourse because through this encounter "a man and woman, in the 'truth' of their masculinity and femininity, become a mutual gift to each other."[116] Only this mode of self-donation incorporates the full significance of conjugal love. All other acts of self-donation lack the full spousal meanings present in sexual intercourse by virtue of the innate language of the body. Likewise procreation takes place only in the act of sexual intercourse because any other act of fertilization is deprived of the meanings and values expressed in the language of the body that distinguish procreation from reproduction.[117] Thus, by virtue of its sexual nature the conjugal act not only unites husband and wife but uniquely unites them, because it facilitates a mode of self-donation and co-subjectivity impossible in other acts, a mode of self-donation and co-subjectivity in which man and woman cleave to one another and become "one flesh".

Just as conjugal love possesses a sacramentality, as an effect of conjugal love conjugal union possesses a sacramentality that should serve as a powerful motivation for the preservation of its integrity. In the order of redemption the union of man and woman in the conjugal covenant "signifies the union of Christ and the Church".[118] The sacrament of matrimony "gives spouses the grace to love each other with the love

---

[116] LF 12.

[117] Cf. DV, II, 4a, and John Paul II, "Human Life": "To eliminate the corporeal mediation of the conjugal act as the place where new human life can originate means at the same time to degrade procreation from cooperation with God the Creator to the technically controlled 're-production' of an exemplar of the species."

[118] CCC 1661.

with which Christ has loved the Church",[119] which in turn establishes a bond between the spouses that signifies the union between Christ and the Church. The union of man and woman can be given this supernatural significance because it possesses in itself a natural symbolism present in the language of the body, a symbolism that is elevated and extended by grace. In other words, the sacramental value of the union of husband and wife depends upon the language of the body that serves as the basis for their union. Because the physical union of man and woman possesses a natural symbolism of love and communion, it can be elevated to the supernatural signification of the union of Christ and the Church. However, if man and woman "unite" in a manner that contradicts the innate language of the body, their union loses its sacramental potential. We understand immediately that a union achieved through anything less than the total, unreserved gift of self cannot signify the union forged in the sacrifice of Christ on the Cross. Thus, man and woman have great reason to preserve the integrity of their union, preserving at the same time its sacramental signification and its greater value to the world around them.

Conjugal Fidelity and Mutual Help

Within the Church's theology of the conjugal act we see an emphasis on the idea of union, yet within the Church's theology of marriage we find the more traditional terms of *conjugal fidelity* (as a good of marriage) and *mutual help* (as a secondary end of marriage). While there are certainly subtle differences among these diverse concepts, mutual help and

[119] Ibid.

conjugal fidelity both find a certain representation in the notion of union because each of the three terms refers to the oneness of husband and wife. Conjugal fidelity, an idea associated with the Augustinian tradition recalled by Pius XI in *Casti connubii*, refers to the preservation of the oneness of the spouses that begins with marital consent. Spouses are faithful to the unity and exclusivity required by marriage, the unity and exclusivity that derives from the spouses "belonging" to each other. Mutual help, on the other hand, has biblical roots and reflects the idea that woman was made as a helper for man.[120] As helpers to each other, man and woman do more than help with the daily tasks of life; they help each other fulfill their personhood through the gift of self. For this reason, God made a complementary person for Adam rather than another man. The creation of Eve is linked directly to the notion of man and woman cleaving to each other and becoming one flesh, a clear reference to the notion of union. Consequently, mutual help has been viewed as the common life of the spouses, that is, the result of their cleaving to one another. Thus, fundamentally both the idea of conjugal fidelity and that of mutual help implicitly refer to the notion of spousal union, and all three relate to the idea of spouses giving themselves to one another in a common life, for the whole of their lives.

3. PROCREATION AND UNION AS *MEANINGS*

In his description of the conjugal act in HV 12, Pope Paul VI referred to "the two meanings of the conjugal act: the unitive meaning and the procreative meaning". By virtue of this

[120] Cf. Gen 2:18–24.

reference, Paul VI introduced a new concept and a new term into the Church's theology of the conjugal act, that of *meaning*. The introduction of the term "meaning" into the Church's theology of the conjugal act constitutes a theological innovation in the truest sense of the word because it brings to the Church's teaching on the conjugal act a new perspective from which to view the conjugal act without displacing those perspectives found in the previous teachings of the Church and in the theological tradition. Viewing the conjugal act from the perspective of its "two meanings" is innovative because it entails viewing the conjugal act in a fresh light, a light that illuminates dimensions of the conjugal act that had not been explicitly articulated by the Magisterium prior to HV. However, the perspective taken by Paul VI in HV 12 not only enhances our understanding of the conjugal act itself but also clarifies the diverse perspectives explicitly utilized in previous magisterial teachings on the conjugal act. Moreover, because of the intrinsic philosophical and theological relationship between the doctrine of HV 12 and the concepts found in the previous magisterial teachings, the new perspective of viewing the conjugal act represented by the term "meaning" serves to confirm the traditional teaching on the conjugal act rather than to displace or preclude the approaches taken in previous magisterial teachings.

Both the Catholic theological tradition and the official teachings of the Church have traditionally described and examined marriage and the conjugal act in terms of the "goods of marriage" and the "ends of marriage". Thus, the Church's theology of the conjugal act relies upon and revolves around the concepts of *good* and *end*. Each of the terms "good" and "end" represents a diverse perspective from which the conjugal act has been viewed, and each corresponds to diverse dimensions of human action. Similarly, the newer term "meaning" represents an additional perspective from which to view the conjugal act and corresponds to a third dimension of human action, a dimension that is related to but not encompassed by those dimensions of the act associated with *good* and *end*. Since it is possible to view the same reality from a variety of perspectives without denying the validity or importance of each, Paul VI's use of the term "meaning" in no way necessitates the abandonment of the more traditional concepts of good and end. On the contrary, because of the intrinsic relationship between the three terms (good, end, and meaning), the diverse perspectives represented by each term are not only compatible with each other but also dependent upon each other and ordered to each other. Thus, rather than running parallel to each other, these diverse perspectives for viewing the conjugal act intersect at key points, and a genuine appreciation of the contribution that each perspective makes within the theology of the conjugal act requires a recognition of both the differences and similarities among them.

In this section I examine the value of viewing the conjugal act from the perspective of its "two meanings" by comparing and contrasting the terms good, end, and meaning according to the manner in which they have been utilized in the Catholic theology of marriage and the conjugal act. On various occasions, the Magisterium has applied all three terms to procreation and union within teachings on the conjugal act. Thus, the first fruit of this examination is a recognition of the fact that each term (good, end, or meaning) describes or designates the realities of procreation and union from a particular perspective. The diverse perspectives represented by these terms correspond to the manner in which procreation and union enter into the various dimensions of the conjugal act as a human act. For this reason, an examination of the relationship between the diverse perspectives from which the conjugal act may be viewed also allows for a clearer understanding of the relationship of the various dimensions of human action.

Procreation and Union as the Goods of the Conjugal Act

The notion of "the goods of marriage" is most closely associated with the Augustinian tradition and serves as the basis for Pope Pius XI's discussion of marriage in the encyclical *Casti connubii*. St. Augustine wrote more on issues of human sexuality and marriage than any of the other Fathers of the Church and exercised great influence on subsequent Catholic theology in these areas. However, in recent years Augustine's contribution in this regard has been judged harshly and often criticized. As Lawler, Boyle, and May point out, "It is fashionable to portray Augustine as something of a villain in the history of the Christian theological reflection on sex, with some even accusing him of a latent Manicheism—that is, of an essentially Gnostic viewpoint which regarded sex as evil."[121] In ironic contradiction to this fashionable portrayal of Augustine, the most prominent and most lasting aspect of Augustine's theology of marriage is his defense of the goodness of marriage and his enumeration of the goods that are proper to marriage.[122]

---

[121] Ronald Lawler, Joseph Boyle, Jr., and William May, *Catholic Sexual Ethics* (Huntington, Ind.: Our Sunday Visitor, 1985), p. 36.

[122] For a balanced review of St. Augustine's teaching on marriage, consult: A. Trapè, "Introduzione generale", in *Sant'Agostino, Matrimonio e verginità* (Rome: Nouva Biblioteca Augustiniana, 1978); Francisco Gil Hellín, *Il Matrimonio e la Vita Coniugale* (Vatican City: Libreria Editrice Vaticano, 1996); Guila Gasparro et al., *The Human Couple in the Fathers* (Boston: Pauline Books and Media, 1999).

Augustine formulated his teaching on the goods of marriage within the context of his defense (primarily against the Manicheans) of the goodness of marriage as a natural institution willed by God in the creation of man and woman. According to Augustine, the goods of *offspring*, *conjugal fidelity*, and the *sacrament* constitute the goods on account of which marriage itself is good.[123] The goods of offspring and conjugal fidelity pertain to the essence of marriage inasmuch as "if either both, or one, of these be wanting, I find not how we can call it [a relationship between man and woman] marriage."[124] Thus, the goods of marriage can be described as the intrinsic and ontological reasons for the goodness of marriage.[125] In other words, the goodness of marriage corresponds to the fact that marriage allows man to participate in or partake of the goods of the procreation of children, conjugal fidelity, and the sacrament. However, inasmuch as these goods are essential to marriage, marriage itself possesses an intrinsic goodness. Thus, for Augustine marriage is good according to our original state,[126] and also in man's fallen state, despite the presence of concupiscence.[127] The Augustinian tradition grounds the inherent goodness of marriage in its intrinsic ordination to offspring, conjugal fidelity, and sacrament, the goods to which marriage tends by its very nature.

---

[123] Cf. St. Augustine, *On the Good of Marriage*, 32.

[124] Ibid., 5.

[125] According to Francisco Gil Hellín, "I beni prole, fedeltà, sacramento non constituiscono, nel pensiero di sant'Agostino, guistificazione estrinseche del matrimonio, ma sono le ragione ontologiche ed intrinseche della sua bontà" (*Matrimonio*, p. 30).

[126] Cf. St. Augustine, *On the Grace of Christ and Original Sin*, bk. 2, chap. 40.

[127] Cf. ibid., chap. 42; St. Augustine, *On Marriage and Concupiscence*, bk. 2, chap. 54.

As Pius XI reminds us, among these goods the child holds the first place.[128] Thus, according to the Augustinian tradition, marriage was instituted by God primarily for the procreation of children.[129] However, while the procreation of children possesses a singular relationship to the institution of marriage, the goodness of marriage does not rest solely upon the good of the child. Augustine sees more in marriage than the procreation of children and defends the goodness of marriage in the cases of spouses who are unable to have children for reasons beyond their control. Augustine states, "And this [the goodness of marriage] seems not to me to be merely on account of the begetting of children, but also on account of the natural society itself in a difference of sex. Otherwise it would not any longer be called marriage in the case of old persons, especially if they had lost sons or had given birth to none."[130] Thus, Augustine rejects the idea that the procreation of children is the sole cause of the goodness of marriage because there is a certain goodness in the natural, marital relationship of man and woman, a relationship that is preserved by their fidelity.[131] Conjugal fidelity, then, is a good of marriage inasmuch as the faithfulness of the husband and wife confirms and preserves the marital society, itself a good. While conjugal fidelity is a good in itself, it also possesses an intrinsic relationship to the good of the procreation and education of children because the marital society (and, therefore, conjugal fidelity itself) is intrinsically ordered to the

[128] Cf. *Casti connubii*, p. 543.

[129] According to St. Augustine, "Marriage itself indeed in all nations is for the same cause of begetting sons, and of what character soever they may be afterward, yet was marriage for this purpose instituted, that they may be born in due and honest order" (*On the Good of Marriage*, 19).

[130] Ibid., 3, 3.

[131] Cf. Gil Hellín, *Matrimonio*, p. 16.

procreation and education of children. As a consequence of this intrinsic relationship, an attack on the good of procreation necessarily destroys the good of fidelity and contradicts the very essence of marriage. According to Augustine, the Manichean rejection of procreation makes of a woman a harlot rather than a wife because "there is no marriage where action is taken to prevent motherhood, and hence no wife."[132] Pius XI also acknowledges the intrinsic connection between procreation and conjugal faith in his analysis of the goods of marriage in *Casti connubii*, stating, "Every sin committed as regards the offspring becomes in some way a sin against conjugal faith, since both these blessings are essentially connected."[133] Thus, while the child holds the first place among the goods of marriage, the Augustinian formulation recognizes the goodness of conjugal fidelity itself and the intrinsic relationship between conjugal fidelity and the procreation of children.

The Goods of the Conjugal Act

In addition to being among the goods of marriage itself, both the procreation of children and the good of conjugal fidelity are related to the conjugal act, an act that is a particular promotion of and participation in the goods of marriage. According to the Augustinian tradition, like marriage the conjugal act is principally ordered to the procreation of children, and the goodness of the conjugal act is inherently linked to the good of procreation. Consequently, sexual intercourse for reasons other than that of procreation lacks its proper perfection because it lacks the proper ordination to the

[132] *On the Morals of the Manicheans*, 18, 65.

[133] *Casti connubii*, p. 566.

principal good of the act.[134] When Augustine considers the possible reasons for sexual intercourse, he clearly holds the procreation of children up as the best and proper reason for engaging in the act.[135] He views other possible motives, such as for the purpose of allaying desire, as lacking in perfection, whereas adultery and fornication are mortally sinful. Additionally, according to Augustine the man or woman who renders the marital debt to a spouse seeking intercourse out of desire chooses a good inasmuch as such a man or woman serves the good of conjugal fidelity.

Lawler, Boyle, and May clarify Augustine's position when they state,

> Many find this teaching of Augustine distasteful or demeaning to marriage. Yet, Augustine's teaching perhaps shows a deeper appreciation of the human reality of marriage than does that of Lactantius, Chrysostom, and Damascene, for in holding that there is some minor fault when spousal relations are sought for the precise purpose of allaying desires and avoiding fornication, Augustine suggests that a basic good of marriage itself is not directly being sought but only indirectly fostered by the avoidance of an activity that is seriously disordered. What is being sought in this type of intercourse is precisely the allaying of a desire and the avoiding of an evil to which the desire may lead. It is hardly an act which precisely expresses conjugal fidelity or, in modern terms, conjugal love. Augustine did clearly teach that the spouse who serves the good of conjugal fidelity by consenting to marital relations to meet the need of the spouse seeking relations for this purpose is choosing something perfectly good, for this spouse is choosing to serve the good of marital

[134] Cf. St. Augustine, *On the Good of Marriage*, 6 and 11.
[135] Cf. ibid.

> fidelity. Marital intercourse in the service of a real good is a good itself.[136]

Two principal ideas emerge from Augustine's analysis of the possible reasons for engaging in the conjugal act: (1) unless sexual intercourse is sought for the purpose of some true good of marriage it lacks its proper perfection, and (2) the goods of marriage to be sought in the conjugal act are *procreation* and *conjugal fidelity*. The conjugal act sought for the purpose of satisfying desire entails a minor fault inasmuch as it is not the direct pursuit of authentic goods but only the indirect fostering of such goods, so long as nothing is done that is contrary to either procreation or conjugal fidelity. On the other hand, acts that either repudiate the good of procreation (contraception) or violate the good of conjugal fidelity (fornication or adultery) are seriously sinful. Thus, the conjugal act maintains its proper perfection (goodness) to the extent to which it is ordered to either the good of procreation, the good of conjugal fidelity, or both.

If there is a deficiency in Augustine's analysis of the conjugal act it is his failure to consider the possibility of spouses engaging in the conjugal act precisely as an expression of their mutual love. However, inasmuch as he does not even consider this possibility, Augustine certainly does not condemn or reject the idea of engaging in the conjugal act for the purpose of expressing love. The standards set by the Augustinian analysis of the conjugal act leave open the possibility of lawfully engaging in the conjugal act as an expression of conjugal love, precisely because the goods of procreation and conjugal fidelity pertain to conjugal love. The Augustinian formulation only requires couples to engage

[136] *Catholic Sexual Ethics*, pp. 39–40.

in intercourse in pursuit of authentic goods beyond the allaying of desire. That is, in order to be "good" the conjugal act must be engaged in for the goods of procreation or conjugal fidelity. Yet, since both procreation and conjugal faith are requirements of conjugal love, the pursuit of either procreation or conjugal fidelity is an act of conjugal love. Therefore, while Augustine does not undertake a discussion of procreation and conjugal faith as expressions of conjugal love in his analysis of the conjugal act, nothing in Augustine's teaching precludes the possibility of seeing them as such. Consequently, his view of the conjugal act is open to the possibility of viewing the act as an expression and perfection of love. In fact, while working on the basis of the Augustinian framework, Pius XI includes the cultivation of conjugal love as a possible good sought in the conjugal act even when conception is thought to be impossible.[137]

The Notion of Goodness

According to the Augustinian tradition the goods of the conjugal act are the procreation of children and the conjugal fidelity of the spouses. The presence of these goods relates directly to the perfection of the act itself, because if they are absent or if they are repudiated by the spouses then husband and wife incur some fault in the act. In other words, the goods of procreation and conjugal fidelity are the goods on account of which the conjugal act itself is good; they are the ontological and intrinsic reasons for the goodness of the act itself. While we have thus identified the goods of the

[137] *Casti connubii*, p. 566.

conjugal act, the significance of something being a good remains unspecified. What does it mean to call procreation and conjugal fidelity the *goods* of the conjugal act?

Goodness is one of the most fundamental of human concepts with a long history in Western philosophy.[138] Though the term "good" is employed in various spheres of life with varying connotations, the notion of goodness itself invariably revolves around being, desirability, and perfection. In a very profound sense goodness and being are really the same thing and differ only in idea.[139] Being is itself good, and anything that preserves or perfects being is good. Yet, the notion of goodness is distinct from being because "goodness adds to being its desirability to an appetite."[140] *Being* is *good* insofar as it is desirable, and the good is that which all things desire.[141] Goodness refers to the idea that being and its perfection can be *desired* and *sought*, not simply *known*. In other words, "being is said to be good insofar as it is desirable, in the same way it is said to be true insofar as it is intelligible."[142] According to St. Thomas, "the essential meaning of the good is that it provides a terminus for appetite."[143] Thus, in a very fundamental sense to be good means to be desirable to an appetite. However, an appetite does not bestow goodness on an object but acknowledges or bears witness to the goodness of an object through the desire produced.

---

[138] For a thorough review of the meaning of the term "good", consult: Servais Pinckaers, *The Sources of Christian Ethics*, trans. Mary Thomas Noble (Washington, D.C.: Catholic University of America Press, 1995), pp. 408–20.

[139] Cf. St. Thomas Aquinas, *Summa Theologica*, I, q. 5, a. 1.

[140] Tomás Alvira, Luis Clavell, and Tomás Melendo, *Metaphysics*, trans. Luis Supan (Manila: Sinag-Tala, 1991), p. 158.

[141] Aristotle, *Nicomachean Ethics*, I, 1 (1094a, 1).

[142] Alvira, Clavell, and Melendo, *Metaphysics*, p. 158.

[143] *Summa Contra Gentiles*, III, chap. 3.

While the notion of goodness expresses the relationship of being to an appetite, the goodness of things depends upon their act of being and not on the movement of an appetite. In other words, goodness is intrinsic to the object of desire and not bestowed upon the object by or in an appetite's movement with regard to the object. Being and the perfection of being give rise to desire, and this desire bears witness to goodness without itself being the source of goodness. Therefore, "Although the good is 'what all desire,' it is good not because of the fact that all desire; rather it is desired by creatures precisely to the extent that it is perfect or is a *being*." [144] Desirability expresses the goodness of an object, but goodness cannot be reduced to desirability alone. Inasmuch as the good is desired, the notion of goodness embraces the idea of perfection "since all things desire perfection".[145] The good is not simply desirable but also perfective and desirable because it is perfective. An object or an activity arouses desire in an appetite inasmuch as it is perceived or apprehended as perfective of the subject of the appetite. Moreover, because everything is perfected according to its own nature, the notion of goodness intrinsically refers to nature.

The notion of goodness, then, pertains to the relationship of an object (or activity) to an appetite that tends to the object or goodness of the object. With regard to the rational appetite or will, the relationship may take various forms depending upon the manner in which the will tends toward the object in which goodness has been apprehended. For example, the good may arouse desire or move the will to desire in such a manner that the will tends to the good "passively", as in the case of attraction or simple desire (that is,

[144] Alvira, Clavell, and Melendo, *Metaphysics*, p. 159.

[145] St. Thomas Aquinas, *Summa Theologica*, I, q. 5, a. 1.

I want). When the will tends to a good by virtue of attraction, we cannot speak of willing in the proper sense, because in "true willing the subject is never passively directed to an object".[146] The relationship between the will and the good in the case of simple desire correlates to the notion of *motivation*, for in this case the good moves or motivates the will rather than the will moving actively toward the good.[147] Attraction consists in the capacity of the good to move the will when the subject apprehends goodness in an object. When the will actively tends to an object, the relationship between the good and the appetite takes on a new character, and willing in the true sense occurs. In the case of active willing, the good takes on the character of an end when it is the object

[146] K. Wojtyla, *The Acting Person*, trans. Andrzej Potocki (Boston: D. Reidel Publishing, 1979), p. 127.

[147] The word "motivation" is employed in a variety of ways in different spheres of discussion. In the context of everyday conversation, motivation often possesses a psychological connotation and refers to what is "driving" a person, and a self-motivating person is one who drives himself without requiring outside encouragement. From this perspective we can also speak of subconscious drives versus conscious drives in determining what motivates a person to act in a particular way. Even in a more philosophical sense, motivation can mean the explanation or reason for the particular behavior of an agent. In the context of this study, however, I do not employ motivation in either of these two senses. Instead, I take motivation in a simpler, perhaps purer, sense as that which moves or causes movement, and this meaning corresponds precisely to the notion of good as desirable. The psychological sense of motivation and the philosophical sense of motivation described above could both fall under the scope of this more general meaning of motivation, but the idea of motivation need not play the substantial role in an act that the psychological and philosophical senses suggest. Thus, for example, some financial benefit connected to a particular activity might be attractive to an agent without being the driving force behind his activity (i.e., it is not a key factor in his decision about the activity) or the explanation for his acting (i.e., the agent desires the financial benefit [as good], but he would engage in the activity even were there no financial benefit connected to the activity).

of intention. By virtue of a decision on the part of a subject, the relationship between the good and the will passes from attraction or motivation to intention, and the good becomes an end precisely to the extent that it is intended or actively willed. Inasmuch as marriage and the conjugal act entail deliberate intention or active willing, the Church speaks of "the ends of marriage" in addition to "the goods of marriage".

Procreation and Union as the Ends of the Conjugal Act

The concept of the "ends of marriage" recalls a metaphysical approach to the institution of marriage as a natural institution and as a juridical entity. As Pius XI reaffirmed in his encyclical *Casti connubii*, God instituted marriage and endowed it with certain ends and laws that govern the pursuit of these ends.[148] The ends of marriage are the purposes for which God instituted marriage and the goals to which spouses tend in marrying, and the ordination of marriage to precise ends corresponds to the fact that as an intelligent agent God could not act without intelligible ends. As the 1944 statement from the Roman Rota clarified, the term "end" in the context of marriage refers to a good (*bonum*) that is meant to be obtained both on the part of nature and by the intention of the agents.[149] The term "end", then, most fundamentally denotes a good to which either nature or an agent tends. Moreover, the ordination of marriage to specific ends determines the very structure of marriage, because "it is always the end that determines the characteristics of any plan."[150]

[148] *Casti connubii*, pp. 542–43.

[149] Cf. Sacra Romana Rota, *AAS* 36 (1944):184.

[150] Ramón García de Haro, *Marriage and Family in the Documents of the Magisterium*, trans. William May (San Francisco: Ignatius Press, 1993), p. 119.

Thus, the ends of marriage enter into the very definition of marriage and give a certain intelligibility to the institution of marriage.

Throughout the theological tradition and with great consistency in the official teaching of the Church, both procreation and spousal union have been identified as ends of marriage.[151] Procreation is the primary end of marriage inasmuch as "the true practice of conjugal love, and the whole structure of family life that results from it, have this aim: that the couple be ready with stout hearts to cooperate with the Creator and Savior, who through them will increase and enrich his family day by day."[152] However, spousal union is also essential to marriage, inasmuch as "marriage was not instituted solely for procreation; rather, its very nature as an unbreakable compact between persons, and the welfare of the children, both demand that the mutual love of the spouses be embodied in a rightly ordered manner, that it grow and ripen."[153] Moreover, man's natural inclination to the ends of procreation and union constitute the basis for the "naturalness" of marriage between man and woman.[154] Finally, the ends of procreation and union are the ends that man and woman pursue jointly as the basis for the joining that is the essence of matrimony itself. As we read in the Supplement to St. Thomas' *Summa Theologica*, "Now things directed to

---

[151] The 1944 statement of the Roman Rota observed that marriage has the primary end of the procreation and education of children and the secondary end of mutual help as "is evident from the Constitutions and numerous encyclicals of the Supreme Pontiffs, from the common doctrine of theologians, canonists, and moralists and from the explicit words of Canon Law" (Sacra Romana Rota, p. 184).

[152] GS 50.

[153] Ibid.

[154] Cf. St. Thomas Aquinas, *Summa Theologica*, Supplement, q. 41, a. 1.

one purpose are said to be united . . . since by marriage certain persons are directed to one begetting and upbringing of children, and again to one family life, it is clear that in matrimony there is a joining . . . and this joining, through being directed to some one thing, is matrimony."[155]

The conjugal act shares with marriage the ordination to procreation and spousal union as ends. Just as procreation and union specify marriage among other human relationships and enter into the very definition of marriage, procreation and union are "essential aspects"[156] of the conjugal act inasmuch as the conjugal act cannot exist apart from the intention of these ends. According to Pope Pius XII, the human sexual faculty is "a natural power, of which the Creator himself has determined the structure and the essential forms of activity, with a precise purpose and with corresponding duties, to which man is subject in every conscious use of the faculty."[157] As the natural operation of the sexual faculty, the conjugal act possesses an intrinsic structure and proceeds "according to laws inscribed in the very being of man and woman".[158] The intrinsic structure of the conjugal act and the laws that govern its actualization derive from an ordination to the purposes or ends that God himself has assigned to the act. As with marriage itself, the ends and essential aspects of the conjugal act are procreation and union.

Inasmuch as procreation and union are *goods* intended by God and by the spouses in marriage, as *ends* procreation and

[155] Ibid., q. 44, a. 1.

[156] HV 12.

[157] Pius XII, "Address to the Micro-biological Union of San Luca, November 12, 1943", in *The Teachings of Pius XII* (New York: Pantheon Books, 1957), p. 43.

[158] HV 12.

union retain the fundamental characteristics of the goods of marriage. As goods of marriage, procreation and union are the intrinsic and ontological reasons for the goodness of marriage inasmuch as they are essential to marriage.[159] Moreover, inasmuch as they are goods, the ends of marriage are desirable and perfective. The desirability and the perfective character of the ends of marriage express the relationship of the realities to an appetite and to the subject of the appetite. Thus, as *goods intended*, procreation and union are desirable and perfective to the spouses. However, the notion of end attributes to procreation and union a character not expressed in the term "good". In addition to desirability and perfection, the term "end" embraces deliberate (intelligent) intention (active willing). As ends, procreation and union are the essential aspects of marriage and the conjugal act that are intended on the part of God and on the part of the spouses. The ends of marriage contribute not only to the intrinsic goodness (that is, the desirability) of marriage and the conjugal act but also contribute to the intelligibility of the various aspects of marriage and the conjugal act and account for their intrinsic structure.

Procreation and union do not lose their status as goods when the term "end" is applied to each of them precisely because the definition of an end includes the term "good". Instead, the term "end" adds a further perspective from which the realities of procreation and union are viewed. While the good relates to the will as that which motivates the will in the case of attraction, an end relates to the will as that which is intended by the will in the case of active willing. As ends, procreation and union retain the character of goods precisely

[159] Cf. Gil Hellín, *Matrimonio*, p. 30.

because the will only intends that which is apprehended as desirable.[160] However, in acquiring the character of ends, procreation and union pass from being that which motivates the will to that which the will intends. The notion of good and end correspond to diverse movements of the will and represent diverse dimensions of a human act in the sense that the good can give rise to an act when it motivates the will, while an end gives the ontological structure to an act when it is intended by the will.

The Concept of End in Human Action

With regard to human action, the *end* is "the first goal of the intention and indicates the purpose pursued in the action".[161] The end of an act constitutes "the principal intention of the agent, without which the act would not be realized".[162] As the object of intention or the purpose of the act, the end is properly the object of the interior act of the will.[163] The *end* of an act comprises one of the three fundamental components of every human act (*actus humanus*),[164]

---

[160] St. Thomas Aquinas writes, "Now every appetite is only of something good. The reason of this is that the appetite is nothing else than an inclination of a person desirous of a thing to that thing" (*Summa Theologica*, q. 8, a. 1).

[161] CCC 1752.

[162] García de Haro writes, "Precisando ulteriormente, il fine è l'intenzione principale dell'agente, senza la quale l'atto non sarebbe realizzato" (*La vita cristiana* [Milan: Edizione Ares, 1995], p. 254).

[163] Cf. St. Thomas Aquinas, *Summa Theologica*, I–II, q. 18, a. 6.

[164] I employ the terms "act" and "human act" in a technical sense that corresponds to St. Thomas' *actus humanus* (see *Summa Theologica*, I–II, q. 1, a. 1). Human acts, then, are those actions that proceed from free will and over which man exercises dominion. According to Martin Rhonheimer, "They are actions, in other words, that man carries out in personal autonomy, in freedom, and with rational consideration: through the will and intellect, man is

along with the *object* of choice (*means*) and the *circumstances* of the act. Each of these components is willed by the agent and thus contributes to the moral character of the act; each must be in accord with right reason in order for an act to be morally good.[165] In every human act, the means, end, and circumstances are willed by the agent. The end, however, is willed differently from the means or circumstances inasmuch as the end is willed in itself while the means and circumstances are willed for the sake of the end. Thus, the end of an act occupies a particular role within the structure of the act and gives to the act its very reason for existence and intelligibility, for the end of an act explains why a particular external activity would be chosen in this particular manner.

Human activity manifests human freedom, a power that is "rooted in reason and will".[166] The very meaning of rational activity includes the ability to act for the sake of an end apprehended as good, and the notion of end is present in every human act as an indication that the human agent acts intelligently. Indeed, as St. Thomas states, "Now, there is no question that intellectual agents act for the sake of an end, because they think ahead of time in their intellects of the things which they achieve through action; and their action stems from such

---

master of his own actions" (*Natural Law and Practical Reason: A Thomist View of Moral Autonomy*, trans. Gerald Malsbary [New York: Fordham Press, 2000], p. 411). Cf. García de Haro, *Vita cristiana*, p. 181: "Pertanto, atto umano o libero è quello che promana dalla volontà illuminata dall'intelligenza. Esso è esclusivo delle creature spirituali, che fruiscono di potenza intellettiva e volitiva, di potenze cioè sono capaci di governare liberamente la propria condotta." Cf. also Wojtyla, *Acting Person*, pp. 25–31.

[165] CCC 1755: "A *morally good* act requires the goodness of the object, of the end, and of the circumstances together."

[166] CCC 1731.

a preconception."[167] The fact that action stems from the preconception of an end signifies the fact that a human act depends upon the end for its very existence, for the object of choice, while pertaining to the essence of the act, is willed for the sake of the end. Though the end is the goal of an act and the terminus of an act, the end is first in the order of intention because the selection of an end precedes the choice of the means of the act. The human agent desires the means and circumstances of a given act inasmuch as he apprehends them to be conducive to an intended end. Thus, the end constitutes the life-giving principle of an act and provides intelligibility to an agent's desire for the means and circumstances of the act.

Along with the object of choice, the end of an action pertains to the essence of the act, representing the "form" of the act whose "matter" is the object of choice.[168] However, whereas man wills the object of choice for the sake of the end or as a means to the end, "the end is willed in itself" as the terminus of the movement of the will.[169] As the *Catechism* states, "The object chosen is a good toward which the will deliberately directs itself."[170] The object or means in a human act pertains to the dimension of active willing inasmuch as the will directs itself toward the means as "a freely chosen kind of behavior" and "the proximate end of a deliberate decision".[171] The end of an action is also a good

---

[167] *Summa Contra Gentiles*, 3, chap. 2.

[168] Cf. St. Thomas Aquinas, *Summa Theologica*, I–II, q. 18, a. 6.

[169] Ibid., I–II, q. 8, a. 3. Cf. also I–II, q. 12, a. 2.

[170] CCC 1751.

[171] VS 78 states, "The object of willing is in fact a freely chosen kind of behavior. . . . By the object of a given act, then, one cannot mean a process or an event of the merely physical order. . . . Rather, that object is the proximate end of a deliberate decision which determines the act of willing on the part of the acting person."

toward which the will directs itself. In the case of an end, however, the good is willed for its own sake by a particular act of the will. The act of the will regarding the means as ordained to an end is called *choice*, and the act of the will regarding an end as achieved by some means is called *intention.*[172] Therefore, the means and the end differ both with regard to the sake for which each is willed and in the manner in which each is willed. Man wills the means for the sake of the end by virtue of choice, whereas the end is willed in itself and is *intended* rather than *chosen*. Both the means and the end are actively willed as good or desirable, yet each is willed in a different manner through different acts of the will.

The intention of the end, then, is the first act of the will with regard to active willing, for intention precedes the other acts of the will concerning a given action, such as choice or consent. However, the intention of the end is not absolutely

[172] Cf. St. Thomas Aquinas, *Summa Theologica*, I–II, q. 13, a. 4. The *Catechism of the Catholic Church* (1752) defines intention as "a movement of the will toward the end: it is concerned with the goal of the activity." Throughout my study of the conjugal act I employ the term "intention" (or "intend") according to this basic definition provided by the *Catechism*. Thus, for example, when I speak of "the intention of procreation and union", I mean "a movement of the will toward procreation and union as the ends or goal of the act". This basic definition of intention leaves open the possibility of various forms or types of intention, such as *actual intention* (the goal is present in the subject's mind in the very performance of the act), *virtual intention* (an act possesses a goal by virtue of a decision on the part of the agent in the initial undertaking of an activity, but the goal of the act does not remain present in the subject's mind throughout the performance of the act), *habitual intention* (an act possesses a goal through a decision made by the agent prior to engaging in the activity; the decision, however, is not renewed at each performance of the act, and thus the goal may not be present in the mind of the subject in each performance of the act). The fundamental characteristic of intention, then, is the movement of the will toward some good(s) as the end or goal of an activity by virtue of a decision on the part of the agent. Without such a movement of the will, an activity ceases to be a "human act" [see footnote 164 above].

the first movement of the will toward the good because attraction precedes intention. The good motivates or attracts an agent inasmuch as said good is desirable. A reality remains simply an apprehended good so long as it merely produces desire in the subject, but such a reality becomes the end of an act when it is intended as the goal of an activity. The reality (that is, the thing desired) itself remains the same, while the relationship between the reality and the will passes from the order of motivation (simple wanting or non-effective willing) to the order of intention. For this reason, the reality itself remains a good throughout, inasmuch as it remains desirable and perfective and *desirable as perfective*. Thus, while the order of intention (and the notion of end) corresponds to a particular relationship between the will and some reality, a relationship in which the reality is intended as the goal of an activity, the intended goal always retains the character of a good. Consequently, while not every good becomes the end of an act (that is, not every good desired is then willed as the goal of a particular activity), every end is a good, and the notion of end adds to the notion of good the idea of intention, the idea of the appetite intelligently or deliberately directing itself to a good as the goal of an activity.

The difference between the order of motivation and the order of intention serves as the basis for the distinction between the term "good" and the term "end" in a description of human action. The term "good" conveys the desirability of an object and corresponds to the level of attraction. In the human act the desired good may become the end of the act if the agent wills such a good as a goal (wills the motivating good for its own sake). As an end, the desired good becomes the principle of the act that gives the act a certain intelligibility and indeed its very reason for existence. On the other hand, a desired good can also merely enter into the circumstances of the act as a foreseeable good consequence of the act rather than becoming its end.[173] When the motivating good becomes part of the circumstances of the act, such a good may possibly contribute to the intelligibility of an act. It does not, however, possess the character of an end for the sake of which the means are chosen.[174] Because motivation pertains to the circumstances of an act, motivation does not pertain to the substance of the act and does not stand as the principle of action. In distinction to motivation, the term "end" specifies the manner in which a good enters into the essence of the act, and thus "end" adds the notion of being intended as a goal to the notion of desirability expressed in the term "good".

As ends of the conjugal act, procreation and union, then, are not simply goods that make the conjugal act attractive or desirable but are also the goals that the spouses intend in the action. The conjugal act results from willing "a freely chosen kind of behavior"[175] for the sake of procreation and union, and the intention of procreation and union provides intelligibility and an intrinsic structure to the act inasmuch

---

[173] Cf. García de Haro, *vita cristiana*, pp. 255–56.

[174] Regarding the sense in which I intend "motivation", see footnote 147 above. García de Haro describes motivations that enter into the circumstances of an act as "accidental motivations" because they do not pertain to the substance of the act precisely because the act would be realized even in the absence of these goods. To illustrate the difference between an intended end and an accidental motivation, he refers to the difference between acting *ex vanitate* and simply acting *cum vanitate* (cf. *vita cristiana*, pp. 255–56). In the context of the conjugal act, physical pleasure represents a good example of a "motivating good" or an "accidental motivation" inasmuch as the pleasure associated with the act makes the act attractive and can contribute to the intelligibility of the act without necessarily becoming an end without which the act would not be realized.

[175] Cf. VS 78.

as procreation and union are the essential aspects of the act.[176] Because procreation and union pertain to the essence of the conjugal act, the conjugal act does not and cannot exist apart from the intention of these two ends. Even while other goods may enter into the circumstances of the act as motivations, the conjugal act remains inseparable from the intention of procreation and union.

Procreation and union pertain to the essence of the conjugal act primarily as the intended ends for the sake of which the act is performed; however, they also enter into the intrinsic structure of the act as the object chosen. In certain actions the intention of the end possesses a particular character when the end is not the product of the act but simply the action itself.[177] The conjugal act is just such an act because spouses do not intend to produce procreation and union by means of a specific kind of behavior but rather simply intend the activities of uniting and procreating as ends in themselves.[178] In other words, procreation and union are both

---

[176] Cf. HV 12.

[177] Cf. St. Thomas Aquinas, *Summa Contra Gentiles*, 3, chap. 2: "Now if an action does in fact terminate in something that is made, the inclination of the agent tends through the action toward the thing that is produced. But, if it does not terminate in a product, then the inclination of the agent tends toward the action itself. So, it must be that every agent in acting intends an end, sometimes the action itself, sometimes a thing produced by the action."

[178] Cf. William May, *Marriage: The Rock on which the Family Is Built* (San Francisco: Ignatius Press, 1995), pp. 95–96: "The marital act is not an act of 'making', either babies or love. Love is not a product that one makes; it is a gift that one gives—the gift of self. Similarly, a baby is not a product inferior to its producers; it is, rather, a being equal in dignity to its parents. The marital act is surely something that husbands and wives 'do'; it is not something that they 'make'. . . . Even when they choose this act with the ardent hope that, through it, new human life will be given to them, the life begotten is not a product of their act." Cf. also Carlo Caffarra, "La fecondazione *in vitro*", *Anthropotes* vol. 6, no. 1 (May 1985), pp. 111–13.

the ends for the sake of which the act is performed and the proximate ends of the deliberate decision that constitutes the object of choice. Inasmuch as the object of choice is not "a process or event of the merely physical order",[179] the object of choice entailed in the conjugal act possesses an ontological identity that can be known and described apart from the physical elements of the behavior. This ontological identity derives from the proximate ends of the will, which in the case of the conjugal act are procreation and union. Thus, there are two senses in which procreation and union are the ends of the conjugal act because procreation and union pertain to the essence of the conjugal act both as the intended ends for the sake of which the act is performed and as the proximate ends that ontologically specify the moral object of the act.

Procreation and union are the ends of the conjugal act inasmuch as spouses intend and choose them as such in the free exercise of the sexual faculty. The ontological structure of the conjugal act derives from the intention and choice of procreation on the part of spouses because the structure of a human act corresponds to the level of active willing and not to the physical components of an action. When, for example, Pope Pius XI speaks of the intrinsic structure of the conjugal act in *Cast connubii*, his comments refer to the structure that derives from the intention and choice necessarily entailed in the conjugal act. Each human act is distinguishable by virtue of the ends intended and the means chosen on the part of the human agent. Thus, two actions may differ with regard to their moral species even though they entail the same physical structure, just as the conjugal act differs from adultery though each entails genital intercourse.

[179] Cf. VS 78.

Procreation and Union as the Meanings of the Conjugal Act

While the notions of the goods of marriage and the ends of marriage both enjoy a long tradition in Catholic theology, the concept of the meanings of the conjugal act gained prominence only with the use of this terminology in HV 12. References to procreation and union as the meanings of the conjugal act do not appear in the writings of St. Augustine, St. Thomas, and the other authors of the theological tradition or in official magisterial teaching prior to the promulgation of *Humanae vitae*. Nonetheless, the idea of procreation and union as the meanings of the conjugal act currently stands at the center of the Church's theology of the conjugal act. The value of the relatively new term "meaning" rests in the manner in which it embraces and builds upon the previously employed terms "good" and "end" while adding to them another significance that furthers the Church's effort to view the conjugal act in the light of an integral vision of man. While the term "goodness" corresponds to human desire and perfection and while the term "end" expresses the human ability to intend goods deliberately, the term "meaning" relates to the human subject's ability to experience his deliberate intentions and to experience himself as the subject of such intentions through consciousness. Thus, meaning includes the human capacity for experience in addition to the human capacity for rational activity that is expressed in the notion of an end. In other words, just as "end" includes and expands upon "good", "meaning" includes and expands upon "end" by viewing procreation and union from the perspective of conscious experience.[180]

---

[180] The term "meaning" as it was used in HV 12 and as it is discussed here should not be confused with the *symbolic meaning* of the conjugal act. The

Within his reflections on HV 12, Pope John Paul II identifies "the ontological dimension" of the conjugal act and the "subjective and psychological dimension" of the conjugal act as two distinct yet closely related dimensions of the one act between the spouses.[181] According to this view of the conjugal act, the ontological dimension consists in the nature and the fundamental structure of the conjugal act as a human act. As such, the ontological dimension corresponds to the intention of procreation and union as ends because the conjugal act receives its intrinsic structure from the ends for the sake of which it is performed.[182] The ontological dimension also refers to the intrinsic structure of the act as it is inscribed in the very being of man and woman because procreation and union are the ends of the sexual faculty according

---

symbolic meaning of the conjugal act, which I discuss in section 1 of chapter 4, derives from the physical structure of the act, which possesses a symbolic value by virtue of the resemblance it bears to certain spiritual realities. The symbolic meaning of sexual intercourse is always present (by virtue of its physical structure) independently and regardless of the intention of the agents. The symbolic meaning of the conjugal act is bound up with what Pope John Paul II calls "the innate language of the body" (FC 32). In the context of HV 12, however, "meaning" refers to the awareness or experience on the part of the man and woman who are engaging in the conjugal act (cf. Karol Wojtyla, "The Teaching of *Humanae Vitae* on Love", in *Person and Community*, trans. Theresa Sandok [New York: Peter Lang, 1993], p. 308) and derives from the actual performance of the act as a human act (*actus humanus*). For this reason, while the symbolic meaning of the conjugal act is present independently of the intention of the agents, the unitive and procreative meanings of the act are directly dependent on the intention of the agents.

[181] Cf. General Audience of July 11, 1984.

[182] As a human act (*actus humanus*), the conjugal act is distinguished from other sexual or genital acts by the intention and choice entailed in the act, not by its physical structure. Thus, the ontological identity of the act derives not from its physical structure but precisely from this movement of the will. I further consider the components of the conjugal act as a human act in section 1 of chapter 4.

to the design that God has given the faculty. The ontological dimension, then, amounts to a view of the conjugal act from the perspective of active willing with regard to the ends intended in the act and inscribed in the nature of the faculty itself. In other words, the ontological dimension corresponds to "conscious acting" or man's capacity for voluntary action based on the cognition of an end.[183]

The subjective and psychological dimension of the conjugal act, on the other hand, refers to that dimension of the act expressed in the notion of meaning. The subjective dimension of the conjugal act directly relates to the ontological dimension because the ontological dimension serves as the basis for the subjective dimension, and in a sense becomes the subjective dimension when it is "carried over into the conscience and the decisions of the acting parties".[184] John Paul II describes the interrelation of these two dimensions in terms of the entrance of the truth of the ontological dimension into the subjective dimension, clarifying that the truth is "first in the ontological dimension ('fundamental structure') and then—as a result—in the subjective and psy-

---

[183] Concerning the idea of "conscious acting", consult Wojtyla, *Acting Person*, pp. 27–31.

[184] General Audience of July 11, 1984. By virtue of this relationship between the subjective dimension and the ontological dimension of the conjugal act, the meanings of the conjugal act are "objective" inasmuch as they derive from the nature of the act as an act of conjugal love. In other words, though the meanings of the act correspond to the level of human experience or awareness, human consciousness does not fabricate the meanings of the conjugal act. Instead, the meanings (i.e., the realities of procreation and union) exist first in the ontological dimension of the act and then, as a result, enter into the subjective dimension of the act. For this reason, we can describe procreation and union as *the meanings of the conjugal act* and not merely as a subject's personal experience.

chological dimension ('significances')".[185] Inasmuch as John Paul II sees a strict correspondence between the meanings of the act and the subjective dimension of the act, a specific relationship between the meanings of the act and the ontological dimension emerges, a relationship in which the meanings of the act are derived from the truth of the ontological dimension. The interrelationship between the ontological dimension and the meanings of the act is possible through the function of the human consciousness.

While the ontological dimension of the act corresponds to man's capacity for *conscious acting*, the subjective dimension corresponds to the notion of *consciousness of acting* whereby man possesses an awareness of his acting consciously. Man becomes aware of his conscious acting through the function of consciousness, which reflects or mirrors the object of cognition and all that man does in his acting. In human action, "consciousness accompanies and reflects or mirrors the action when it is born and while it is being performed".[186] Inasmuch as human action is born in the deliberate intention of an end and is performed through free choice, consciousness mirrors or reflects both intention and choice. However, as Wojtyla points outs, "consciousness not only reflects but also interiorizes in its own specific manner what it mirrors, thus encapsulating or capturing it in the person's ego".[187] The manner in which consciousness reflects and interiorizes intention and choice allows man to experience intention and choice and to experience them as his own.

The function of reflection and interiorization performed by man's consciousness explains how the two meanings of

[185] General Audience of July 11, 1984.

[186] Wojtyla, *Acting Person*, p. 31.

[187] Ibid., p. 34.

the conjugal act are derived from its ontological dimension. As ends in the ontological dimension of the conjugal act, procreation and union become the two meanings of the conjugal act when husband and wife experience them as the object of intention and choice through the awareness provided by consciousness. Procreation and union are cognized and intended as ends first, and then they are interiorized as meanings through the functioning of consciousness. If consciousness and meaning function in this manner in human action, then procreation and union are meanings of the conjugal act only to the extent that they are ends of the conjugal act. Moreover, spouses cannot have an authentic experience of procreation and union unless they intend procreation and union. If the subjective dimension of the conjugal act derives from the ontological dimension of the act, only the intention of procreation and union yields the experience of procreation and union as the meanings of the conjugal act.

Does this understanding of *meaning* in turn imply that spouses who do not experience themselves as intending procreation and union have no procreative or unitive meaning in their conjugal act? The ontological dimension of the conjugal act derives from the active willing of husband and wife because a human act (*actus humanus*) possesses its structure from the movement of the will, not from a physical process or event. Thus, there is no conjugal act apart from the intention/choice of procreation and union. Consequently, the meanings of the conjugal act cannot exist apart from the intention/choice of procreation and union. Moreover, because procreation and union are the ends (essential aspects) of the act and of the sexual faculty itself, the meanings are truly *the meanings of the act*, not mere fabrications of human consciousness.

Yet, how many couples have an experience of procreation and union during the conjugal act? Certainly, many couples may not experience themselves intending procreation and union as such during the conjugal act but instead know these realities under another name: *conjugal love*. Because procreation and union relate intrinsically to conjugal love and indeed are the fruit of conjugal love, they can be encompassed by the larger notion of conjugal love. With regard to the conjugal act, procreation and union are essential components of the movement of the will associated with conjugal love. Consequently, when spouses intend conjugal love and experience conjugal love in the conjugal act, they necessarily intend and experience procreation and union under the larger concept of conjugal love, precisely because *by intending the whole one intends its essential parts*. Thus, in an authentic conjugal act spouses experience procreation and union either as ends as such or as contained in the larger notion of conjugal love, provided they have intended authentic conjugal love in their sexual encounter.

Can spouses ever experience union without intending union as it is understood by the Church? Some couples may experience a type of "union" in their sexual relations even if they have not intended union by the complete gift of self (for example, if they are using contraceptives). However, such an experience is not authentic and amounts ultimately to delusion. Most likely such a couple experiences the recognition of union as a good that motivates them and attracts them. In other words, they experience their attraction to the notion of union through sexual intercourse. Without ever intending union, however, they cannot have the experience of an act that is genuinely unitive. To experience a non-unitive act as unitive is nothing more than illusion; they are experiencing something that is not really there. This is made possible because the attraction to union is present. Yet, being attracted and acting are quite different realities, and the experience of each is radically different. The illusion of meaning results from an over-concentration on motivation rather than intention. Thus, to experience union or procreation authentically, spouses must actually procreate and unite. In other words, the meanings of the conjugal act are only present in the conjugal act, which proceeds from a specific intention and choice.

4. THE INDISSOLUBLE CONNECTION

The doctrine of the indissoluble connection between the procreative and unitive meanings of the conjugal act (henceforth IC), initially formulated in HV 12, stands at the center of Catholic sexual ethics and has "great importance on the anthropological and moral planes".[188] As a doctrine with implications on both the anthropological and ethical levels, the doctrine of the IC essentially affirms a morally relevant anthropological fact. Viewed from this perspective, the IC belongs principally to the metaphysics of the human person and secondarily to the field of sexual ethics. Thus, a proper understanding of the IC requires first an understanding of the manner in which the doctrine is anthropological and also an idea of how anthropological facts possess implicit but nonetheless real moral significance.[189] As anthropological fact, the IC comprises part of the moral criteria "drawn from the

[188] DV, II, 4c.
[189] DV, intro., 3.

nature of the human person and human action" in the light of which matters of sexual ethics are examined.[190]

The Indissoluble Connection as an Anthropological Fact

When I initially considered the doctrine of the IC in section 1 of chapter 2, I noted the descriptive character of the doctrine, describing HV 12 as a set of affirmations or a statement of fact. Here I return to this line of thought in order to clarify the manner in which the doctrine of the IC is a fact and, more precisely, the sense in which it is an anthropological fact. What does it mean to say that the IC is an anthropological fact? First, as a statement of fact the doctrine of the IC is not directly normative but rather descriptive. That is, the doctrine of the IC states what the case *is* rather than what it *ought to be*. It is a fact that there is an indissoluble connection between the procreative meanings/aspects of the conjugal act. The IC is not something that ought to be established by man in his actions. The principle of inseparability does not state that man ought to maintain or observe the connection between the unitive and procreative meanings of the sexual act. Instead, independently of human volition, the very nature of the conjugal act entails the IC. Both the language of HV 12 and the very definitions of union and procreation suggest the factual nature of the IC.

The factual nature of the IC is essential to an understanding of the doctrine, and it clarifies the criteria for establishing the veracity of the doctrine. Factual statements are verified differently from normative or value statements. The statement "there is an indissoluble connection between the unitive and

[190] GS 51.

procreative meanings of the marital act" differs fundamentally from the statement "you ought to love your neighbor" or even "it is wrong or immoral not to love your neighbor." Normative and value statements center around the idea of moral goodness, while descriptive statements refer to being as such. The doctrine of the IC falls into the latter category inasmuch as it concerns being directly. The truth, then, of the doctrine of the IC is a matter of the speculative intellect. This truth, however, has practical and ethical implications.

The exact relationship between facts and normative statements remains complex and often debated,[191] yet we can at least acknowledge that certain facts have serious ethical implications, and more specifically that ethical differences often stem from diverse concepts of the human person. The very idea of ethics (that is, of discussing the moral quality of human acts) proceeds from a prior though often unarticulated anthropological conclusion that man acts freely and thus

---

[191] A consideration of the relationship between facts and values or normative statements often arises in the context of discussions of natural law and the formulation of universal moral norms. The relevance of theoretical facts for ethical conclusions has received renewed interest in the English-speaking world in recent decades due, at least in part, to the efforts of Germain Grisez, John Finnis, and Joseph Boyle to develop a natural law theory that does not proceed from the basis of theoretical knowledge. Examples of this line of thought can be found in: John Finnis, *Natural Law and Natural Rights* (Oxford: Clarendon Press, 1983), and Germain Grisez, "The First Principle of Practical Reasoning: A Commentary on the Summa Theologiae, 1–2, Question 94, Article 2", *Natural Law Forum* 10 (1965). For further considerations of the relationship between fact and value, see, for example: Alasdair MacIntyre, "Hume on 'Is' and 'Ought'", *The Philosophical Review* 67 (1959); Ralph McInerny, "The Principles of Natural Law", *American Journal of Jurisprudence* 25 (1980); and Henry Veatch, "Natural Law and the 'Is-Ought' Question", *Catholic Lawyer* 26 (1980–1981). For a summary and analysis of these diverse positions, consult: Robert A. Gahl, Jr., *Practical Reason in the Foundation of Natural Law according to Grisez, Finnis, and Boyle* (doctoral diss., Roman Athenaeum of the Holy Cross, 1991).

responsibly. Many anthropological conclusions of this type logically precede ethical discussion. Other anthropological facts more directly relate to ethical discussion because they help to determine the course of the discussion. For example, once the purpose of a faculty is grasped, this knowledge of what the faculty's purpose *is* cannot be divorced from the discussion of how the faculty *ought* to be employed. Whatever the relationship between fact and value or normative statements, the doctrine of the IC certainly possesses ethical implications of great importance. The manner in which the IC stands at the center of magisterial teaching on contraception, artificial fecundation, and other issues of sexual ethics manifests the ethical significance of the doctrine.

Moreover, the doctrine of the IC does not simply state one fact among millions of facts about the created universe but rather regards an anthropological fact of considerable importance; it regards the substantial unity of man as body and soul. While the IC ostensibly concerns the sexual act, the doctrine of the IC primarily regards what it means to be a human person in the exercise of one's sexual faculty. More specifically, it represents a statement of or affirmation of the unity of the human person. As M. Rhonheimer states, "It is an anthropological principle expressing the fundamental unity of human persons as compound beings of body and spirit." [192] The connection between the unitive and procreative meanings of the conjugal act derives from and expresses the unity of the human person.[193] In one sense the doctrine of the IC is known from the proper definitions of procreation and conjugal union. These are accurately known, however, only in

[192] M. Rhonheimer, "Contraception, Sexual Behavior, and Natural Law", in "*Humanae vitae*"*: 20 anni dopo*, p. 87.

[193] Cf. DV, II, 4a.

the light of an integral vision of man, the subject of both procreation and union. The IC and the inseparability principle derive from the nature of the human person as a composite of body and soul. The IC becomes apparent only from the anthropological perspective that views man as a composite unity. In turn, the IC testifies to this unity of the human person and helps us to understand that "the body is a constitutive part of man, that it belongs to his being and not his having."[194]

The doctrine of the IC testifies to the substantial unity of the human person, and thus the personal nature of the body, at the moment of sexual intercourse. Some analyze the sexual act in such a way as to distinguish and even isolate its various meanings, such as those that are biological or physical from those that are spiritual or personal, or those that are conscious and intentional from those that are subconscious and non-intentional. However, such an approach to the conjugal act erects artificial barriers between spheres and dimensions of the act that are interrelated and integrated by their nature. The sexual act possesses these various aspects because the human person encompasses these various dimensions and has the potential to execute an act that contains these various elements. The biological and spiritual aspects of the act correspond to the human person's potential to operate on both the spiritual and bodily planes. Man has the capacity for both spiritual love and bodily operations. These diverse spheres meet most prominently in the sexual faculty of man because sexuality pertains to the biological, psychological, and spiritual dimensions. In and through the sexual faculty, physical expressions signify and effect a profound love and

[194] John Paul II, *Discourse to Priests*.

spiritual communion.[195] By virtue of the unity of the person, physical intercourse "is meant to become a type of language by which husband and wife are able to express to each other all that they wish to say in the way of love and spiritual union".[196] Thus, the diverse values of sexual intercourse are interrelated because they correspond to the diverse aspects of the human person that are interrelated by virtue of the unity of body and soul.

The various aspects and values of the sexual act can be considered distinctly on the theoretical or conceptual level, just as the various aspects of the human person can be considered individually on the theoretical or conceptual level. However, the conjugal act itself consists in the unity and interpenetration of its various components just as the human person consists in a unified totality of body and soul. Man is essentially a composite of body and soul, with various faculties and capacities that belong to the body and the soul. Yet, the human person comprises the totality of the unity of body and soul and their respective capacities. The human person cannot be relegated or reduced to any single element of the human composite. The person is both "a soul which expresses itself in a body and a body informed by an immortal soul".[197] Likewise, the human person cannot be reduced to one of his faculties or functions; they all equally pertain to the person even if some more clearly distinguish man from the other animals. In a similar manner (indeed, because of this unity of the person), the sexual act possesses various aspects and meanings, yet the unity, the coming together of these various aspects and meanings, constitutes the act itself.

---

[195] Cf. Pius XII, "Address to Midwives", p. 171; GS 49; CCC 2360.

[196] Quay, *Christian Meaning*, p. 36.

[197] FC 11.

Because the human person is an integrated whole, each component of the human composite manifests itself in some manner in every human act. Thus, it is not possible to say that here the body is the subject of this act and there the soul is the subject of that act. Rather, as Rhonheimer states, "Human acts are always, although in different ways, acts of body *and* spirit *cooperating*. Human acts therefore are . . . always acts of a *body*, though of a *spiritually informed* body . . . always acts of a *spirit*, although a *bodily bound* spirit." [198] Every human act represents the unity and integration of the human person, body and soul. Otherwise, one is forced to embrace a dualistic anthropology or a fragmented notion of the human person in which isolated aspects could be the subject of acts. Unfortunately, some modern approaches to human action, including so-called fundamental option theories and proportionalism, tend toward fragmentation and disintegration. In particular, those who embrace a fragmented view of the person tend to reduce the body to a raw datum devoid of personal value and to reduce the person to consciousness and conscious experiences. However, the Church has rejected such dualistic and fragmentary anthropological approaches and their implications for human action, affirming instead the integrity of the person as a unified totality.[199]

Love and Friendship

The substantial unity of the human person possesses particularly important implications within the area of love and

[198] Rhonheimer, "Contraception", p. 88.

[199] See, for example, John Paul II, VS 48. For a concise description and critique of the fragmentary or "disintegrative" view of the human person, consult: William May, *Marriage*, pp. 75–80.

friendship. Friendship or love, which can seem to be a wholly spiritual or non-material reality, involves both the bodily and spiritual aspects of the human person. The very nature of friendship requires the subjects of the friendship to possess a manner in which to be present to each other and the ability to communicate with each other. No matter how lofty or "spiritual", every friendship requires this presence and communication. Human persons are present to each other and communicate with each other through their bodies because the body expresses the person and makes interpersonal communion possible. At the same time, it is only because man has an interiority that he can be the subject of friendship and that bodily gestures have personal significance. Therefore, in a particular way, acts of friendship are always acts of body and soul cooperating. Therefore, "man is called to love and self-giving in the unity of body and soul"[200] because he is "a soul which expresses itself in a body and a body informed by an immortal spirit".[201]

In addition to being the subject of friendship, the human person is also in a particular way the content and object of acts of love and friendship. All love and friendship tends toward union and the gift of self. Inasmuch as friends unite through self-donation, they are the subjects and objects of acts of love, for it is they who give and receive and they themselves who are given and accepted. This is particularly true of the conjugal friendship because of the quality and degree or extent of self-donation required by the very nature of conjugal love. Conjugal love, based upon a total giving and receiving on the part of the spouses, effects a union by which "the two become one flesh." Self-donation in conjugal

[200] Pontifical Council for the Family, *Truth and Meaning*, 10.
[201] FC 11.

love embraces the good of the whole person, thus, the whole person becomes the content of the gift of love. Because of the substantial unity of the human person, this gift necessarily includes both the bodily and spiritual aspects of the person, including in a special way one's sexuality, which constitutes the *means* of or the principle for the giving and receiving that occurs in the conjugal friendship. Sexuality is the foundation or means of this giving and receiving by virtue of the complementarity of masculinity and femininity, a sign of the human person's ordination to gift and communion.

The unity of the human person possesses clear implications for the sexual self-donation required by conjugal love, inasmuch as this unity requires such donation to be "an act that is inseparably corporal and spiritual".[202] How, though, does the unity of the human person effect or necessitate an indissoluble connection between the two essential meanings/aspects of the conjugal act? The unity between the two essential meanings of the conjugal act derives from the unity of the human person, who is both the subject and the object of the act, as a sexual person. In a particular way, the intrinsic relationship of procreation and union derives from the fact that each pertains to the same human faculty, the sexual faculty. The sexual faculty of the human person is a complex power in that it is ordered to two ends: union and procreation. As the actualization of the potential of this faculty, union and procreation are the one complex object of the sexual act. Therefore, in the sexual act, one can no more isolate procreation and union from each other than one can fragment human sexuality. Sexuality permeates the entire human person, and as such it cannot be fragmented without

[202] DV, II, 4a.

the fragmentation of the human person. The sexual faculty is one complex faculty of the human person that penetrates the spiritual and bodily aspects of the person, and its actualization is one complex reality that involves the spiritual and bodily aspects of the person.

Because of the manner in which the doctrine of the IC is often presented, it can appear as though the ultimate source of the connection between the unitive and procreative meanings of the marital act is simply the structure of the act itself. That is, the connection seems to be the result of the structure or the nature of the conjugal act, or even the structure of the sexual organs themselves. The IC is intimately related to the "structure" of the marital act and also to the nature of the sexual organs; however, the relationship is not one of cause and effect. Instead, the relationship is one of final cause to formal cause. The twofold end of procreation and union determines the intimate structure or inherent design of the conjugal act, for it is always the end that determines the characteristics of any plan. The source of the connection between these essential meanings is not the structure of the act, but rather the structure of the act manifests an ordination to these ends in accord with the nature of the realities themselves. Thus, the conjugal act possesses an intrinsic structure by virtue of its ordination to these ends, but it receives its ordination to these ends from the nature of conjugal love and marriage.

What, then, is the source of the connection between these two realities? The true source of this connection lies in the metaphysical structure of the human person and the nature of human sexuality. Procreation and union are indissolubly linked because man's capacities to procreate and to enter into conjugal communion are indissolubly linked. In turn, these capacities are linked by virtue of the substantial unity of the person, which has far-reaching implications in the area of conjugal love. By virtue of the substantial unity of body and soul, the body expresses the person and serves as the basis of interpersonal relationships. In the conjugal friendship, the body serves a special purpose because it makes possible the total gift of self required by conjugal love and expresses this self-donation in the language of the body. In other words, a union achieved outside the body cannot be a conjugal union because it lacks the spousal significance uniquely expressed in the language of the body in sexual intercourse. By virtue of the substantial unity of the person, the body becomes a "constituent element"[203] of conjugal union, not an instrument with which conjugal union is achieved and expressed.

For its part, the body possesses an inherent procreative potential that must be included in the mutual self-donation of the spouses. The human intellect discovers an ordination to the fruitfulness of the transmission of life inscribed in the body. The designations *male* and *female* signify the diverse manners in which the human body manifests this ordination to fruitfulness through the transmission of life. The biological terms *male* and *female* express primarily a genital difference. Therefore, if the body cannot be left out of the total donation of self, neither can the body's ordination to fruitfulness through the transmission of life be left out of the total donation of self. Put another way, the fruitfulness, of which maleness and femaleness are manifestations, cannot be excluded from the total gift of self anymore than one's maleness or femaleness can be; one's maleness or femaleness cannot be excluded anymore than one's body can be; and one's body cannot be excluded anymore than one's soul. The

---

[203] John Paul II, General Audience of November 21, 1979.

fruitfulness through the transmission of life, one's being male or female, one's body and one's soul are all essential and united in the self because of the basic unity of the body and the soul.

However, procreation and union are not indissolubly connected by virtue of the substantial unity of body and soul because procreation pertains to the body and union pertains to the soul. The Catholic position does not argue that procreation and union are intrinsically linked by virtue of the substantial unity of the person inasmuch as procreation = body and union = soul. Rather, the unity of the body and soul prevents either union or procreation from being relegated to the realm of either body or soul.[204] If man were such that he could fragment himself or isolate certain aspects of himself, then it would be possible to have a human friendship or sexual union that was not both bodily and spiritual. However, as a unified totality, man cannot fully give himself to another in sexual union without that donation encompassing the spiritual dimension of his personhood, his body, and his being male or female with its ordination to procreation.

This understanding of the relationship between the substantial unity of the person and the intrinsic link between union and procreation hinges primarily on a "specifically human meaning of the body"[205] and a particular understanding of man's dominion over his own body. The relationship between union and procreation derives from the fact that "man is not the owner and absolute lord of his body, but only its usufructurary".[206] Man exercises a stewardship over

---

[204] Cf. Rhonheimer, "Contraception".

[205] VS 50.

[206] Pius XII, "Address to the Micro-Biological Union of San Luca".

his body, but his use of the body is orientated and limited by the immanent teleology of the body and its faculties. Man and woman express and realize conjugal union through the body, but they do not *use* the body as an instrument. Instead, they speak with the body, in the language of the body, in accord with its inherent finalities. If they reject these inherent finalities, the body fails to express union because such a rejection contradicts the innate language of the body. In the physical expression of conjugal love man and woman are confronted with the "insurmountable limits to the possibility of man's domination over his own body and its functions".[207] In turn, these limits derive from the substantial unity of the body with a spiritual soul, a unity that distinguishes it from the rest of the visible universe and draws it into the realm of the personal.[208] Ultimately, then, the link between union and procreation derives from and bears witness to the fact that "the body is a constitutive part of the person, that it belongs to his being and not to his having."[209]

The Indissoluble Connection

The idea of the IC refers principally to a mutual relationship between procreation and union in the conjugal act. It also pertains, however, to the very nature of the realities themselves. The IC recognizes the intrinsic relationship between the two meanings of the conjugal act, stating that they are indissolubly bound to each other. Yet, insofar as procreation and union are linked to each other by their very definitions, the doctrine of the IC belongs to the very definitions of the

[207] HV 17.
[208] Cf. DV, intro., 3.
[209] John Paul II, *Discourse to Priests.*

essential aspects of the conjugal act. The "connection" itself possesses certain characteristics that follow from the manner in which it belongs to the definitions of procreation and union. These principal characteristics of the connection between union and procreation are: (1) the connection is indissoluble and exceptionless; (2) the connection is intrinsic to the two meanings/aspects of the conjugal act; (3) the connection exists in the existential level, not merely the conceptual or theoretical level; and (4) the connection is self-evident in a qualified sense.

The connection between the two essential meanings/aspects of the conjugal act is exceptionless and indissoluble. This exceptionless and indissoluble character implies two essential things about the connection. First, the connection is exceptionless and indissoluble to the extent that any attack on or negation of one meaning is necessarily an attack or negation of the other. As Cormac Burke states, "one cannot annul the procreative aspect or the procreative reference of the marital act without necessarily destroying its unitive function and significance.... In other words, if one deliberately destroys the power of the conjugal act to give life, one necessarily destroys its power to signify love."[210] The refusal to procreate prevents conjugal union inasmuch as it is a refusal to give oneself and is a contradiction of the innate language of the body through which conjugal union is established.[211] Likewise, the conception of a child outside the context of true conjugal union is not an act of procreation because it remains deprived of the spousal meanings expressed in the language of the body in the conjugal act, spousal meanings

[210] C. Burke, "Marriage", pp. 154–56.

[211] Cf. John Paul II, *Discourse to Priests*, and FC 32.

that are essential and defining characteristics of procreation.[212] Procreation and union interpenetrate each other such that neither can be annulled or suppressed independently of the other.

In turn, the exceptionless and indissoluble character of the connection means that neither procreation nor union exists individually, and thus, no act contains solely one of the meanings. There is never an instance of procreation without the union of spouses, and there is never a union of spouses that is devoid of the procreative meaning. As Bartholomew Kiely states, "Each of the two meanings is preserved in its integrity only if the two remain united."[213] Man cannot fully give himself to another while attempting to exclude the procreative aspect of his personhood, nor is the conception of a child procreation if it is not in the context of conjugal donation and union. Martin Rhonheimer writes, "Procreation considered independently from spiritual love *is not the same thing anymore.* And spiritual love tending to bodily union between male and female considered apart from its procreative meaning *is not the same thing anymore either.* This is precisely what follows from man's substantial body-soul unity."[214] Union and procreation exist as one complex whole, or not at all.

The idea of an indissoluble and exceptionless connection between procreation and union may seem to stand in direct contradiction to simple observation. Many situations appear to represent either procreation without union or union without procreation. Two simple examples are the case in which

---

[212] Cf. DV, II, 4.

[213] B. Kiely, "Contraception, In Vitro Fertilization and the Principle of Inseparability", in "*Humanae vitae*": *20 anni dopo*, p. 330.

[214] Rhonheimer, "Contraception", pp. 90–91.

a rape victim becomes pregnant and the case of a married couple that has been medically diagnosed as sterile. The lack of a loving union between a rapist and his victim is obvious to all. The question remains, then, if there can be an act of procreation in this act of violence. Because of the exceptionless nature of the connection between procreation and spousal union the answer must be no, but the real reason behind the negative answer lies in the definition of procreation, examined in section 1 of this chapter. While an act of rape may result in the *conception* of a child, it is never an act of *procreation*, man's cooperation with the creative love of God. Similarly, if a couple is sterile and remains childless throughout their marriage, does the exceptionless nature of the connection between procreation and union imply that there is also no unitive meaning in their conjugal acts? No, the physical sterility of a couple does not necessitate the absence of the procreative meaning from their conjugal acts. Again, this is grasped only in the light of a proper understanding of procreation that recognizes the greater meaning of procreation above the *conception* of a child. Apparent contradictions to the exceptionless nature of the IC are generally dispelled through an adequate definition and understanding of the two meanings themselves, precisely because the IC is intrinsic to the definitions of procreation and union.

The indissoluble connection between the two essential meanings/aspects of the conjugal act is intrinsic to the meanings/aspects. The source, and guarantor as it were, of the exceptionless nature of the indissoluble connection is the intrinsic nature of the connection. That is, because the connection is intrinsic to the realities themselves (that is, belongs to the very definition of each) there can be no exceptions to the connection. For that reason, the word "connection" describes the relationship of procreation and union only when it is used in a qualified sense, and understanding this qualification is necessary to understanding the idea itself. We can speak of a "connection" between procreation and union, yet because the bond belongs to the definition of the realities themselves, it is not something that unites two otherwise individual meanings or ends. Procreation and union of their very natures are connected because of what each reality is, and this again is a reflection of the substantial unity of the human person.[215]

The connection that exists between the meanings of the conjugal act can, therefore, be contrasted with the bond that unites husband and wife. The bond between husband and wife is similar to the connection between the meanings of the conjugal act in that it is indissoluble. Furthermore, the marriage bond fully unites the husband and wife such that they become "one flesh" just as procreation and union become the one twofold end of the conjugal act. However, the marriage bond is not intrinsic to husband and wife as the IC is to procreation and union. Man and woman exist outside the marriage bond prior to entering it. Each has an independent intelligibility prior to the bond's formation. The

---

[215] Rhonheimer writes, "Thus for a correct and exhaustive understanding of the Inseparability Principle it seems to be decisive to recognize that these two meanings are neither two meanings solely 'added' to one another nor merely two conjoined or accumulated 'functions' of which each has its full intelligibility independently from the other. Rather, I should say, each one receives its full intelligibility as a human reality—its full human meaning—precisely from the other. . . . If we consider things in this perspective of an anthropology which takes seriously the substantial unity of body and spirit then the reason why these two meanings are inseparably connected becomes obvious: by separating them we would alter both the meaning of human procreation and the meaning of marital loving union. Both meanings are not extrinsically, but intrinsically connected: the very connection constitutes the specifically human content of both meanings" (ibid.).

same is not true of procreation and spousal union. Both their existence and their intelligibility are bound together by the very nature of the realities themselves. One can have neither procreation nor union without the other, and one cannot sufficiently define or understand procreation or union without reference to the other.

Therefore, the term "connection" must be employed in a qualified sense to designate the relation of procreation to spousal union. The IC does not constitute a bridge or connector that serves as the principle for the unity of these two realities. Rather, the principle of unity between procreation and union is found in the respective natures of the realities themselves. The intrinsic relationship between procreation and union pertains to the very definition of each. The idea of a "connection" between the two refers to a certain aspect of the definition of each rather than to a third reality. Thus, as the connection belongs to the definition of procreation and conjugal union, an adequate understanding of this term is not possible apart from the definitions of the meanings/aspects themselves. The mutual relationship between union and procreation should be considered as a defining characteristic of each rather than a third entity in itself. In other words, rather than isolating the relation in itself, concentrating on the manner in which procreation and union mutually enter into each other by definition yields a better understanding of the indissoluble connection itself. In this line of thought, Rhonheimer states that the indissoluble connection signifies the "*reciprocal inclusive correlation*" of the two meanings of the conjugal act.[216] The intrinsic nature of the IC derives from the fact that the relationship between procreation

[216] Ibid., p. 90.

and union results from the fact that each term includes the other in its definition. For this reason, the term "connection" should only be used in a qualified sense because it can convey the idea of a third reality that extrinsically unites procreation and union.

However, there are various possible phrases to describe the manner in which procreation and union are related to each other, and "indissoluble connection" (*nexu indissolubili*) not only remains valid but also reflects the Magisterium's own language to describe this relationship. Rhonheimer's phrase "reciprocal inclusive correlation" seems particularly insightful and concise because it reflects the intrinsic character of the relations. The same is true of William May's approach in which he describes procreation and union as "inherently and indissolubly interrelated".[217] Any similar terminology is helpful inasmuch as it clarifies the intrinsic character of the relationship. The intrinsic nature of the IC is crucial to this doctrine because it serves as the basis of its indissoluble character. The intrinsic character of the connection requires one to "cut the very heart out" of the realities in any attempts to separate or isolate them from each other, destroying both in the process. The intrinsic character of the mutual penetration of procreation and spousal union also places the principle of their unity within the realities themselves such that they are not dependent on a third factor (for example, the intention of the spouses or the structure of the act) for their unity.

A third essential characteristic of the IC is its existential character. As noted in chapter 2, some perceive a certain "existential lack of harmony" between the doctrine of the IC and

---

[217] William May, "An Integrist Understanding", in *Dimensions of Sexuality*, ed. Dennis Doherty (New York: Doubleday, 1979), p. 107.

what man experiences in daily sexual life. This misperception often results in a notion of the IC that relegates it to the purely conceptual level and makes it an ideal, denying its practical significance. According to this approach, there is clearly a conceptual relationship between procreation and union because the concept of procreation is necessarily linked to spousal union and vice versa. However, on the existential level it is possible, because "the conditions in which human beings live conspire at times to separate the two functions existentially", to have an instance of one of the meanings isolated from the other.[218] The indissoluble connection becomes then an ideal on the existential level while remaining the standard on the conceptual level. While the ideas of procreation and union are clearly connected, in the actualization of these two realities, they co-exist only occasionally under the right conditions. Thus, it is an ideal to have both together, but this ideal is not always possible.

Clearly, the Church intends the doctrine of the IC as more than a theoretical ideal, as is evident from the context of *Humanae vitae* in which the doctrine was originally formulated. Moreover, it would seem that the answer to this line of thought could be found in the exceptionless character of the connection, because if there are *no exceptions* to the IC, then the existential plane is not exempt from manifesting this connection. However, this avoids the more specific question of whether the exceptionless and indissoluble character of the IC extends to the existential level or whether the IC is only a conceptual ideal to which man can aim. The answer to this question emerges from the definitions of procreation and conjugal union, definitions that indicate that

[218] James P. Hanigan, *What Are They Saying about Sexual Morality?* (New York: Paulist Press, 1982), p. 33.

these two realities are more radically connected in the practical order than they are on the conceptual level. That is, procreation and conjugal union can only be distinguished as concepts while they remain completely integrated as objects of choice. Procreation and union can be distinguished as diverse meanings/aspects of the conjugal act, but it is not possible to actualize either as *the* meaning of the act. Instead, the meaning of the conjugal act encompasses both. In other words, while we can conceive of each as a distinct meaning related to the other, as Wojtyla points out, "These aims can . . . only be realized in practice as a single complex aim."[219] On the existential level, procreation and spousal union become a single, complex object of choice; they exist as one complex actualization of man's potential for sexual union, never as independent realities. Thus, the doctrine of the IC pertains to the existential level more strictly than to the conceptual level.

Unfortunately, certain contemporary theologians commonly deny the existential, intrinsic connection between procreation and conjugal union. As a review of the antithesis of the doctrine of the IC reveals, the roots of this denial often stem from an inadequate understanding of procreation, which in turn results from more serious anthropological errors. The following pre-*Humanae vitae* statement from Rosemary Radford Ruether represents this mode of thought: "We must then make clear that the procreational and the relational aspects of the sexual act are two semi-independent and interrelated purposes which are both brought together in their meaning and value within the total marriage project, although it is not only unnecessary but even biologically impossible that

[219] Wojtyla, *Love and Responsibility*, p. 68.

both purposes be present in every act."[220] This line of thinking hinges primarily on a poor understanding of procreation, an understanding of procreation that is fundamentally biologistic.[221] Notice that the supposed impossibility of each purpose being present in every conjugal act derives from *biological* reasons. This mistaken view of the conjugal act represents not only a failure to recognize the intrinsic relationship of union and procreation but also a failure to recognize the personal nature of procreation, something affirmed throughout the official teachings of the Church.

This common misconception of procreation results from a faulty anthropology. The anthropology operating in this line of thought allows for aspects of the human being, such

[220] "Birth Control and the Ideals of Marital Sexuality", in *Contraception and Holiness* (New York: Herder & Herder, 1964), p. 73.

[221] Many so-called "revisionist" theologians embrace a reductive and physicalistic notion of procreation indicative of a dualistic anthropology. Thus, Ruether refers to "the biological cause and effect that produce the child" ("Birth Control" p. 75), and Richard McCormick argues, "It is not the sexual organs which are the source of life, but the person" ("Notes on Moral Theology", *Theological Studies*, vol. 29, no. 4 [December 1968], p. 730). A more recent example of this line of thought is found in Lisa Sowle Cahill, "Accent on the Masculine", in *Understanding "Veritatis Splendor"*, ed. John Wilkins (London: SPCK, 1994), where Cahill describes the Church's emphasis on procreation as the "sacralisation of physical processes" (p. 57) and speaks of the "procreative function" (p. 57) as though the transmission of human life were merely a bodily function. Each of these authors embraces the idea that a child is the product or effect of his parents, locating the source of human life in "the person" (McCormick) and implicitly denying the fact that God is the source of human life, indeed the Author of Life. If the soul is the principle of life and if God creates the soul immediately (CCC 366), then the human person is not the source of life. Moreover, this being the case, the child is not produced by a "biological cause and effect" (Ruether) and the transmission of life is not a "physical process" (Cahill) to be sacralized. The physicalistic notion of procreation expressed by these authors (and others) diverges greatly and fundamentally from the Catholic concept of procreation (summarized in section 1 of chapter 3) and betrays, in my opinion, an unfortunate empiricism.

as the potential for procreation, to be merely biological realities. Such an anthropology is dualistic inasmuch as it isolates the *personal* from the *bodily*. Conversely, an integral vision of man, one that rejects such dualism, does not allow for such a fragmentation of the human person and recognizes both the bodily and spiritual aspects of the person as "personal". The biologistic understanding of procreation that is the heart of the antithesis of the doctrine of the IC results from an anthropology that does not fully understand, or accept, that the body is a constitutive part of the person, even (perhaps especially) in its procreative faculties. The rejection of the doctrine of the IC betrays a faulty anthropology, because if one begins with an adequate anthropological vision and a correct understanding of conjugal love, the doctrine of the IC is self-evident. This brings us to the final essential characteristic of the IC.

The doctrine of the IC is self-evident in itself. The doctrine of the IC "has to be shown rather than demonstrated" because it cannot be proven deductively.[222] The doctrine of the IC is known in the knowledge of its fundamental terms. For this reason, while the doctrine of the IC is not self-evident to man, it is self-evident in itself. If one knows the definitions of the terms involved in the doctrine of the IC, the truth of the doctrine is self-evident. In other words, the very definitions of procreation and union contain the idea of an intrinsic connection between them. And because these definitions are known only in the light of a proper anthropological vision, a lack of knowledge of the IC stems not only from a faulty notion of procreation and union but also from an inadequate anthropological reference point. When these real-

[222] Rhonheimer, "Contraception", p. 87.

ities are viewed in the proper light, the IC becomes self-evident.

CONCLUSION

Within her theology of the conjugal act the Church affirms that the conjugal act is both procreative and unitive in its essential aspects and in its meaning. The relevance of this affirmation gains its greatest significance in a careful reflection on the definitions of "procreation" and "union" and on the significance of the concept of "meaning" in human action. A proper understanding of procreation reveals the profound and sacred character of the conjugal act insofar as procreation entails man's cooperation with God in the transmission of life. The conjugal act allows man to receive from God perhaps the greatest gift he bestows in the natural order, the gift of life. In addition to a profound and complex character, procreation brings to the conjugal act the basis of love insofar as it is a common good around which husband and wife form a communion of persons. As a common good, procreation relates intimately to spousal union, both necessitating union by its very definition and entering into the conjugal character of spousal union. The presence of these two goods transforms sexual intercourse into the conjugal act, into an act of love. Yet, procreation and union not only bring the dimension of love to the conjugal act but also allow the act to share in a very special form of friendship: the conjugal friendship. Thus, procreation and union possess a twofold significance for a theology of the conjugal act: (1) they make the act an act of love, and (2) they give the act its conjugal character. Conversely, apart from these goods sexual intercourse is neither an act of genuine love nor conjugal.

The presence of the term "meaning" in the Church's theology of the conjugal act signals the manner in which procreation and union remain at the heart of a concept of the conjugal act when it is viewed from diverse perspectives. Procreation and union are not only the essential aspects of the conjugal act in the order of intention but also the meanings of the act in the order of human awareness and experience. As a human act, the conjugal act is born in the intention of procreation and union, for these ends give both life and intelligibility to the act. Moreover, through the functioning of human consciousness husband and wife are able to experience their intention of procreation and union. Thus, in light of the role of procreation and union in confirming the conjugal act as an act of love, husband and wife are able to experience their love for one another in the conjugal act so long as they preserve the meanings of the act through the intention of procreation and union. This approach to the conjugal act reveals the manner in which each dimension of the conjugal act intrinsically relates to the other dimensions of the act. Beginning with the intention of procreation and union, the conjugal act entails an experience of love, a symbolic expression of love, and the sacramental representation of God's love for humanity and Christ's love for the Church. Yet, if spouses take the intention of procreation and union away from sexual intercourse, they lose the essence of the act and consequently its meaning and sacramental significance.

In the final chapter of my study I consider the conjugal act in its diverse and interrelated dimensions in order to identify the intrinsic relationship between each dimension and each dimension's ultimate dependency on the intention of procreation and union. Drawing upon the fundamental components of the Church's theology of the conjugal act, I consider the conjugal act as a human act that proceeds from intention and choice, as a symbolic act that utilizes the language of the body, and as a sacramental act that shares in the sacramentality of the conjugal covenant. In each of its dimensions the conjugal act centers on the notion of personal union formed around the common goods of procreation and union. In the second part of the final chapter I summarize the principal anthropological tenets that provide the necessary theological framework and ultimate rationale for the Church's theology of the conjugal act. Here I concentrate not only on the manner in which each of these anthropological tenets contributes to a theology of the conjugal act but also on the manner in which this anthropological vision confirms the conjugal act as a truly "personal" act.

Chapter Four

The Conjugal Act as Personal Act

The idea of the conjugal act as personal act signifies a conviction that the conjugal act is "personal" because it draws upon and incorporates the defining characteristics of the human person. In other words, the conjugal act is the type of activity that only human persons can engage in because it relies upon specifically human traits in its very performance. In this chapter I reflect on the nature of the conjugal act and also the manner in which it relies upon and fulfills man's potential as a person. I begin with a consideration of the conjugal act as a human act proceeding from rational intention and deliberate choice, and also consider the conjugal act in its symbolic and sacramental dimensions. Each of these approaches to the conjugal act centers on the notion of personal union through the intention/choice of procreation and union as an act of conjugal love. In the subsequent section of the chapter I review the anthropological tenets that provide the inner rationale and ultimate coherency for the Catholic concept of the conjugal act as a human, symbolic, and sacramental act. Here I concentrate on the unity of body and soul in the person, freedom understood as *theonomy*, the role of conscience and consciousness in human action, and man's potential for co-subjectivity. These various anthropological tenets converge to create a vision of man that provides an adequate framework for the theology of the conjugal act as personal act.

1. THE CONJUGAL ACT CONSIDERED IN ITS VARIOUS DIMENSIONS

The Conjugal Act as a Human Act

The conjugal act is a singular and irreplaceable act of love between husband and wife. In and through the conjugal act man and woman give themselves to one another,[1] express and perfect their love for each other,[2] participate in the goods of marriage, and consummate their marriage.[3] The conjugal act is an utterly unique human act precisely because of its *conjugal* character or the fact that it entails a singular expression of conjugal love through the pursuit of the goods of marriage.[4] By their very definitions, procreation is inseparable from the conjugal act, and spousal union finds its full-

---

[1] Cf. FC 11 and LF 12.

[2] Cf. GS 49.

[3] Cf. *Code of Canon Law*, can. 1061, § 1.

[4] According to William May, "The marital act is an utterly unique kind of human act; it is a collaborate, personal act carrying out the choice of the spouses to actualize their marriage and participate in the goods perfective of it" (*Marriage: The Rock on Which the Family Is Built* [San Francisco: Ignatius Press, 1995], p. 95). Cormac Burke writes, "What makes marital intercourse express a unique relationship and union is not the sharing of a sensation but the sharing of a power: of an extraordinary life-related, creative, physical, sexual power. . . . Other physical expressions of affection do not go beyond the level of mere gesture; they remain a symbol of union desired. But the conjugal act is not a mere symbol. In marital intercourse, something *real* has been exchanged, with a full gift and acceptance of conjugal masculinity and femininity" (*Covenanted Happiness* [Princeton: Scepter Press, 1999], p. 91).

est expression in the conjugal act, by which husband and wife become one flesh. In addition to allowing for a singular participation in the goods of marriage, the conjugal act (and only the conjugal act) consummates a marriage constituting the marriage in its full reality,[5] and the inability to engage in the conjugal act is an impediment to marriage.[6] The uniqueness of the conjugal act derives, then, from the fact that it affords husband and wife the opportunity and the fullest means for self-donation, for the actualization of the goods of marriage, and for the embodiment of the words of matrimonial consent.[7]

The conjugal act possesses such a wealth of significance by virtue of its bodily and sexual nature. As a human act (*actus humanus*), however, the conjugal act cannot be reduced to the genital encounter of man and woman. Instead, as with all human acts, the conjugal act is distinguishable by

---

[5] Cf. Pope John Paul II, General Audience of January 5, 1983: "The coming into being of marriage is distinguished from its consummation, to the extent that without this consummation the marriage is not yet constituted in its full reality. The fact that a marriage is juridically contracted but not consummated (*ratum–non consummatum*) corresponds to the fact that it has not been fully constituted as a marriage. Indeed the very words 'I take you as my wife—my husband' refer not only to a determinate reality, but they can be fulfilled only by means of conjugal intercourse. This reality (conjugal intercourse) has moreover been determined from the beginning by institution of the Creator."

[6] According to canon law, "Antecedent and perpetual impotence to have intercourse, whether on the part of the man or of the woman, which is either absolute or relative, of its very nature invalidates marriage" (*Code of Canon Law*, can. 1084, § 1).

[7] Regarding this final point, Bartholomew Kiely writes, "In marrying the spouses give them*selves* to each other. Consent is always required for the validity of marriage. In the conjugal act, this self-giving is expressed in a unique way. The spouses are not sharing a function or a satisfaction, but them*selves*" ("Contraception, In Vitro Fertilization and the Principle of Inseparability", in *"Humanae vitae": 20 anni dopo. Atti del II Congresso Internazionale di Teologia Morale* [Milan: Edizione Ares, 1989], p. 331).

the intention and choice of the agents, not the physical components of the act. Apart from a pursuit of or participation in the goods of marriage, the genital encounter in itself does not yield the conjugal act.[8] The genital encounter is an essential element of the conjugal act, inasmuch as the conjugal act does not and cannot take any other physical form, but the genital encounter does not suffice for the conjugal act (thus, with respect to the conjugal act, the genital encounter is *necessary but not sufficient*). The necessary presence of the genital encounter derives from the fact that the goods of procreation and spousal union are not found apart from this physical encounter. However, it is the goods of procreation and spousal union themselves that specify the conjugal act and pertain to its essence, while the genital encounter is essential to the conjugal act only secondarily and by virtue of its relationship to these goods. The goods of procreation and spousal union do not exist apart from genital intercourse, and inasmuch as procreation and union belong to the essence of the conjugal act, so too does the genital encounter. However, because the genital encounter can take place apart from the goods of procreation and union (such as in the cases of fornication, adultery, or rape), the genital encounter does not stand at the center of the concept of the conjugal act as a human act.

[8] William May writes, "the marital act considered precisely as a human, personal act, is more than a genital act between a man and a woman who simply happen to be married. It is an act that inwardly participates in their one-flesh, marital union and in the 'goods' or 'blessings' of marriage . . . the goods of loving fidelity and children. The *marital* act, therefore, as distinct from a merely *genital* act, is one that is (1) open to the communication of spousal love and (2) open to God's gift of human life" ("Anthropological Advances in *Humanae Vitae*", in *"Humanae vitae": Servizio profetico per l'uomo* [Rome: Editrice Ave, 1995], p. 379).

While the genital encounter of man and woman does not necessarily constitute the conjugal act, such an encounter becomes the conjugal act to the extent that the man and woman intend the ends of procreation and union. As with every genuinely human act, the essence of the conjugal act concerns the movement of the human will more than the physical movement entailed in the act. HV 12 identifies procreation and union as "essential aspects" of the conjugal act, indicating that the essence of the conjugal act derives from the movement of the will toward these goods. In light of this consideration, the "intimate structure" of the conjugal act mentioned in HV 12 refers to the ontological structure of the act, not the physical structure of the act. In other words, understood as a human act the term *conjugal act* describes certain movements of the will, undeniably related to external movements, rather than an event or a process of the physical order.[9] The intention and choice of procreation and union on the part of the spouses give rise to the conjugal act and establish its ontological structure while at the same time confirming the genital encounter as a personal encounter and an act of conjugal love.

Inasmuch as it necessitates the genital encounter of man and woman, the conjugal act presents the opportunity for a personal encounter because the sexual faculties of man and woman cannot be isolated from the human body, which is "a constitutive part of the person who manifests and expresses

[9] According to St. Thomas, the species of a human act derives from the object of choice. Cf. *Summa Theologica*, q. 18, a. 2. Pope John Paul II affirms that the object of an act "cannot mean a process or an event of the merely physical order". Instead, the object is "the proximate end of a deliberate decision which determines the act of willing on the part of the acting person" (VS 78).

himself through it".[10] According to Pope John Paul II, "in the body and through the body, one touches the person himself in his concrete reality." [11] Thus, in the genital encounter of man and woman, as the two bodies touch, two human persons touch and encounter each other. This basic fact of two persons touching each other serves as the initial basis for co-subjectivity in the conjugal act because each person is a subject possessing free will and capable of self-determination. However, the basic fact of two persons touching represents only an opportunity for co-subjectivity, for the physical encounter itself cannot ensure that each subject is relating to the other as a subject as opposed to an object of use. Instead of co-subjectivity, the genital encounter may entail the instrumentalization of the other or the abuse of the other. In fact, experience reveals a particularly strong temptation to such instrumentalization and abuse in the sexual encounter of man and woman, a use and abuse related to the pleasure available through sexuality. While the physical dimensions of the genital encounter cannot preclude instrumentalization and abuse, man and woman can avoid this use and abuse when they direct themselves and subordinate themselves to a common aim in their acting.[12]

In order to actualize the inherent potential for co-subjectivity in the genital encounter, man and woman must

---

[10] DV, intro., 3.

[11] *Discourse to the Members of the 35th General Assembly of the World Medical Association*, October 29, 1983, in *AAS* 76 (1984):393.

[12] Karol Wojtyla writes, "How is it possible to ensure that one person does not then become for the other—the woman for the man, or the man for the woman—nothing more than the means to an end—i.e., an object used exclusively for the attainment of a selfish end? To exclude this possibility they must share the same end" (*Love and Responsibility*, trans. H. Willets [San Francisco: Ignatius Press, 1993], p. 30).

share a common end to which they direct themselves, for in the pursuit of a common good each person views the other as an equal and as one who shares his or her good and not one who leads to an individually experienced good.[13] In the sexual sphere, procreation and union, the ends of marriage itself, present themselves to man and woman as common ends to which they can direct themselves in accordance with the nature of the sexual faculty. According to Wojtyla, "These objective purposes of marriage create in principle the possibility of love and exclude the possibility of treating a person as a means to an end or as an object for use." [14] Inasmuch as it essentially entails the intention to procreate and unite, the conjugal act always entails the pursuit of a common good and co-subjectivity, transforming the genital encounter into a personal encounter. Moreover, through the co-subjectivity of the conjugal act man and woman unite to each other, bound in and through the common good they pursue, and thus their personal encounter effects a personal union between them.

When the genital encounter is ordered to the (common) ends of procreation and union, we discover in this intimate mode of touching the notion of co-subjectivity, the pursuit of common goods, and personal union, all of which pertain to the realm of love or friendship. Conversely, apart from the intention to procreate and unite, the genital encounter remains devoid of love and deteriorates to the realm of exploitation. Addressing specifically the indispensability of procreation, Karol Wojtyla writes, "Unwillingness for

[13] According to Wojtyla, "When two different people consciously choose a common aim this puts them on a footing of equality, and precludes the possibility that one of them might be subordinated to the other" (ibid., p. 29).

[14] Ibid., p. 30.

parenthood in a man and a woman deprives sexual relations of the value of love, which is a union on the truly personal level, and all that remains is the sexual act itself, or rather reciprocal sexual exploitation."[15] Through the movement of their wills, through their intention and choice, man and woman transform their physical movements in the genital encounter into either an act and an expression of love or into an act of use and exploitation. The genital encounter embodies love when the physical intimacy of the act derives from the intention of procreation and union, common goods to which man and woman subordinate themselves.

The intention of procreation and union inserts the value of love into the genital encounter, precisely because such an intention requires two fundamental, interwoven elements of true love or friendship: the pursuit of a common good and the gift of self. The pursuit of a common good creates a bond between persons, bringing individuals into a unity that, without destroying their singularity as persons, transforms individuals into a greater whole, into a new reality. Therefore, in order to pursue a common good with others, human persons must be willing to give themselves into this new reality, this greater whole that transforms their individuality. The gift of self does not mean, then, a simple exchange of persons (something that is in fact impossible). Instead, each member of the friendship gives himself or herself to the other by willingly joining to the other in co-subjectivity ordered to some authentic common good. Inasmuch as the pursuit of a common good always effects such a joining, the pursuit

---

[15] Ibid., p. 249. In the same section of his work, Wojtyla states that man and woman truly procreate when their marital relations entail a personal union. Thus, he indicates that his emphasis on the indispensability of procreation includes an equal emphasis on union. See pp. 248–49.

of a common good requires the free gift of self into the unity that arises from this joining.[16] Essentially love of friendship is this gift of self to another in the pursuit of a common good. According to their very definitions, both procreation and union necessitate and entail the gift of self in co-subjectivity with another; thus, by intending these ends man and woman commit themselves to the gift of self and to love.

While all true friendship involves the gift of self in and through the pursuit of a common good, friendships vary greatly from one another in terms of their quality and depth by virtue of the common good around which the friendship is formed.[17] In a certain sense, the good to which friends order themselves specifies the friendship or love that they share. When man and woman give themselves to each other with the intention of procreation and union they share "a very special form of personal friendship"[18] that stands apart from all other forms of human association. Procreation and union pertain to a unique kind of friendship known as conjugal friendship, a manner of friendship distinguished by its totality, permanence, and fruitfulness.[19] Thus, inasmuch as it essentially entails the gift of self and the pursuit of a common good, the conjugal act is by its very nature an act of love, and because the common good in question pertains to

---

[16] In the Supplement to St. Thomas' *Summa Theologica*, we read, "A joining denotes a kind of uniting, and so wherever things are united there must be a joining. Now things directed to one purpose are said to be united in their direction thereto, thus many men are united in following one military calling or in pursuing one business, in relation to which they are called fellow-soldiers or business partners" (q. 44, a. 1).

[17] Cf. Aristotle, *Nicomachean Ethics*, books 8 and 9; St. Thomas Aquinas, *Summa Theologica*, I–II, q. 26, a. 4; Wojtyla, *Love and Responsibility*, pp. 84–88.

[18] HV 9.

[19] Cf. ibid.

conjugal love, the conjugal act is necessarily an act of conjugal love. Moreover, because this unique act of touching embraces the goods of procreation and union in an unparalleled manner, the genital encounter of man and woman with the intention of procreation and union is not only *an* act of conjugal love but *the* act of conjugal love or *the conjugal act*.

The conjugal act, then, results from a genital encounter of man and woman who express their love by the intention to procreate and unite in and through the bodily manifestations of their masculinity and femininity. Because the authentic intention of procreation and spousal union is inseparable from conjugal love (that is, such an intention presupposes conjugal love and is an act of conjugal love), the intention of procreation and union presupposes and requires the institution of marriage, for the institution of marriage is "an interior requirement of the covenant of conjugal love".[20] As an act of conjugal love, the conjugal act is inseparable from marriage, and only a husband and a wife can engage in the conjugal act. William May describes the conjugal act as "an act participating in the marriage itself and one made possible only because of the marriage: marriage, in short, *enables* husband and wife to engage in the marital act."[21] May further states that, while nonmarried men and women can engage in genital acts, only "husbands and wives, who have freely chosen to give themselves the identity of irreplaceable and nonsubstitutable spouses, are capable of the conjugal or spousal act—of giving and receiving. And they are capable of doing so precisely because of their marriage."[22]

---

[20] FC 11.

[21] William May, *Marriage*, p. 27.

[22] Ibid.

Marriage enables husband and wife to engage in the conjugal act by virtue of the choice that spouses make in consenting to marry, and in turn marital consent finds its completion in the conjugal act. Marital consent consists in a human act by which man and woman mutually give themselves to one another.[23] According to the *Catechism*, "This consent that binds the spouses to each other finds its fulfillment in the two 'becoming one flesh.' "[24] While spouses initially express their consent in spoken words, marital consent is ordered to the physical expression of self-donation, for "it is in their bodies and through their bodies that spouses consummate their marriage."[25] Thus, a marriage is consummated "if the parties have performed between themselves in a human manner the conjugal act which is per se suitable for the generation of children, to which marriage is ordered by its very nature and by which the spouses become one flesh".[26] The conjugal act consummates marriage because the self-donation at the heart of procreation and spousal union images and completes the self-donation by which spouses institute their particular marriage in the act of marital consent.

Considered as a human act, the conjugal act consists of several indispensable and intrinsically related components. The conjugal act derives above all from the intention to procreate and unite, for these are the ends of the act, and the end is always first in the order of intention. The pursuit of these two goods specifies the conjugal act, giving both structure

---

[23] Cf. CCC 1627; GS 48; *Code of Canon Law*, can. 1057, § 2, which states, "Matrimonial consent is an act of the will by which a man and a woman, through an irrevocable covenant, mutually give and accept each other in order to establish marriage."

[24] CCC 1627. Cf. John Paul II, General Audience of January 5, 1983.

[25] DV, II, 4b.

[26] *Code of Canon Law*, can. 1061, § 1.

and intelligibility to the act. Because the pursuit of these goods necessarily entails genital intercourse, genital intercourse constitutes a necessary component of the conjugal act by virtue of its relationship to the goods of marriage. However, the physical structure of the act remains secondary to the ontological structure, and the act is identified more with the intention and choice of the spouses than with its physical component. Inasmuch as the pursuit of procreation and union entails self-donation and co-subjectivity, the conjugal act is an act of love by its very nature. As conjugal love is the life-giving principle of marriage, conjugal love vivifies and informs the conjugal act, determining the form and value of the act in and through the intention of procreation and union. Conjugal love, however, never exists apart from the institution of marriage. Therefore, in their expression of conjugal love through the pursuit of procreation and union, spouses "actualize their marriage and participate in the goods perfective of it".[27] As a unique expression of spousal love, the conjugal act is also a unique actualization of marriage, one by which spouses consummate their marriage, embodying the mutual gift of self expressed in matrimonial consent.

The Conjugal Act as a Symbolic Act

The conjugal act possesses a fundamental structure composed of the various elements that contribute to its essence as a human act, a fundamental structure by which we can distinguish the conjugal act from other acts of love. This fundamental structure of the conjugal act consists of a mixture or a composite of physical elements (deriving from the bodily

---

[27] William May, *Marriage*, p. 95.

nature of the act) and spiritual elements (related to love and human willing). Through the interrelation of the physical components and the spiritual components of the act, the conjugal act possesses a particular type of signification whereby the material dimension of the act points to and manifests that which is occurring on the spiritual level. By virtue of this signification, the conjugal act acquires a particular type of sign-value or a *symbolic* meaning, and "the physical intimacy of the spouses becomes a sign and pledge of spiritual communion."[28] Additionally, the symbolic meaning inscribed in the conjugal act serves as a reminder of the spiritual realities that should accompany the sexual union of husband and wife, guiding the mind to a greater understanding of what the act is meant to entail.

The human person is a composite of matter and spirit, and all modes of human communication utilize matter to express ideas that are apprehended by the mind. The material reality that communicates an idea or leads one to knowledge constitutes a sign. While all signs are material realities that direct the mind to a certain idea, not all signs function in the same way.[29] For example, *conventional signs* direct the mind to a certain idea on the basis of a mutual agreement between those who employ the conventional signs, while the material realities utilized are in fact otherwise unrelated to the ideas themselves. In the case of conventional signs, the human mind has assigned a particular signification to the matter utilized. Words, whether written or spoken, are conventional signs understood only by those who are educated in

---

[28] CCC 2360.

[29] In my description of the various types of signs employed in human communication, I follow and summarize the ideas of Paul Quay in *The Christian Meaning of Human Sexuality* (San Francisco: Ignatius Press, 1985) pp. 14–16.

the language to which the words pertain. In contrast to conventional signs, *images* and *symbols* possess a certain sign-value by virtue of a resemblance between the material component of the sign and the idea to which it directs the mind. An image is a type of sign that signifies a material reality by virtue of some resemblance to that reality. A symbol, on the other hand, possesses a sign-value by virtue of its resemblance to a spiritual reality. Paul Quay writes, "the material sign that we call a symbol has a sign-value not only by some sort of convention or by material similarity but by virtue of the fact that its material form, structure, action, or appearance is similar to or like the immaterial thing it signifies."[30] The conjugal act possesses a *symbolic* meaning because it acquires its sign-value by virtue of the similarity between its material components and the spiritual communion to which it points.

The material dimension of the conjugal act consists in a physical oneness that is achieved by the joining of two complementary bodies, precisely with regard to the faculty by which they are most radically complementary. The spouses' bodies literally fit together, one (partially) entering the other and one (partially) surrounding the other, because they differ in such a way as to complete or fulfill the potential of each other. Complementarity essentially refers to a difference ordered to completion in union. On the basis of their physical complementarity, husband and wife become one flesh in an act of genital intercourse. When it bears its full fruit, their act of intercourse may entail the physical union of their respective generative cells resulting in the conception of a child. In such a case, the physical oneness of spouses yields a

[30] Ibid., p. 16.

physical fruit. Finally, within their physical union spouses may also experience a considerable degree of arousal and pleasure derived from the intimate touching entailed in the conjugal act. These various aspects of the physical dimension of the conjugal act (the union, the fruitfulness, and the pleasure and excitement) possess symbolic value inasmuch as they correspond to and resemble certain spiritual dimensions of the act.

The physical union of husband and wife in the conjugal act symbolizes the personal union they achieve through "a total personal self-giving, in which the whole person, including the temporal dimension, is present".[31] While achieving a physical oneness, spouses also unite their very persons in such a way that their souls "are joined together more directly and more intimately than their bodies".[32] During the act of intercourse, husband and wife share their bodies with each other, granting to each other an unparalleled degree of access. Their physical openness and joining symbolize "the intimate partnership of life and love"[33] that they share by virtue of their irrevocable, mutual gift of self made at the moment of matrimonial consent. Spouses share their bodies with each other in the conjugal act because they share something greater, a common life, by virtue of their conjugal covenant with each other. Just as spouses unite their bodies by means of the complementarity of their respective sexual faculties, the common life of the conjugal covenant arises out of the complementarity of masculine and feminine persons. As persons man and woman were created together and willed for each other, and their

[31] FC 11.

[32] Pope Pius XII, *Casti connubii*, 542.

[33] GS 48.

complementarity derives from and corresponds to their ordination to union on a personal level.

The conjugal act inherently possesses the potential to generate new human life through the physical conception of a child, and the child himself, as the physical fruit of the act, possesses symbolic value inasmuch as he represents the love of husband and wife and their desire for parenthood. According to *Donum vitae*, "parents find in their child a confirmation and completion of their reciprocal self-giving: the child is the living image of their love, the permanent sign of their conjugal union, the living and concrete expression of their paternity and maternity."[34] A child conceived in the conjugal act symbolizes the will of the spouses that the goodness of each spouse be preserved and continued in another like them. The conception of a child also signifies a married couple's commitment to a common life together because the child conceived must also be nurtured and cared for over a number of years. The child, then, symbolizes a love that embraces the good of the whole person and bears witness to the common life to which spouses commit themselves in marriage.

Even the sexual arousal and physical pleasure that accompany sexual intercourse possess symbolic meaning and point to certain dimensions of the spiritual communion of husband and wife. The physical arousal experienced in conjunction with sexual intercourse physically prepares each spouse for the physical union achieved in intercourse. The preparation for physical intercourse in turn symbolizes the emotional and spiritual readiness of each spouse for their union on the spiritual level. As physical oneness in inter-

---

[34] DV, II, 1. Cf. also FC 14.

course symbolizes a couple's spiritual communion, sexual arousal symbolizes their readiness and willingness to enter into this communion of mind and heart. For its part, the pleasure given and received in the act symbolizes the joy and the delight that the spouses find in each other as persons. The bodily sensations produced in the act call to mind the joy of spirit and the warmth of heart that each spouse experiences in the other precisely as a person. In and through their physical excitement and pleasure, spouses reveal to each other the joy and excitement of spirit that each evokes in the other and that their oneness evokes in them both.

Viewed as a symbolic act, the material dimension of the conjugal act directs the mind to a wealth of profound spiritual realities, such as the spiritual communion of marriage, the total love of the spouses, and the joy that spousal love evokes in man and woman. In order to live conjugal chastity, spouses cannot remain indifferent to the symbolic dimension of the conjugal act.[35] Instead, husband and wife must recognize and practice the truth that intercourse signifies, incorporating its symbolism into their own expressions of love, utilizing its symbolism to convey that which they experience on the spiritual level. In other words, "intercourse is meant to become a type of language by which husband and wife are able to express to each other all that they wish to say in the way of love and spiritual union."[36]

---

[35] Cf. John Paul II, General Audience of October 24, 1984. Here the Pope describes conjugal chastity, in contrast to continence, as "a singular capacity to perceive, love and practice those meanings of the language of the body which remain altogether unknown to concupiscence itself. Those meanings progressively enrich the marital dialogue of the couple, purifying it, deepening it, and at the same time simplifying it."

[36] Quay, *Christian Meaning*, p. 36.

When they understand it properly and engage in it honorably, spouses are able to express the most profound aspects of their love for one another through the symbolism of intercourse, aspects of love that exceed the limitations of the conventional signs of which human languages are composed.

Within the symbolic dimension of the conjugal act, spouses discover a wealth of meaning by which they can express and perfect their love for one another. However, spouses also discover within the symbolic language of intercourse certain boundaries that direct them and confine them to a specific message, the message of conjugal love. The boundaries of the language of intercourse derive from the symbolic nature of the language itself, which relies on the resemblance between the material aspects of intercourse and the spiritual realities to which they point. In sexual intercourse, spouses encounter symbols, not conventional signs, and therefore the meanings of the various physical aspects of the act are discovered by the human mind, not assigned by the human mind. Inasmuch as the conjugal act possesses a determined physical content (determined by the nature of the goods to which the act is ordered), the act contains a determined (or objective) symbolic meaning.

In addition to discovering a determined symbolic meaning in the act of intercourse, spouses also discover in the language of intercourse a determined mode of communication by which the bodies speak on behalf of the spouses through the so-called "language of the body". The symbolic language of sexual intercourse relies upon a more fundamental anthropological condition by which the body expresses the person. As a constitutive part of the person, the body manifests the person and expresses the person. The body, however, never becomes an *instrument* by which man communicates with others. In other words, because the body belongs to man's *being* and not his *having*,[37] the body speaks as man or on behalf of man with his personal authority.[38] In sexual intercourse the body "speaks" a particular message of self-donation and conjugal love. Husband and wife make the message of the body their own when they actually intend the message of the body by virtue of the intention and choice to procreate and unite through their genital intercourse. In such a case the conjugal act possesses its full symbolism. However, by the very structure of sexual intercourse the body speaks its message of love and self-donation even in the absence of a corresponding intention on the part of the man and woman. When the body expresses love and self-gift apart from a corresponding intention, sexual intercourse that is not an act of conjugal love produces a sexual "lie" because the body says something on behalf of the person that is simply not true.[39] Thus, in order to utilize the inherent symbolism of sexual intercourse and to avoid falsifying the sexual act, husband and wife must conform their intention to the message of love communicated through the body.

As a symbolic act the conjugal act possesses a wealth of significance by which husband and wife can express the most profound dimensions of their love and affection for each other. However, the symbolic meaning of the act corrupts when

---

[37] Cf. John Paul II, *Discourse to Priests Participating in a Seminar on "Responsible Parenthood"*, September 17, 1983, in *Insegnamenti di Giovanni Paolo II*, 6, 2 (1983).

[38] According to John Paul II, "man—male or female—does not merely speak with the language of the body. But in a certain sense he permits the body to speak 'for him' or 'on his behalf,' I would say, in his name with his personal authority" (General Audience of January 26, 1983).

[39] Cf. Quay, *Christian Meaning*, pp. 64–67; Pope John Paul II, FC 32 and General Audience of January 26, 1983.

the physical components of the symbolism exist apart from their corresponding spiritual realities. Instead of a profound form of expression and communication, the sexual act becomes an exercise in illusion and falsehood apart from the intention of procreation and spousal union. For this reason, the symbolic meaning of the conjugal act depends upon or relies upon the fundamental structure of the act as a human act. Only the conjugal act actualizes and possesses the symbolic expression available in the genital encounter of man and woman. Apart from the various components of the conjugal act as a human act (such as the intention of procreation and union, conjugal love, co-subjectivity, and so on), sexual intercourse remains empty from the symbolic point of view and becomes an occasion of instrumentalization instead of union, an occasion of deception instead of love, and an occasion of disappointment instead of joy and delight. Sexual intercourse lacks all meaning or value as a symbolic act unless it results from the human act identifiable as the conjugal act.

The Conjugal Act as a Sacramental Act

In addition to its natural symbolism of love and union, the conjugal act possesses a sacramentality whereby the act reveals and manifests something beyond the relationship of the couple performing the act. According to Paul Quay, "This sacramental symbolism involves all that is present in the marital relationship but gives it a fuller meaning at a level of communion where there is no possibility, even, of sexual union."[40] The sacramental signification of the sexual relationship of husband and wife, then, incorporates and pre-

[40] *Christian Meaning*, p. 56.

serves all that exists in the relationship by its very nature while extending the significance of the relationship to spiritual realities beyond the sexual union of man and woman. This sacramentality pertains above all to the conjugal covenant of husband and wife and secondarily to the conjugal act inasmuch as the conjugal act embodies conjugal love and participates in marriage and the goods perfective of it. In other words, the conjugal love of husband and wife possesses a certain sacramental symbolism that the conjugal act shares precisely as an act of conjugal love. The sacramental symbolism of the conjugal covenant refers to the order of creation for all true marriages and also to the order of redemption for the marriages of those baptized into the Christian mystery. In both respects, the sacrament of marriage and the sacramentality of the conjugal act center upon the idea of personal loving communion.

A sacrament (in the broad sense of the word) fundamentally accomplishes a certain manifestation and realization of a mystery in the world through a material sign.[41] The sacrament "announces" a mystery (a profound spiritual truth) to the world through a material sign on the basis of symbolism (a resemblance to the mystery) while also making that very mystery present through the material sign. Thus, a sacrament directs the mind to some truth and makes present what it signifies. Materiality and symbolism enter into the very notion of a sacrament. A sacrament, however, differs from a mere symbol because a sacrament not only resembles a spiritual reality but also makes that reality present in the world. The sacramental signification of the conjugal act derives from both its material (bodily) dimension and from the

[41] Cf. John Paul II, General Audience of February 20, 1980; General Audience of July 28, 1982; and General Audience of September 8, 1982.

spiritual values (the love and communion) that are truly present in an authentic act of conjugal love. In and through their bodies spouses are able to announce and make present profound spiritual mysteries precisely because in and through their bodies they share a love and personal communion of the most profound character.

In the order of creation (that is, according to its essence as a natural institution), the conjugal relationship of man and woman sacramentally signifies the love and communion of the Trinity as well as the love of God for humanity. Reflecting upon the conjugal covenant of husband and wife, Pope John Paul II has described the conjugal relationship as the human reality that most perfectly images the unity and communion found in God.[42] The Triune God, who is Love, "lives a mystery of personal loving communion".[43] Within this personal loving communion, the Persons of the Trinity share the fullness of the nature that they possess except for that which constitutes them as Father, Son, and Holy Spirit. God created humanity in his image and likeness by creating man and woman and by giving them the capacity for personal loving communion based on their common human nature and the complementary modes in which each is human. The image of God (as Trinity) inscribed in humanity "is manifest in the sexual difference and in the sexual union of man and woman".[44] When they love each other on the basis

---

[42] Homily of December 30, 1988, Feast of the Holy Family: "Non c'è al mondo un'altra immagine più perfetta, più completa di ciò che è Dio: unità, communione. Non cè un'altra realtà umana che corrisponda meglio a questo mistero divino."

[43] FC 11.

[44] Emiliano Jimenez Hernández, *Uomo e donna, immagine di Dio* (Naples: Grafite Editrice, 1998), p. 8: "L'immagine di Dio si manifesta nella *differenza e nella comunione* sessuale degli uomini."

of their sexual complementarity, sharing all they are and possess in a common life, man and woman actualize their potential to image the personal loving communion lived by God. As *the* act of conjugal love, the conjugal act most perfectly symbolizes the personal loving communion of the Trinity by virtue of the total self-giving and all-embracing union at the heart of the act.

The conjugal covenant of man and woman also symbolizes the love of God for humanity and the covenant that God makes with his people. According to John Paul II, "The communion of love between God and his people, a fundamental part of the revelation and faith experience of Israel, finds a meaningful expression in the marriage covenant which is established between a man and a woman."[45] When spouses faithfully live out the marriage covenant, "their mutual love becomes an image of the absolute and unfailing love with which God loves man."[46] The symbolism of conjugal love is vivid enough for Old Testament prophets such as Hosea, Jeremiah, and Ezekiel to use spousal imagery to describe God's relationship with his people and their infidelity to the covenant, and the prophets' use of spousal imagery sheds light on the nature of conjugal love.[47] Moreover, as the mystery of the New Covenant in Christ fulfills God's original covenant with his people, the covenant sanctioned in the blood of Christ elevates and perfects the original symbolism of marriage. Thus, through the New

---

[45] FC 12.

[46] CCC 1604.

[47] Cf. CCC 1611: "Seeing God's covenant with Israel in the image of exclusive and faithful married love, the prophets prepared the Chosen People's conscience for a deepened understanding of the unity and indissolubility of marriage."

Covenant in Christ the conjugal covenant gains greater, renewed sacramental significance.

By virtue of their entrance into the Christian mystery through baptism, Christian spouses sacramentally represent and enter into the covenant of Christ and the Church in and through their conjugal covenant. Through baptism Christians are "sacramentally assimilated to Jesus",[48] and by virtue of this sacramental assimilation Christian marriage is assumed into the covenant of Christ and the Church.

> Indeed, by means of Baptism, man and woman are definitively placed within the new and eternal covenant, in the spousal covenant of Christ with the Church. And it is because of this indestructible insertion that the intimate community of conjugal life and love, founded by the Creator, is elevated and assumed into the spousal charity of Christ, sustained and enriched by His redeeming power.[49]

As a sacrament in the order of redemption, Christian marriage not only directs the mind to the everlasting, self-sacrificial love of Christ for the Church but also "gives spouses the grace to love each other with the love with which Christ has loved his Church".[50] The natural conjugal love of husband and wife is "assumed into the spousal charity of Christ", thereby being transformed, perfected, and supernaturalized by God's grace.[51] Because the conjugal act embodies conjugal love and proceeds directly from conjugal love, the physical intimacy of Christian spouses in the conjugal act benefits from this perfection and supernaturalization of conjugal love.

---

[48] CCC 537.

[49] FC 13.

[50] CCC 1661.

[51] Cf. CCC 1642 and 1661.

While sacramentally representing the union of Christ and the Church, the conjugal union of husband and wife makes present in the world a "supernatural, tender, and fruitful love" [52] that finds its source in the "new and eternal covenant sanctioned in the blood of the cross".[53] By transforming man and woman in baptism, the grace of God gives man and woman new hearts, rendering them capable of loving one another as Christ has loved the Church. Consequently, the conjugal act, the act by which husband and wife consummate and fulfill their love, not only acquires a greater symbolic meaning but also becomes the sacramental embodiment of the everlasting, self-sacrificial love of Christ on the Cross. More than an act of conjugal love, by virtue of its sacramentality the conjugal act becomes an act of *conjugal charity*.[54]

Love stands at the center of the notion of sacramentality in the conjugal act. The conjugal covenant and the conjugal act symbolize and realize in history the divine love of God within the Trinity, toward his Chosen People, and for his Bride, the Church. In other words, the conjugal union of husband and wife announces and realizes the personal loving communion effected by divine love. Though the conjugal covenant and the conjugal act are intrinsically bodily, sexual forms of love, the sacramental symbolism of the conjugal act derives from the embodiment of love found in the act rather than from the bodily or sexual union itself. The personal loving communion lived by God is not based on sexual

---

[52] CCC 1642.

[53] FC 13.

[54] According to John Paul II, in Christian marriage, "Conjugal love reaches that fullness to which it is interiorly ordained, conjugal charity, which is the proper and specific way in which spouses participate in and are called to live the very charity of Christ who gave himself on the Cross" (FC 13).

complementarity between the Persons of the Trinity. Yet, the conjugal act can sacramentally represent non-sexual forms of personal loving communion precisely because the conjugal union of husband and wife extends beyond their bodies to their very humanity, to their persons.

If the conjugal act were merely a form of bodily and sexual union, its sacramental signification would not reasonably correspond to its nature; that is, there would be no symbolic basis for its sacramentality because it would lack the requisite resemblance found in all symbols. Mere sexual union does not resemble the personal loving communion lived by the Triune God because the relationship of the Persons of the Trinity is not based on sexual complementarity. However, the sexual union of husband and wife resembles and images the personal loving communion of the Triune God because for husband and wife sexual union in the conjugal act is necessarily and essentially (by virtue of the intention of procreation and union) a form of personal loving communion. The material dimension of the conjugal act allows for its symbolic and sacramental character (all sacramental symbols are composed of matter), and the personal union effected through the act possesses the requisite resemblance. The sexual dimension of the conjugal act pertains to the essence of the act, inasmuch as there could not be a non-sexual conjugal act, but it enters into the act as a specifically human mode of personal communication and self-donation; sexual union is not the defining characteristic of the act but only a dimension of the act necessitated by the nature of the human person and the goods to which the act is ordered. Thus, the bodily and sexual union of husband and wife in the conjugal act resembles the personal loving communion lived by God precisely because the human body and human sexuality are *personal*. In other words, two *human persons* constitute the *matter* of the sacramental symbol of the conjugal act. In the context of the conjugal act, human, bodily union signifies personal loving communion because for husband and wife such a union effects and perfects the personal loving communion of the conjugal covenant.

2. AN INTEGRAL VISION OF MAN

Among the various ideas contained in the Catholic theology of the conjugal act, certain anthropological tenets emerge that sustain the inner logic of this concept of the conjugal act while also revealing the greater relevance of the act for the human person. Utilizing "criteria drawn from the nature of the human person and human action",[55] the Catholic concept of the conjugal act not only describes the marital relations of husband and wife but also reveals a specific vision of husband and wife as human persons. Ultimately, the Catholic concept of the conjugal act depends upon this anthropological vision for its coherency, for certain aspects of the conjugal act are comprehensible only within the framework of this anthropological vision. Without fully examining their profound significance, in this section of my study I identify the principal tenets of the anthropological vision that underlies the concept of the conjugal act described in the preceding sections of the work, seeking also to indicate the manner in which the conjugal act is eminently human or *personal*. Among the components of this anthropological vision, I refer specifically to the substantial unity of body and soul, freedom understood as theonomy, the significance of the human conscience and human consciousness,

[55] GS 51.

and the human capacity for co-subjectivity and the pursuit of a common good.

Man as a Unity of Body and Soul

By his very nature man is a corporeal and spiritual being, possessing a body and a soul in a unified whole.[56] Not merely extending to both the spiritual realm and the material realm, each human person constitutes the integration of matter and spirit or "the compenetration of the life of the body with the life of the soul".[57] Within the human composite of body and soul, matter and spirit "are not two natures united, but rather their union forms a single nature".[58] As "an incarnate spirit", the human person consists in a "unified totality" of body and soul bound together in a mutual relationship by which the soul informs the body and the body expresses the soul.[59] The term "soul" refers to the innermost aspect of man, his spiritual principle, and the animating form of the

[56] Cf. CCC 362 and St. Augustine, *City of God*, 13, 24: "This is indeed true, for the soul is not the whole man; it is the better part of man, and the body is not the whole man; it is the lower part of him. It is the conjunction of these two parts that is entitled to the name of 'man.'"

[57] John Paul II, "Families, God Calls You to Holiness!", *L'Osservatore Romano* (English ed.), October 8, 1997, p. 1. Cf. also Michael Healy, "Man: A Unity of Body and Soul", in *Creative Love: The Ethics of Human Reproduction*, ed. John Boyle (Front Royal, Va.: Christendom Press, 1989), pp. 107–16, which contains a critique of the dualism represented by Joseph Fletcher, *Morals and Medicine* (Boston: Beacon Press, 1960).

[58] CCC 365. Cf. also GS 14 and Dionigi Tettamanzi, *L'uomo, immagine di Dio* (Casale Monferrato: Edizione Piemme, 1992), pp. 48–53.

[59] FC 11. Cf. John Paul II, LF 19. According to Martin Rhonheimer, "man's corporeality is fully integrated into the structure of spiritual life; it is 'informed' by spiritual life, becoming however itself the *subject* or 'carrier' of spiritual acts" (Martin Rhonheimer, "Contraception, Sexual Behavior, and Natural Law", in *"Humanae vitae": 20 anni dopo*), p. 88.

body.[60] The human body is the matter that the soul animates and informs by virtue of a substantial unity. Thus, giving life to the body, the human soul makes the body to be a human body. The resulting composite of matter and spirit is a unique type of being in God's creation: the human being. Pope John Paul II describes the creation of man as a "union of body and spirit" and "a decisive innovation in the process of creation. With the human being, all the greatness of the visible creation gains a spiritual dimension."[61]

By virtue of its "substantial union with a spiritual soul", the human body "is a constitutive part of the person who manifests and expresses himself through it".[62] More than a conglomeration of tissue and functions, the human body is an integral part of the human person. John Paul II has forcefully reaffirmed that "each human person, in his absolute unique singularity, is constituted not only by his spirit, but by his body as well. Thus, in the body and through the body, one touches the person himself in his concrete reality."[63] Man does not possess his body as an instrument or a vehicle of his spiritual soul. Instead, "corporeality forms an essential part of man."[64] In other words, the human body belongs to man's *being* and not to his *having*.[65] As a constitutive, essential

[60] Cf. CCC 363, 364, and 365.

[61] "Families", p. 2.

[62] DV, intro., 3.

[63] *Discourse to the Members*, p. 393.

[64] Ramón Lucas Lucas, *L'uomo spirito incarnato* (Cinisello Balsamo: Edizione Paoline, 1993), p. 195.

[65] Cf. John Paul II, *Discourse to Priests;* Dionigi Tettamanzi, "Reflections on *Veritatis Splendor*: Only the Son Brings True Freedom", *L'Osservatore Romano* (English ed.) October 27, 1993, and *I due saranno una carne sola* (Turin: Elle Di Ci, 1986), p. 268, where he writes, "Il rapporto che si dà tra l'uomo e il suo corpo non è identico al rapporto che si dà tra l'uomo e le cose ch'egli possiede e usa . . . l'uomo non *ha* il corpo, bensì *è* il suo corpo."

part of the person, the human body expresses the person and shares the dignity of the person.

The body *expresses* the person in a twofold manner inasmuch as it manifests the person in the visible world and also reveals the identity of the person through its sexual dimension. The human body differs from other bodies because, rather than being something entirely exterior, "the human body is the exteriorization of something that is essentially interior."[66] The human person lives an interior life on the basis of cognition and volition,[67] and the human body expresses this inner life in a concrete manner, expressing the person, making him present in the visible world. By making the person present in and to the world, the human body capacitates man for interpersonal communication. Indeed, all forms of human communication rely upon the body and its ability to express the person. Moreover, by means of the language of the body, the body can also "speak" on behalf of the person, thus expressing profound personal, spiritual truths.

Through its sexual characteristics, the human body also expresses the person by manifesting his particular mode of being human while also revealing the other-directedness of all human persons. Each human person possesses a sexual identity; that is, exists as either a masculine person or a feminine person. When the body expresses a person's sexual identity, it reveals "a fundamental component of the personality, one of its modes of being, of manifestation, of communi-

---

[66] Ramón Lucas Lucas, *L'uomo spirito incarnato*, p. 197: "Il corpo umano differisce essenzialmente dal corpo non-umano, non per la composizione chimica, ma perché il corpo non-umano è tutto esteriorità, mentre il corpo umano è *inoltre* esteriorizzazione di un qualcosa essenzialmente interno."

[67] Cf. Wojtyla, *Love and Responsibility*, p. 22.

cating with others, of feeling, of expressing and living human love".[68] Therefore, by manifesting sexual characteristics, the body reveals certain fundamental truths about a particular person. By virtue of its sexual aspects, the human body also reveals the identity of the human person as ordered to self-gift and personal communion. The sexual faculty of the male body remains incomprehensible apart from knowledge of the female body, just as the female sexual faculty remains incomprehensible apart from knowledge of the male body. Moreover, the life-giving potential of the male and the female bodies is actualized only in their interrelation. Thus, both theoretically and practically, the male and the female body complete or complement each other in their sexual aspect. Since the body is a constitutive part of the person, the complementarity of the male and female bodies expresses a complementarity of persons, revealing the other-directedness of each person. In turn, this other-directedness of the person reveals an ordination to self-gift to a complementary other and reveals the essence of personhood as existing with and for another.[69]

Because it is a constitutive part of the person, the human body not only expresses the person but also shares the dignity that is proper to the human person. In other words, the body is personal (acquires a certain dignity) by virtue of its substantial union with a spiritual soul. In accord with its personal dignity, man does not exercise an unlimited dominion over his body and its functions. Instead, there are "insurmountable limits to the possibility of man's dominion over

[68] Congregation for Catholic Education, *Educational Guidance in Human Love* (November 1, 1983), 4.

[69] Cf. John Paul II, General Audience of January 9, 1980.

his own body and its functions".[70] As Pius XII affirmed, "Therefore, man is not permitted to order his life and the functions of his organs according to his desire, in a way contrary to the internal and inherent purposes assigned to them. . . . Man is not the owner and absolute lord of his body, but only its usufructurary."[71] As the steward of his own body, man exercises a limited dominion over the body in which he is guided by the natural finalities of the body and its faculties. These inherent finalities of the body and its faculties direct man to authentic goods of the person precisely because these finalities result from the creative intention of God. God himself created the human body, ordering its functions and prescribing and limiting its use. Thus, instead of merely limiting man's dominion over the body, the personal dignity of the body perfects man's freedom by directing him to authentic personal goods.

The doctrine of the substantial unity of man's body and soul unfolds into various anthropological tenets that are particularly relevant in the area of conjugal relations. By virtue of its substantial unity with man's spiritual soul, the body is a constitutive part of the person, manifesting and expressing the person in the visible world. This fact, in turn, provides the rationale of sexual, bodily union as a personal union in the conjugal act. As a constitutive part of the person, the body is able to serve as the substratum or context for the intimate expression of conjugal love. Moreover, in accord with its personal dignity, the finalities of the body guide husband and wife in their expression and actualization of conjugal love. The finalities of the sexual faculty reveal the

[70] HV 17.

[71] Pius XII, "Address to the Micro-Biological Union of San Luca".

indissoluble connection of the procreative and unitive aspects of conjugal love because the body possesses a certain dignity. Ultimately, the body both capacitates man for conjugal love and defines the manner in which spouses embody conjugal love and confirm their conjugal covenant in the conjugal act.

Human Freedom as Theonomy

The idea of a prescribed form or act of love seems to eliminate the very notion of freedom, consequently precluding the possibility of true human love. How can spouses love each other freely if they are obliged to follow a specific form? How can love flourish amidst obligations and limitations? Certainly, love demands freedom, for conjugal love would not be human were it not free, and the conjugal act would not be a human act if it were not the result of free will. Conversely, the greater one's freedom, the greater one's ability to love fully and to act in a truly human manner. While a skewed view of man considers obligations and direction as the enemies of freedom, freedom properly understood finds its authentic and complete fulfillment and perfection precisely in the acceptance of the law and the obligations and forms that the law prescribes.[72] Thus, inasmuch as the laws governing the performance of the conjugal act enhance, promote, and protect freedom, the intrinsic structure of the conjugal act enhances, promotes, and protects the love of husband and wife. Yet, love flourishes under the guidance of the law

[72] Cf. VS 35.

only in the context of a proper notion of freedom, freedom as *theonomy*.[73]

The conjugal act is a *prescribed* form or act of love inasmuch as the meanings of the conjugal act are *inscribed* in the very being of man and woman[74] and inasmuch as the act proceeds according to laws *inscribed* in the being of man and woman.[75] As a human act, the conjugal act possesses an identifiable essence or ontological structure that corresponds to laws inscribed in human nature. These laws govern man's pursuit of and participation in the goods of procreation and union. In other words, in their pursuit of the goods of marriage and in their consequent acts of conjugal love, spouses are not free to proceed completely at will, as if they could determine in a wholly autonomous way the honest path to follow. Instead, husband and wife must conform their activity to the creative intentions of God, expressed in the very nature of marriage and of its acts.[76] In their performance of

---

[73] I take the terms "theonomy" and "participated theonomy" directly from VS 41, where they are mentioned briefly as a proper way of understanding the relationship between God's law and human freedom. Thus, I included this understanding of freedom as part of John Paul II's anthropological vision in chapter 2, section 2. For a more detailed description and discussion of the concept of theonomy or participated autonomy, consult Martin Rhonheimer, *Natural Law and Practical Reason: A Thomist View of Moral Autonomy*, trans. Gerald Malsbary (New York: Fordham Press, 2000). Rhonheimer's treatment of autonomy, valuable in many respects, is particularly so because of the manner in which he clearly links the notion of "participated theonomy" to the idea of man as *imago Dei*. See in particular pp. 234–56.

[74] Cf. FC 32.

[75] Cf. HV 12.

[76] Cf. HV 10, which refers explicitly to the good of procreation: "In the task of transmitting life, therefore, they are not free to proceed completely at will, as if they could determine in a wholly autonomous way the honest path to follow; but they must conform their activity to the creative intention of God, expressed in the very nature of marriage and its acts, and manifested by the constant teaching of the Church." Cf. also GS 50 and 51.

the conjugal act, husband and wife do not act in a wholly autonomous way, yet, nonetheless, they remain free. Freedom in such a case can only mean autonomy that is genuine though not absolute. Such a notion of freedom corresponds to what *Veritatis splendor* describes as theonomy, or participated theonomy.

In contrast to a concept of freedom that grants man an absolute sovereignty (including the ability to decide what is good and evil), Pope John Paul II describes a vision of freedom in which man is genuinely autonomous though ruled by God through the natural law that is written on his heart.[77] According to the Holy Father, "Man's genuine moral autonomy in no way means the rejection but rather the acceptance of the moral law, of God's command."[78] God governs man is such a way as to preserve his autonomy by giving him a participation in his own wisdom and providence. Human persons, like all creatures, are ruled by God, for nothing escapes his rule. God, however, rules human persons in such a way that they are not only ruled but also rulers of themselves.[79] Because God rules man we can speak of theonomy, yet because God grants man a share or participation in his own ruling, *theonomy* is not a *heteronomy*.[80] God does not

[77] Cf. VS 31–53.

[78] VS 41.

[79] Cf. St. Thomas, *Summa Contra Gentiles*, 3, chap. 1: "God, Who is in all ways perfect in Himself, and Who endows all things with being from His own power, exists as Ruler of all beings, and is ruled by none other. Nor is there anything that escapes His rule, just as there is nothing that does not receive its being from Him. . . . Of course, the result of this rule is manifested differently in different beings, depending on the diversity of their natures. For some beings so exist as God's products that, possessing understanding, they bear His likeness and reflect his image. Consequently, they are not only ruled but are also rulers of themselves."

[80] Cf. VS 41.

rule man from the outside, through a law that is extraneous to the human person. Instead, God rules man from the inside by inscribing his law on man's heart and by allowing man to make this law his own.[81] By writing the natural law upon man's heart, God directs man to the good, yet man's freedom remains the genuine source of the actions by which he pursues the good referred to in the law.

By inscribing his law on the heart of man, God gives to man a particular identity in addition to governing his actions. That is, God's law comprises part of man's very being and contributes to him a certain identity. In biblical terms, man is identified as "the image and likeness of God" present in visible creation. As an integral part of his specifically human identity, God "inscribed in the humanity of man and woman the vocation, and thus the capacity and responsibility, of love and communion".[82] Thus, man not only possesses a certain identity (essence or nature) but also a summons or call to develop this identity in a particular manner by virtue of the vocation inscribed in his very humanity. Man's role in the universe derives from who he is, and his role represents the dynamic and existential development of who he is. Man comes into existence with capacities and responsibilities interwoven in the form of an identity that contains a vocation.[83] From this perspective, man's freedom becomes the ability to undertake the dynamic and existential development of his identity, thus embracing this identity and ful-

---

[81] Cf. VS 43: "He cares for man not 'from without,' through the laws of physical nature, but 'from within,' through reason, which, by its very natural knowledge of God's eternal law, is consequently able to show man the right direction to take in his free actions."

[82] FC 11.

[83] In this line of thought, I apply John Paul II's ideas (in FC 17) on the family to the individual person.

filling his vocation. For their part, the various precepts of the law become the reiteration of man's identity/vocation, a reference point or guiding light for freedom.

Freedom understood as theonomy means that human freedom never exists in an existential vacuum. Instead, man exercises freedom in the context of an identity and a vocation. This context of identity/vocation gives freedom a particular role as "a force for growth and maturity in truth and goodness".[84] Human freedom is the ability to undertake the existential development of one's identity, the ability to be the source of one's growth in maturity by responding to the vocation to love. Human freedom does not bestow an essential identity on man; this identity he receives from God. Instead, freedom gives man the ability to accept his identity in his actions under the guidance of God's law. Because the law does not operate like a computer program encoded in the person, freedom calls for "that creativity and originality typical of the person".[85] Moreover, though man cannot change his essential identity and vocation through freedom (that is, he cannot cease to be human), the exercise of freedom demands great responsibility because human actions do give moral definition to the person by virtue of their immanent dimension.[86] However, every step of the way, man's identity/vocation serves as the fundamental reference point for freedom; man's moral character reflects either the proper use of

[84] CCC 1731.

[85] VS 40.

[86] Cf. VS 71: "Human acts are moral acts because they express and determine the goodness or evil of the individual who performs them. They do not produce a change merely in the state of affairs outside of man but, to the extent that they are deliberate choices, they give moral definition to the person who performs them, determining his profound spiritual traits."

freedom to cultivate his identity or the abuse of freedom and the blurring of his identity.

An understanding of human freedom as the existential development (under the guidance of God's law) of man's identity provides the rationale for a prescribed act of love within the conjugal covenant. In the very creation of man and woman, God orders the human sexual faculty to specific goods (union and procreation principally) that specify the faculty itself and provide the context for its free exercise. Man and woman are ordered to these goods in diverse modes, and these diverse modes of participating in the goods of sexuality correspond to the sexual identity of man and woman as masculine and feminine persons. The sexual identities of man and woman are further specified in marriage as they become husband and wife respectively. As a vocation, marriage actualizes and concretizes the capacity of man and woman to fulfill their innate, human vocation to love and communion. Their identities and vocation as husband and wife provide man and woman the context in which they freely exercise their sexual faculty in order to undertake the existential development of their sexual identity. By conforming their intentions to those of the Creator, man and woman truly love each other as spouses. In performing the conjugal act according to God's intentions for human sexuality expressed in the law, man and woman embrace and develop their identities as husband and wife.

Just as God governs man in the development of his identity as a person by means of the natural law written on his heart, God governs husband and wife in their expression of conjugal love through laws inscribed in their very beings. In other words, God governs man's existential development of his sexual identity (directs man to the goods of marriage) by means of laws inscribed in the very being of man and woman as an integral part of directing man's existential development of his human identity (directing man to the good in general) by means of the natural law. The laws that govern the pursuit of the goods of marriage consist of those precepts of the natural moral law that pertain to the free exercise of the sexual faculty. A prescribed form of conjugal intercourse results from these precepts, along with the various other rights and obligations of the married state. In fact, it would be somewhat perplexing if God had authored marriage as a natural institution without including a prescribed form of the marital act. When he authored marriage (in the very creation of man and woman) independently of the will of man, God quite coherently included a prescribed form of conjugal intercourse without denying human freedom its proper role in the married life and in the performance of the conjugal act. In the preservation of freedom within marriage, God's law preserves the possibility of love between husband and wife in the conjugal act.

Within the framework of freedom as theonomy, God preserves man's freedom by directing him to the good in such a way that allows man a share or participation in his own governance.[87] God's law, existing in man (written on his heart), becomes man's own law. Consequently, the human person governs himself according to a law that he does not himself author. In the context of conjugal love, man directs himself to the goods of marriage according to the manner that God's law points out for him, while at the same time making this manner his own. Thus, the prescribed, objective act of conjugal love becomes the personal, intimate expression of love

[87] Cf. Wojtyla, *Love and Responsibility*, p. 27: "If God intends to direct man towards certain goals, he allows him to begin to know those goals, so that he may make them his own and strive towards them independently."

between husband and wife. The universal mode of pursuing the goods of marriage becomes a couple's particular way of participating in the goods of marriage. Directed to the conjugal act by laws inscribed in their very being, husband and wife find the conjugal act to be a perfectly fitting and sublime manner of sharing themselves with each other, of sharing their love for each other, and of generating a family together. *The conjugal act*, though prescribed by the law, truly becomes *their conjugal act*. This appropriation and personalization of the conjugal act on the part of spouses occurs through the functioning of conscience, the aspect of man by which he perceives God's law and makes it his own.

The Role of the Human Conscience and Consciousness

Participated theonomy is possible because man discovers in himself a law that he has received from the Creator. In turn, the discovery of God's law is possible through the functioning of the human conscience, by which man knows God's law and assimilates its truth. In the context of conjugal love, the human conscience allows spouses to apply God's law to their particular expression of love in the conjugal act, ensuring that their action conforms to their identity as spouses and to the truth of conjugal love. Human consciousness relates directly to the functioning of the conscience because it enables man to experience himself as the subject of his acts (thus reminding him of his responsibility for his acts) and provides man with an awareness of what he is doing/willing in a particular action (that is, gives him an experience of the diverse components of the act). Human consciousness contributes a particularly human character to human action, reminding man of the responsibility he bears as an acting subject and enabling him to *experience* his action.

The understanding of freedom as participated theonomy contained in *Veritatis splendor* relies upon the possibility of an interaction between freedom and God's law, an interaction in which God rules man while preserving his genuine autonomy. The relationship between human freedom and God's law is lived in the moral conscience of each person, for the conscience brings the law to bear on the acts that proceed from freedom.[88] Employed in this sense, *moral conscience* refers to "man's most secret core and his sanctuary"[89] or the heart of the person. In the depths of his conscience, in the depths of his being, "man detects a law which he does not impose on himself, but which holds him to obedience."[90] The authority of man's moral conscience, its ability to hold him to obedience, derives from its ability to witness to God's law, its ability to be the *locus* of contact between God and man.[91] Thus, Pope John Paul II describes conscience as "the witness of God himself, whose voice and judgement penetrate the depths of man's soul".[92] The moral conscience, then, provides man with an awareness of God's law (thus establishing a context for freedom) by bearing witness to God's voice, by allowing God to speak to man in the depths of his being.

---

[88] Cf. VS 54: "The relationship between man's freedom and God's law is most deeply lived out in the 'heart' of the person, in his moral conscience."

[89] GS 16.

[90] Ibid.

[91] Cf. CCC 1777: "When he listens to his conscience, the prudent man can hear God speaking."

[92] VS 58; Cf. John Paul II, General Audience of August 17, 1983: "Moral conscience does not close man within an insurmountable and impenetrable solitude, but opens him to the call, to the voice of God. In this, and not in anything else, lies the entire mystery and dignity of the moral conscience: in being the place, the sacred place where God speaks to man."

When he speaks to man through the functioning of the moral conscience, God provides man with an awareness of general moral principles that serves as the basis for a judgment of conscience regarding a particular action. Thus, the notion of conscience "includes the perception of the principles of morality"[93] and the ability to formulate a judgment about human action on the basis of these principles. Though man can make erroneous judgments of conscience through ignorance, "no one is deemed to be ignorant of the *principles* of the moral law, which are written in the conscience of every man."[94] Thus, every man carries God's law (the natural law) within him inasmuch as it "is written and engraved in the soul of each and every man".[95] The judgment of conscience results from the application of these moral principles (the first of which is the conviction that one must love and do good and avoid evil) to a particular, concrete act. The judgment of conscience is a judgment of reason that "makes known what man must do or not do"[96] whereby "the human person recognizes the moral quality of a concrete act that he is going to perform, is in the process of performing, or has already completed."[97] The judgment of conscience indicates the *good* on the basis of the awareness of the principles of morality known through the witness of conscience. Man places his confidence in the judgment of

[93] CCC 1780. This awareness or perception of moral principles corresponds to Aquinas' notion of *synderesis*. Cf. St. Thomas, *Summa Theologica*, I, q. 79, a. 12.

[94] CCC 1860 (emphasis added).

[95] Cf. Pope Leo XIII, *Libertas præstantissimum*.

[96] VS 59: "The judgment of conscience is a practical judgment, a judgment which makes known what man must do or not do, or which assesses an act already performed by him."

[97] CCC 1778.

conscience because it ultimately results from his inner dialogue with God.

The judgment of conscience directs man to the good and helps him avoid evil by bringing the natural law to bear on particular acts, enabling man not only to know the law but also to *appropriate* and *assimilate* the truth contained in the law, making this truth his own. By applying the law to a particular act, the conscience "transforms" the universal and objective moral law into the proximate and personal norm. The Holy Father explains, "whereas the natural law discloses the objective and universal demands of the moral good, conscience is the application of the law to a particular case; this application of the law becomes an inner dictate for the individual."[98] Conscience discloses the good in a particular case with the authority of the natural law and formulates the "proximate norm of personal morality".[99] As the proximate norm of morality, the truth contained in the natural law becomes man's own truth, his own understanding of the good. According to John Paul II, "The acting subject personally assimilates the truth contained in the law. He appropriates this truth of his being and makes it his own by acts and corresponding virtues."[100] Consequently, though guided by the natural law (that is, ruled by God), man becomes his own guide (that is, rules himself) by appropriating or assimilating the truth contained in the law,

[98] VS 59.

[99] Ibid.

[100] VS 52. Cf. Carlo Caffarra, *Living in Christ: Fundamental Principles of Catholic Moral Theology* (San Francisco: Ignatius Press, 1987), p. 109: "Moral conscience constitutes and institutes the *personalization* of moral values and norms—it is what enables the human person to realize himself in his unrepeatable individuality according to *the truth* of moral values and norms."

by uniting his own inner voice with the voice of God that "echoes in his depths".[101]

Far from constricting man's freedom, the witness and judgment of conscience keep man free by enabling man to identify accurately the good, the true object of freedom. Considering "the more one does what is good, the freer one becomes",[102] conscience truly enhances and increases man's freedom inasmuch as it discloses the good in each particular case. In the context of conjugal love, conscience preserves freedom and authentic love by allowing husband and wife to identify and intend the goods around which their communion of love forms. The communion of persons at the heart of conjugal love forms on the basis of specific common goods. The conjugal act embodies conjugal love and participates in the conjugal communion inasmuch as it is ordered to these specific goods of conjugal love. Conversely, sexual intercourse fails to embody conjugal love apart from the intention of the goods of marriage. As the aspect of man by which he identifies the good of each situation, conscience enters the domain of conjugal love as the guardian of love by ensuring that husband and wife order their acts of love to the goods of marriage. Rather than constricting or limiting the expression of love, conscience ensures the authenticity of the marital embrace, giving spouses the freedom to love each other "conjugally". Moreover, because conscience entails the appropriation of the truth of the law, by *following* their consciences in their sexual relations, spouses *direct* themselves and *order* their actions according to their own truth. Thus, the fundamental structure of the conjugal act preserves and promotes the love of husband and wife when they perceive and

[101] Cf. GS 16.

[102] CCC 1733.

embrace the truth of this prescribed form of love through the operation of their consciences.

While conscience guides man to the good through the judgment of conscience, the full relevance of conscience derives from the functioning of human consciousness, which enables man to experience his own subjectivity. The judgment of conscience, based upon man's awareness of general moral principles, enables man to recognize the moral quality of a particular action before, during, and after its performance. Because conscience applies the objective universal law in such a way as to formulate the proximate norm of personal morality, the judgment of conscience possesses the authority of the natural law and the character of a personal recognition of the truth. While the judgment of conscience applies specifically to particular acts, conscience also enables man to recognize his own moral character or state insofar as consciousness allows man to experience particular actions as his own. Because consciousness accompanies and reflects or mirrors action,[103] each human subject experiences his acts as *his own* by experiencing the manner in which they proceed from his exercise of free will. According to Wojtyla, "Consciousness allows us not only to have an inner view of our actions (immanent perception) and of their dynamic dependence on the ego, but also to *experience these actions as actions and as our own.*"[104] Thus, consciousness enables man

[103] Cf. K. Wojtyla, *The Acting Person*, trans. Andrzej Potocki (Boston: D. Reidel Publishing, 1979), p. 31: "Consciousness accompanies and reflects or mirrors the action when it is born and while it is being performed; once the action is accomplished consciousness still continues to reflect it, though of course it no longer accompanies it. The accompanying presence of consciousness is decisive in making man aware of his acting rather than in making his acting conscious."

[104] Ibid., p. 42.

to experience the intimate relationship between himself and his acts, thereby enabling him to take responsibility for his own acts and to share in the moral quality of the act as its subject. In other words, inasmuch as consciousness enables man to experience his responsibility for his acts, consciousness enables man to recognize the judgment of his acts as a judgment of himself.

The accompanying presence of consciousness not only plays a critical role in allowing man to experience the development of his moral character through his action but also gives human action a particularly *human* quality. A human act (*actus humanus*) results from the movement of free will in terms of intention and choice. In this sense, the attribute "human" derives from the presence of deliberation and choice that give human action its rational nature. Actions that proceed from intention, deliberation, and choice (and the rationality upon which they depend) are unique to humans among the visible creatures of the universe. Yet, consciousness is also a uniquely human trait among visible creatures, and it adds its own human character to action by enabling the person to *experience* himself as the subject of particular acts. Through consciousness the person experiences himself as a subject, not simply the moral quality of his acts or his moral state. Consciousness allows the person to experience his own subjectivity by accompanying the act as it proceeds from free will. Thus, the human subject experiences the action itself (the movement of the will) and his role in the action (himself as the source of the movement of the will).

Whereas the function of the human conscience allows husband and wife to appropriate the conjugal act as their own personal form of expressing conjugal love, human consciousness enables spouses to experience their conjugal act as their own act of love. By conforming their activity to the dictates of conscience, husband and wife ensure the authenticity of their acts of love. Conscience, then, promotes and protects the love of husband and wife by bringing the truth of the law inscribed within them to bear on their acts of love. Consciousness, on the other hand, reveals the spouses' responsibility for the authenticity of their expression of love by giving husband and wife an experience of their role in the performance of the act. Consciousness confirms for husband and wife the conjugal act as their own manner of loving each other by enabling them to experience their own subjectivity in the act. Because the conjugal act entails co-subjectivity, consciousness enables husband and wife to experience the conjugal act as an act of love precisely by providing them with an experience of their roles as co-subjects of the act. Such an experience, however, requires a husband and wife actually to act as co-subjects because consciousness itself does not create experiences but allows man to encounter reality in an experiential way. Thus, apart from the pursuit of a common good the authentic experience of co-subjectivity, and hence love, remains impossible. Since love itself cannot exist without the pursuit of a common good, the authentic experience of love requires co-subjectivity in the pursuit of a common good.

Co-Subjectivity and the Pursuit of a Common Good

In considering the conjugal act, we encounter one action performed by two persons, for both husband and wife are acting, yet only one act results. The idea of one act proceeding from two agents reveals a particular use of freedom by which man is not merely the subject of his own act but the co-subject of a shared act. An analysis of human subjectivity reveals the foundations of human freedom in the ability to act deliberately for the sake of an end. Co-subjectivity emerges from man's ability to act deliberately with another for the sake of a common end. More than acting in the same place and at the same time, co-subjectivity enables man to act *with* another, which in turn presupposes a common end that is shared with the other precisely as a common end. Man's capacity for co-subjectivity provides the basis for love in the conjugal act and reveals the particularly personal nature of the act.

The term *love* most fundamentally means to will the good for the beloved.[105] However, there are various types and degrees of love. For this reason, we speak of *true love* or love in the truest sense, which is also called friendship. K. Wojtyla refers to the love of friendship when he states, "Love is the realization of a certain kind of communion based upon a common good."[106] Anytime persons direct themselves to one purpose a certain bond arises between them because they are united in purpose.[107] In this manner a certain partnership develops between soldiers, businessmen, or teammates who dedicate themselves to the accomplishment of a common goal. However, true love or friendship forms between those seeking a common good when each person recognizes the common good as the good of the other and as his own good, and consequently friendship involves seeing the good of the other as one's own good. Viewing another's good as one's own good creates a bond between friends, and they seem to become two halves of a greater whole. Thus, Aquinas states, "when a man loves another with the love of

---

[105] Cf. CCC 1766; St. Thomas Aquinas, *Summa Theologica*, I–II, q. 26, a. 4: "To love is to will the good of another."

[106] Wojtyla, *Love and Responsibility*, p. 300 (n. 37).

[107] Cf. St. Thomas Aquinas, *Summa Theologica*, Supplement, q. 44, a. 1.

friendship, he wills good to him, just as he wills good to himself: wherefore he apprehends him as his other self, insofar, to wit, as he wills good to him as to himself." [108] Love in the truest sense, then, means becoming one with the beloved in such a way that the lover acts for the sake of the beloved as if it were his own sake.[109]

Becoming one with another entails a certain loss of one's individuality, and in this loss of individuality the notion of *self-gift* enters into the realm of love. Self-donation does not and cannot mean an exchange or transfer of selves between persons precisely because the very notion of personhood entails the incommunicability of the person.[110] Instead, the gift of self means giving up one's strict individuality by becoming the other half of the beloved and by seeing the beloved as the other half of oneself. In a certain sense love enables the "I" of the beloved to become the "I" of the lover inasmuch as the good of the beloved becomes the good of the lover. A communion results from this aspect of love that enables each friend to transcend the level of the individual; that is, from the union of one "I" with another "I" a "we" results. However, such a union requires the gift of self because a strict defense of the "I" prevents the formation of a "we". In friendship I give myself to the beloved to the extent that I allow the beloved to view me as another half of himself and my good as his good and to the extent that I broaden my understanding of myself and my good to include him and his good. Such a communion requires a common good that can be *our* good rather than simply *my* or *his*

[108] Ibid., I–II, q. 28, a. 1.

[109] Cf. ibid., a. 2.

[110] Cf. Wojtyla, *Love and Responsibility*, pp. 24, 96–97.

good, and conversely the pursuit of a common good entails the gift of self into this communion.

The gift of self, however, never entails the loss of self even if it requires one to transcend the category of individual, and herein lies a specific capacity or characteristic of personhood: the capacity for distinction in unity. In order to love another with the love of friendship, I must give myself into a communion with another in such a way that we mutually become the other half of each other. Within the context of the friendship our identities become bound up with each other, and yet we remain distinct as persons precisely because he sees *me* as his other half and I see *him* as my other half. Though friends become *one* common subject, as it were, of the friendship (it could never be my friendship or his friendship; it is always our friendship), they remain *two* persons. In becoming the other half of my friend I am never reduced to his other half; I also remain myself. In other words, personhood allows for the possibility of radical unity in conjunction with radical distinction, as the roots of the notion of personhood clearly reveal.[111]

In the conjugal friendship self-donation and the resulting communion reach a singular quality and degree, a quality and degree marked by the idea of husband and wife cleaving to one another so that they become one flesh.[112] The one flesh terminology applies to no other human friendship, and only in marriage do two persons share themselves in such an

[111] The concept of "person" as it is currently employed in theology and philosophy originated with the efforts of the early Christians to formulate certain doctrines concerning the Trinity. It corresponds, therefore, most fundamentally to the idea of relationship and unity and distinction. For an account of this development, consult: J. Ratzinger, *Introduction to Christianity*, trans. J./R. Foster (San Francisco: Ignatius Press, 1990), pp. 114–37.

[112] Cf. Gen 3:24.

all-encompassing and permanent way. Only husband and wife *belong* to each other.[113] The unique self-donation and communion of persons found in marriage derive from the unique nature of the common good to which marriage is ordered: the procreation and education of children. No other friendship is based on the human potential for parenthood, and thus no other friendship includes the total gift of self. In other words, only the conjugal friendship requires sexual self-donation for the whole of one's life because only the conjugal friendship is ordered to the procreation and education of children. Herein lies the indispensability of procreation in marriage: procreation makes the spousal friendship *conjugal* inasmuch as procreation makes it *human*, *total*, *sexual*, *fruitful*, *bodily*, and *permanent*.[114] The relationship of man and woman is never a conjugal friendship apart from the communion of persons formed around the procreation and education of children.

Though husband and wife are radically and uniquely united in marriage, their unity remains a moral unity, not an ontological unity. When man and woman "become one" in marriage, they do not become one person but rather one common subject, as it were, of the conjugal life. According to Pope John Paul II, spousal unity "is therefore a question of unity, not in the ontological sense, but in the moral sense—unity through love".[115] In a certain sense, the "I" of the wife becomes the "I" of the husband, and she becomes his own flesh. Thus, in his Letter to the Ephesians, St. Paul says, "He

[113] Cf. 1Cor 7:4: "A wife does not belong to herself but to her husband; equally a husband does not belong to himself but to his wife."

[114] Cf. HV 9 for a description of conjugal love.

[115] General Audience of September 1, 1982.

who loves his wife loves himself."[116] Commenting on this passage, John Paul II writes, "Love not only unites the two subjects, but allows them to be mutually inter-penetrated, spiritually belonging to one another to such a degree that the author of the letter can affirm: 'He who loves his wife loves himself' (Eph 5:28). The 'I' becomes in a certain sense the 'you' and 'you' the 'I' (in a moral sense, that is)."[117] Spousal love unites husband and wife in such a way that they mutually interpenetrate and spiritually belong to each other, becoming one in the moral sense. The moral sense of spousal unity corresponds precisely to the notion of co-subjectivity. Husband and wife are one subject without ceasing to be two persons. Such a oneness, such co-subjectivity, is possible only in the pursuit of a profound common good, and thus once again we come to the indispensability of procreation and union for conjugal relations.

Conjugal relations depend upon the capacity of husband and wife to be one common subject while remaining two distinct persons, and in its relationship to the human capacity for co-subjectivity the conjugal relationship fulfills the potential of the human person, fulfilling man's fundamental and innate vocation. According to Pope John Paul II, love is "the fundamental and innate vocation of every human being."[118] Here the Holy Father refers to love in the sense by which man and woman image God, who in himself "lives a mystery of personal loving communion".[119] Thus, God calls

---

[116] Eph 5:28.

[117] General Audience of September 1, 1982.

[118] FC 11.

[119] Cf. ibid.: "God is love and in Himself He lives a mystery of personal loving communion. Creating the human race in His own image and continually keeping it in being, God inscribed in the humanity of man and woman the vocation, and thus the capacity and responsibility, of love and communion."

man and woman most fundamentally to the formation of a communion of persons. More than a task given to man, the call to communion through the gift of self reveals the very essence of personhood. In a sense, being the subject of intelligent, deliberate action reveals man's humanity, while being a co-subject reveals his personhood. The personal dimension (communion) requires and relies upon the human dimension (freedom, intelligence, conscience, and so on) and yet adds something to it. The conjugal act is personal, then, precisely because it draws upon man's capacity for communion, allowing man to fulfill his innate vocation, allowing husband and wife to image God.

CONCLUSION

Whether considered as a human act, a symbolic act, a sacramental act, or a personal act, a consideration of the conjugal act invariably returns to the goods of procreation and union. The conjugal act constitutes a singular and irreplaceable moment in the conjugal life of husband and wife, uniquely embodying their love and personal union. The conjugal act allows for a particular expression and communication of conjugal love through its symbolic dimension. Moreover, as a sacramental act the conjugal act shares in the richness of the sacramental symbolism of the conjugal covenant, enabling spouses to represent sacramentally the love of God for humanity and the love of Christ for the Church in their own expression of love. The personal dimension of the conjugal act corresponds to and fulfills man's potential for co-subjectivity and communion insofar as it allows husband and wife to become one while also remaining two persons. However, the conjugal act's wealth of significance derives from its two essential aspects, procreation and union, for apart from these goods the sexual intercourse corrupts into sexual exploitation. These common goods stand at the center of the conjugal act, and the intention of procreation and union transforms genital intercourse into an act of love, possessing symbolic, sacramental, and personal significance. Thus, spouses forfeit such a wealth of significance and value when they preclude either of these essential aspects. For this reason the Church faithfully exhorts spouses to preserve procreation and union in their sexual relations as a means of preserving their love and the sacred symbolism of their love.

When the Church exhorts spouses to preserve and foster the procreative and unitive aspects of sexual relations, the notion of a "prescribed" act of love emerges, insofar as the Church says the sexual act should possess this content rather than another. Yet, far from constricting the expression of spousal love, such exhortation directs the consciences of husband and wife to the truth inscribed in the very being of man and woman, a truth that enables them to love each other as persons. The Church's concept of the conjugal act (that is, that it is necessarily procreative and unitive in its essence and meaning) seems to run counter to most popular notions of the sexual relations of man and woman. However, the very idea that the sexual relationship can have an objective and universal content represents an even greater and more fundamental divergence from popular discussions of sexuality precisely because it contradicts the contemporary exaltation of freedom that suggests that man and woman can give any meaning to the sexual act. Many popular views of freedom and conscience require the person to decide for himself how and for what purpose the sexual faculty will be used. Consequently, the idea of a universal and objective concept of the conjugal act seems to offend the very dignity of the person, whose freedom and conscience enable him to proceed autonomously. Therefore, the idea of a prescribed or universal and objective expression of conjugal love requires the support of an adequate anthropology.

Throughout her development and articulation of a theology of the conjugal act, the Church has provided and clarified the anthropological framework upon which her teaching in the area of marriage and sexuality relies. An understanding of freedom as *theonomy* stands at the forefront of this anthropological vision because it allows for the idea of loving freely without proceeding in a wholly autonomous way. Husband and wife retain and perfect their freedom (and hence their capacity for love) by conforming to the truth because human freedom finds its fulfillment in the acceptance of God's law.[120] Husband and wife find an objective reference point for the exercise of their freedom in their sexual identities as man and woman and as husband and wife. The proper functioning of conscience allows husband and wife not only to perceive the truth but also to appropriate the truth, transforming the universal, objective law into the proximate norm of personal morality. A correct understanding of conscience provides the rationale for the idea of a universal, prescribed form of love becoming the personal, intimate expression of love. Consequently, in the light of an integral vision of man the moral demands of the truth become the guardian and promoter of love.

When husband and wife conform their activity to the truth disclosed by the conscience, they preserve the truly personal nature of the conjugal act by confirming it as an act of love. As a human act, a symbolic act, and a sacramental act the

[120] Cf. VS 35.

conjugal act is an act of love and personal union by virtue of the intention of procreation and union. Since the capacity for love and communion is a true hallmark of the person, the conjugal act emerges as a personal act in all its various dimensions. The very idea of personhood rests upon the ability to live with another and for another without losing one's personal identity; persons are able to be simultaneously united and distinct. The conjugal act draws upon this aspect of personhood because it entails co-subjectivity and requires husband and wife to become one flesh while remaining ontologically distinct. The conjugal act effects a true oneness between husband and wife though they remain two persons. This two-in-one aspect of the conjugal act results from the co-subjectivity made possible by the intention of procreation and union and confirms the conjugal act as a truly personal act.

GENERAL CONCLUSION

In *Familiaris consortio* Pope John Paul II describes the difference between the practice of contraception and periodic continence (NFP) as "a difference which is much wider and deeper than is usually thought, one which involves in the final analysis two irreconcilable concepts of the human person and of human sexuality".[1] These words from the Holy Father equally apply to the difference between the Catholic concept of the conjugal act and the prevailing popular view of sexual relations. While my study of the conjugal act was not aimed at an examination and comparison of these two diverse and irreconcilable concepts of the human person, I have endeavored to show that the Catholic concept of the conjugal act emerges from and intrinsically entails a specific concept of the human person, while at the same time taking the Church's teaching on the conjugal act as an opportunity to examine the interaction and integration between sexual ethics and anthropology.

As a way of investigating the relationship between anthropology and the Catholic concept of the conjugal act, I began my study of the conjugal act with two principal goals: (1) to examine and present the Catholic Church's profound and beautiful concept of the conjugal act and (2) to investigate the larger theological framework within which the Church articulates her theology of the conjugal act. Each of these goals essentially coincides with the other because the Church's

[1] FC 32.

theology of the conjugal act emerges from the context of her doctrines on the conjugal life and from the context of Christian anthropology and remains comprehensible only within the convergence of these two foundational theological frameworks. The Catholic concept of the conjugal act, then, presents the act as a personal act, proceeding from reason and will, that shares the procreative and unitive aspects of the conjugal life in accord with the nature of man and woman as sexual persons composed of body and soul and endowed with freedom and conscience.

As a conclusion to my study of the conjugal act, I summarize here the Catholic concept of the conjugal act and its most prominent elements and also the foundations of this concept of the conjugal act, which are located in the Church's teachings on the conjugal life and in the Catholic vision of the person. These concluding remarks not only account for the theoretical basis of the Church's uniquely profound understanding of marital relations but also point to the reason why the Magisterium of the Church possesses both the capacity and the obligation to instruct spouses with regard to their sexual relationship.

The Catholic Concept of the Conjugal Act

Certainly, the Catholic view of the conjugal act transcends the level of biology, sexual instinct, and subconscious drives insofar as the conjugal act results from the deliberate intention and choice of specific ends. Sexual intercourse between husband and wife differs greatly from animal unions, though it physically resembles them, because it relies upon human intelligence and free will. The presence of free will in the conjugal act accounts for the specifically human character of the act but does not quite capture the sense in which the act is a personal act. The conjugal act is a personal act by virtue of the manner in which it relies upon specific traits of the human person. According to Catholic teaching, the conjugal act incorporates the language of the body and its nuptial meaning, the potential for parenthood, and man's capacity for co-subjectivity and friendship. Not every free act incorporates these various aspects of the person. Thus, the conjugal act is a human act (*actus humanus*) and yet something more: a personal act. In its personal dimension, the conjugal act enables husband and wife to fulfill their fundamental vocation to form a loving personal communion in accord with their identity as the image and likeness of the Triune God. By viewing the conjugal act as a personal act, the Church promotes both the dignity of the act and the dignity of the person.

Yet, the beauty and the profundity of the Church's understanding of the conjugal act derive not only from her description of the manner in which the act unfolds as a human and personal act but also from the specific goods that the Catholic position sees as the essence and meaning of the conjugal act. In other words, by focusing her description of the conjugal act on the intention and choice of procreation and union, the Church provides the basis for a deep appreciation of the act precisely because these goods at the heart of the conjugal act account for the profound significance of the act. Procreation enables husband and wife to cooperate with the omnipotent power of God the Creator in actively receiving his gift of new life. In procreating, husband and wife place themselves at the service of life in accord with God's design for human sexuality. Their cooperation with God also requires husband and wife to become co-subjects and to give themselves to each other on the basis of sexual complementarity, for spouses find the potential for parenthood only when they become co-subjects in the sexual domain. The co-subjectivity of procreation provides the basis for spousal union in the conjugal act. In the conjugal act spouses are able to become one in a truly personal union through the bodily union of genital intercourse. Their physical joining in the conjugal act signifies and confirms the spouses' common life together. The conjugal act, then, consummates and embodies the words of love expressed in marital consent by which husband and wife belong to each other all the days of their lives.

Can we overestimate the profundity and significance of an act that allows husband and wife to cooperate with the omnipotent power of God in the transmission of life while embodying the commitment of a lifelong personal loving communion? Because procreation and union imbue sexual intercourse with such a wealth of beauty and significance, by insisting on the indispensability of procreation and union in the conjugal act the Church preserves a great treasure that would otherwise be forfeited and substituted with the pursuit of erotic pleasure or the gratification of an urge.

In addition to asserting the indispensability and centrality of procreation and union in the conjugal act, the Catholic concept of the conjugal act contains a sophisticated understanding of the manner in which these realities enter into the act as *goods*, *ends*, and *meanings* of the act. As goods of the conjugal act, procreation and union are the intrinsic reasons for the goodness of the act, making the conjugal act both inherently desirable and perfective of husband and wife. Yet, more than simply attractive aspects of the conjugal act, procreation and union are also the ends of the act as a human act proceeding from free will. As ends of the conjugal act, procreation and union are the goals intended in the act, the goals for the sake of which the activity is being performed.

Finally, the teachings of the Church also describe procreation and union as the meanings of the conjugal act. The concept of meaning corresponds to the level of human awareness or the level of experience that accompanies the performance of an action. Thus, procreation and union are the meanings of the conjugal act inasmuch as husband and wife possess an awareness of procreation and union as the ends of the conjugal act. These three ways of describing the place of procreation and union in the conjugal act (good, end, meaning) represent diverse modes of viewing the same realities in the context of human action. Yet, inasmuch as the concepts of good, end, and meaning are all intrinsically interdependent, none of the three modes of viewing procreation and union precludes or displaces the other two. Moreover, by accounting for these diverse dimensions of human action, the teachings of the Church assert the indispensability and centrality of procreation and union in each dimension of the conjugal act.

When describing the place of procreation and union in the conjugal act, the Catholic position not only emphasizes the intrinsic relationship of each reality to the nature of the act but also emphasizes the intrinsic relationship between procreation and union as such. In other words, procreation and union are not merely the goods, ends, and meanings of the same human act but rather the indissolubly connected goods, ends, and meanings of the conjugal act. The Church's doctrine of the indissoluble connection between procreation and union, initially formulated in HV 12, posits an intrinsic and unbreakable bond between procreation and union by virtue of the very definitions of the realities. The connection between procreation and union follows from the unity of the human person (from the fact that man's body belongs to his being and not to his having) and is, therefore, an anthropological fact.

In turn, this connection means that procreation and union can be actualized only as one complex aim because "the one is activated with the other and in a certain sense the one by means of the other."[2] By virtue of the indissoluble connection between procreation and union, which results from the substantial unity of the person, husband and wife can pursue and experience procreation and union as the ends and meanings of the conjugal act only when they do so as one complex reality.

The Foundations of the Catholic Concept of the Conjugal Act

In consistently describing the conjugal act as a personal act inherently ordered to the goods of procreation and spousal union, the teachings of the Catholic Church express an utterly unique understanding of the sexual relationship of husband and wife, an understanding that appreciates and promotes the most profound aspects of the sexual act without neglecting any genuinely human dimension of the act. However, as my study has confirmed, we can never reduce this uniquely profound understanding of the conjugal act to a particularly insightful consideration of the sexual act. The Church does not *merely* possess a deeper understanding of sex. Instead, the Church possesses the only adequate basis upon which to discover the integral meaning of the human sexual faculty and its exercise. In other words, the uniquely profound character of the Church's theology of the conjugal act derives, not from some particular insight into sexuality, but rather from the utterly unique vantage point from which the Church views the sexual relationship: her doctrines on the conjugal

[2] John Paul II, General Audience of August 22, 1984.

life according to Christian anthropology. Thus, the beauty and depth of the Church's understanding of the conjugal act manifest an equally unique, beautiful, and profound understanding of the conjugal life and of the human person. Conversely, the popular, superficial view of sexuality betrays an equally inadequate and superficial understanding of the conjugal life and of the human person.

On the basis of her theology of marriage, the Church penetrates the conjugal character of the act, recognizing the manner in which the conjugal act manifests the fundamental dimensions of the conjugal life (institution, friendship, and sacrament). Precisely as *conjugal*, the conjugal act incorporates and manifests each of the fundamental dimensions of the conjugal life. As part of the institution of marriage the conjugal act possesses a specific content (that is, structure, ends, goods, laws) that is inscribed by God in the very being of man and woman. The conjugal act consummates marriage insofar as it embodies the act of marital consent that brings the institution of marriage into existence. Husband and wife cooperate with God in the conjugal act by conforming their activity to his creative intention for sexuality, thereby enjoying a particular realization of the goods of marriage. The conjugal act also manifests the conjugal friendship, perfecting and confirming the love of husband and wife on the basis of the so-called language of the body. As an act of conjugal love, the conjugal act possesses the essential characteristics of conjugal love. Therefore, the conjugal act entails the total gift of self through the complementarity of masculinity and femininity in a bodily act that issues from reason and will by which husband and wife cooperate with God in the transmission of life. Thus, in line with the nature of the conjugal life, the conjugal act is ordered to procreation and union as the specific common goods around which husband and wife form a communion of persons in the act. The personal union at the heart of the conjugal act provides the basis for the sacramentality of the act. As a sacramental act sharing in the sacramentality of the conjugal covenant, the conjugal act sacramentally represents the personal loving communion of the Trinity, God's love for humanity, and Christ's love for the Church.

The Church's doctrines on the conjugal life account for the indispensability of procreation and union in the conjugal act. In a certain sense the Church's theology of the conjugal act has been developed in order to affirm that the finalities of the conjugal life pertain to the conjugal act itself and not merely to the ensemble of conjugal life.[3] According to the Church's theology of the conjugal act, because they both "pertain to the intimate truth of the conjugal act",[4] procreation and union are the indispensable essential aspects and meanings of the conjugal act. As such, spouses cannot intend or experience the conjugal act unless they direct themselves to these two goods, goods that are intrinsically linked by their very definitions. Since the Church's approach to the conjugal act considers the act as a human act (*actus humanus*), the Church describes the act in terms of intention and choice rather than the physical element of the act. Thus, the indispensability of procreation and union refers to the order of active willing, the level of intention and choice.

[3] In *Humanae vitae* Pope Paul VI explicitly addressed the question, "Could it not be admitted . . . that the finality of procreation pertains to the ensemble of the conjugal life, rather than to its single acts?" In his response to this question, Paul VI laid the foundations for a profound theology of the conjugal act, affirming that every conjugal act must remain open to the transmission of life since procreation and union belong to its essence and meaning as a human act of love. See, HV 3, 11, and 12.

[4] John Paul II, General Audience of August 22, 1984.

Ultimately, the intention and choice of procreation and union provide the basis for conjugal love in the act. Insofar as procreation and union are common goods, the intention of procreation and union makes the conjugal act an act of love or friendship, and as goods of the conjugal life, procreation and union make the conjugal act an act of *conjugal* love. However, apart from the intention of procreation and union, genital intercourse is neither conjugal nor an act of love.

In the light of Christian anthropology, the teachings of the Church account for the diverse dimensions of the conjugal act as a human act, a symbolic act, and a sacramental act that proceeds from the use of reason and will in the intention and choice of procreation and union and that effects a personal union through self-donation and co-subjectivity. The Catholic understanding of the body as a constitutive part of the person, of freedom as *theonomy*, and of conscience as a witness to the truth provides the foundations of an understanding of the conjugal act as the objective, universal expression of conjugal love appropriated and lived by husband and wife in their free acts. According to these fundamental principles of Christian anthropology, in the sexual expression of their love husband and wife "are not free to proceed completely at will, as if they could determine in a wholly autonomous way the honest path to follow; but they must conform their activity to the creative intention of God, expressed in the very nature of marriage and its acts."[5] In other words, while spouses freely engage in the conjugal act, they never act in a wholly autonomous way. Instead, they must conform their act to the creative intention of God (the truth about sexuality) expressed in the law, manifest in the

---

[5] HV 10.

inherent finalities of the body, and disclosed by man's conscience. Moreover, inasmuch as acting freely implies the intention of an end, in conforming "their activity" to God's creative intention, husband and wife must conform their intention and choice, not simply their physical activity, to the truth. Thus, the Church can identify a specific intention that must occur in the conjugal act without negating freedom in the act. Freedom properly understood enables spouses to embrace (through intention and choice) the truth of the conjugal act, yet they never possess the ability to determine its essential content and meaning.

Together these two foundational frameworks (the theology of marriage and Christian anthropology) supply the basis for an understanding of the conjugal act as a personal act by which husband and wife fulfill their innate vocation to love and communion in accord with the truth of their being as man and woman. Thus, we can locate the basis of the Church's profound appreciation of the sexual relationship of husband and wife in two converging, fundamental theological frameworks: (1) the Church's doctrine on the conjugal life and (2) the Church's doctrine on the human person as a free and responsible agent.

The Church's position on the conjugal act represents the organic development of these more fundamental doctrines on the conjugal life and on the human person. Conversely, those who fail to see the profound significance of the conjugal act invariably also deviate from the Church's position on these more fundamental questions. Those who view the conjugal life as merely an intimate friendship between two persons or merely the convenient product of cultural evolution reduce the conjugal act to a mere display of sentiment or to a culturally sanctioned satisfaction of the sexual urge. Likewise those who exalt freedom and conscience and deny man's fundamental relationship to God's law subject the essence and meaning of the conjugal act to the whims of man. Finally, if the body is not a constitutive part of the person, then the body and its faculties become raw data open to manipulation in the search for heightened sexual experiences. Ultimately these misguided approaches to the conjugal act empty the act of its most profound significance in the name of romance, sociology, or personal sovereignty.

The unique vantage point of the Church in sexual matters, then, seems to result primarily from a multi-faceted approach to the conjugal life that accounts for its various dimensions as an institution, a friendship, and a sacrament and from an appreciation of authentic personal freedom that harmonizes genuine personal autonomy with the demands of the truth. These foundational teachings on the conjugal life and anthropology rely upon the more fundamental idea of an objective truth about man (and thus sexuality) that the human intellect discovers through the revelation of Christ and to which the human will conforms. The Christian mystery brings this objective truth to light, while the nuptial meaning of the human body expresses the same truth and the human conscience, echoing the voice of God, brings this truth to bear on human action in the sexual domain. Thus, the Church's position runs counter not only to the modern exaltation of free will, which claims an unlimited autonomy in action, but also to the modern exaltation of the human intellect, which portrays the individual intellect as the defining source of the "truth" about the human person. The Catholic theology of the conjugal act differs so greatly from the popular view of sexual relations precisely because it emerges from a view of the human person and personal liberty that rejects the modern presupposition that states, "At the heart of liberty is the right to define one's own concept of existence, of meaning, of the universe, and of the mystery of human life."[6] The Church, grounding her theology of the conjugal act in meanings "that God the Creator has inscribed in the very being of man and woman and in the dynamism of their sexual communion",[7] simply reiterates and unfolds the objective truth about sexuality as it becomes clear in the light of the Christian mystery by virtue of the conviction that man cannot create the truth but must conform himself to the truth.

The Catholic theology of the conjugal act manifests a fundamental conviction about man's inability to define the meaning of his own sexuality, a meaning that he discovers as a norm for his own behavior in the sexual realm. In turn, this fundamental conviction points to something greater, something more profound, and something equally forgotten by the popular approach to sexuality: the Christian God is a personal God who loves man enough to relate to him, to cooperate with him, and to direct him to the good. Man has not been placed in the universe and left to flounder to make sense of his life. Man has been called into existence *through love* and *for love*.[8] Unlike the "modern" man, the Christian does not suffer from an identity crisis; the Christian knows that he has been created in the image and likeness of God and called to loving personal communion through the sincere gift of self. The Christian enjoys this self-understanding by virtue of the Christian mystery, for "only in the mystery of the Incarnate Word does the mystery of man take on light. . . . Christ, the new Adam, in the very revelation of the

[6] United States Supreme Court, *Planned Parenthood of SE Pennsylvania v. Casey*, April 22, 1992.

[7] FC 32.

[8] Cf. FC 11.

mystery of the Father and His love, fully reveals man to himself and brings to light his most high calling."[9]

A Summary of the Major Ideas Identified in the Study

My consideration of the conjugal act was ordered to a threefold methodological goal inasmuch as it proposed to investigate the conjugal act itself, the nature of the conjugal relationship, and the Church's vision of man. In order to summarize the results of my study, I refer to the following points as the most important ideas to have emerged through the course of my investigation of these three areas of concern. Each of the ideas listed here constitutes a fundamental element of the interlocking theoretical framework that comprises the Catholic concept of the conjugal act.

Regarding the Conjugal Act:

- The conjugal act proceeds from rational intention and choice ordered to specific goods as ends. As a human act (*actus humanus*), the conjugal act must be described and considered in terms of free will (volition) and can never be reduced to a physical or material event.
- The finality of marriage and conjugal love pertains to each and every conjugal act.
- In the creation of man as male and female God determined the structure, goods, ends, meanings, and laws of the conjugal act, inscribing the nature/meaning of the act in the very being of man and woman as sexual persons.

[9] GS 22.

- In performing the conjugal act, husband and wife remain free but do not proceed in a wholly autonomous manner.
- Procreation and union are essential/indispensable aspects of the conjugal act that account for the conjugal character of the act and that make it an act of love inasmuch as they are common goods.
- As an act of conjugal love, the conjugal act necessarily entails co-subjectivity and the mutual self-donation of the spouses to each other by virtue of the common goods of procreation and union that are essential aspects of the act.
- There is an indissoluble connection (willed by God) between procreation and union by the very definitions of the two realities as a consequence of the substantial unity of the human person. By virtue of this indissoluble connection, any attack on one of these goods necessarily also regards the other, and neither good ever exists apart from the other precisely because the one is activated with the other and by the other.
- The procreative and unitive meanings of the conjugal act derive from an experience of the act, thus relying upon consciousness for the possibility of experience and on the nature of the act for the authenticity of the experience.
- In addition to possessing a natural symbolism through the language of the body, the conjugal act participates in the sacramentality of the conjugal covenant, thereby signifying the personal loving communion of the Trinity, the love of God for humanity, and the love of Christ for the Church.
- The natural symbolism and the sacramental symbolism of the conjugal act are dependent upon the intrinsic

structure of the act inasmuch as both of these types of symbolism corrupt when sexual intercourse ceases to be an act of personal union.

Regarding the Conjugal Life:

- The conjugal life entails a natural institution, a personal friendship, and a sacrament, and the notion of vocation encompasses all of these diverse dimensions of the conjugal life (that is, husband and wife are called by God to live out each of these three dimensions of the conjugal life).
- The structure, goods, ends, meanings, and laws of the conjugal life are determined by God and inscribed in the nature of man and woman as sexual persons.
- In living the conjugal life, husband and wife remain free, but they always act as cooperators with God, conforming their activity to God's plan for marriage.
- Procreation and union are indispensable/essential aspects of the conjugal life as the ends of marriage and as the common goods upon which the conjugal communion forms.
- The conjugal life possesses a sacramentality by which it images the personal communion of the Trinity and signifies God's love for humanity and Christ's love for the Church.

Regarding Christian Anthropology:

- The human person exists as a composite of matter and spirit by virtue of the substantial union of body and soul. For that reason, the body is a constitutive part of the person and "expresses" the person. The substantial unity of the person accounts for the indissoluble connection between procreation and union and also allows for the expression of personal union through bodily union.

- The natural moral law is God's law "written on the heart of the person". The precepts of the natural law reiterate man's vocation to love, with certain precepts of the natural law referring specifically to the vocation to marriage. This understanding of the natural law accounts for the manner in which the nature of conjugal love and marriage and the conjugal act are inscribed in the being of man and woman.
- Freedom understood as participated theonomy preserves man's genuine moral autonomy without granting him an absolute sovereignty. The notion of participated theonomy allows man to love freely while also conforming his activity to the creative intention of God. According to this understanding of freedom, the moral requirements of the conjugal life in no way constrict or hinder the ability of husband and wife to love each other freely.
- An understanding of conscience that allows man to identify the true, objective good as indicated by God's law while at the same time appropriating as his own the truth of the law provides the necessary point of contact between God's law and human freedom. This understanding of conscience allows husband and wife to identify the goods upon which their love is based and enables them to appropriate the objective, universal content of the conjugal act, making the act their own personal expression of love.
- An understanding of consciousness by which man can experience the meaning of an act he is performing (without fabricating the experience) provides the necessary basis for describing procreation and union as

the meanings of the conjugal act in addition to the goods and ends of the act. This notion of consciousness and meaning accounts for the integration of the ontological dimension and the subjective dimension of the conjugal act, indicating the need to preserve the intrinsic structure of the act in order to have an authentic experience of union and procreation.

- An action theory that describes human acts according to intention and choice provides the basis for understanding acts as metaphysical and moral realities beyond their merely physical components. Such an action theory necessitates a consideration of the conjugal act according to volition and highlights the importance of the goods of procreation and union within a description of the conjugal act inasmuch as they provide the terminus for volition.
- The human capacity for co-subjectivity and self-donation in the pursuit of a common good provides the basis for the love of friendship between persons. The concepts of co-subjectivity and self-donation confirm the conjugal act as an act of love inasmuch as it inherently entails co-subjectivity and self-donation by virtue of being ordered to the common goods of procreation and union, and they also account for the indispensability of procreation and union for conjugal love and for the conjugal act as a specific act of conjugal love.

The Basis of a "Catholic" Concept of Sexuality and Marriage

Each of the fundamental ideas listed above points in its own way to the integration of the Catholic understanding of sexuality and the Catholic concept of the person. In turn, an emphasis on this integration helps us to realize more clearly that "doubt or error in the field of marriage or the family involves obscuring to a serious extent the integral truth about the human person." [10] By rejecting or dismissing the Church's teaching on sexuality, one necessarily takes a stand against the Christian understanding of the human person. In addition to clarifying the serious implications of rejecting the Church's teaching on sexuality, the integration between the Church's doctrine on sexuality and her concept of the person serves as the basis of a specifically Catholic understanding of sexuality, placing issues concerning sexuality clearly within the scope of Christian doctrine.

In a certain sense the universality and the naturalness of marriage and the conjugal relationship would seem to preclude the need for or value of a Christian reflection on the sexual life of husband and wife. Sex seems to be something that falls outside the scope of Christian doctrine. Marriage and sexual intercourse long preceded the Church. Husbands and wives have been transmitting life and expressing love through sexual intercourse for an entire history. Moreover, sexuality and the sexual act appear across the spectrum of the animal world, thus revealing their naturalness. Given sexuality's naturalness and universality, why would couples need the Church to "teach" them how to love each other sexually and how to transmit life? How could something as natural and seemingly simple as sexual intercourse become the subject of Christian doctrine, a body of truths that bases itself in divine revelation?

While the universality and naturalness of sexual intercourse can initially lead to such questioning, understood cor-

[10] FC 31.

rectly this universality and naturalness provide the key to understanding why the Church can teach man and woman about sexuality and how the Church arrives at a specific (that is, beyond the popular) concept of sexual relations between husband and wife. Marriage and sexual intercourse possess a certain universality and naturalness precisely because these realities derive from human nature, not from human culture. Sexuality and marriage belong to the very nature of man and woman as human persons. And since Christ fully reveals man to himself,[11] the integral components of human nature find their clearest explanation in the context of Christian doctrine. Because it belongs to the nature of the human person, sexuality (and its exercise) becomes truly comprehensible only in the context of the Christian mystery and consequently falls within the scope of Church teaching.[12] Thus, we arrive at a specifically Catholic concept of sexuality because we begin with a specifically Catholic concept of the human person, and we possess a specifically Catholic concept of the person by viewing man in the light of Christ.

Yet, the Church does not simply possess a "different" or "specific" concept of human sexuality. Instead, the Church offers the world a particularly insightful and profoundly dignified understanding of sexuality and the sexual act by virtue of the theological framework within which the Church's theology of the conjugal act has been developed. The context

---

[11] Cf. GS 22 and RH 8 and 10.

[12] Paul Quay writes, "We can get a right picture of human sexuality—or anything else in our nature—only insofar as it is contained in Christ. In Him alone will we find unfallen nature and in its absolute fullness, as it was intended by God from the beginning. It follows, since integral human nature is understood only in Christ, that integral human sexuality is a mystery of faith" (*The Christian Meaning of Human Sexuality* [San Francisco: Ignatius Press, 1985], p. 10).

of Christian anthropology allows the Church to penetrate the vast wealth of significance inherent in sexuality and the sexual act, shedding light on both the beauty and the gravity of sexual relations. Above all, the Christian mystery opens the way to an appreciation of the sacred and sacramental character of conjugal relations. The sacramental dimension of the conjugal life not only adds value and meaning to the conjugal act but also ultimately explains why such great care and responsibility must be taken in the sexual domain. The world benefits greatly from the sacramental manifestation of God's love provided by spouses who live out their conjugal relationship according to the truth. What a great loss when ignorance of the truth or disdain for the truth prevents or precludes this manifestation of love.

In the light of Christ, human sexuality becomes a matter of faith, a subject of divine revelation, taking on the gravity that the very word "sacrament" should evoke in us. For this reason, the Church possesses not only the capacity but also the duty to instruct spouses with regard to their sexual relationship. The Church faithfully exhorts husband and wife to preserve the full value and integral meaning of the conjugal act out of love for the precious goods (both natural and supernatural) at stake in the sexual domain. The Church unwaveringly reaffirms her doctrines on sexual ethics, unwilling to see the beauty and significance of the conjugal act cast aside in the name of convenience or erotic pleasure. Promoting the meaning and value of sexuality according to its most profound and sacred aspects, the teachings of the Church can pose a considerable challenge to married couples. Preserving the full meaning of conjugal love in the sexual relationship often requires self-sacrifice, self-mastery, and a willingness to transcend the level of individual pleasure. Yet, these challenges are simply part of the nature of marriage as a Christian vocation, a call and a path to holiness. In preserving the full meaning of their sexual relationship, spouses not only preserve the beauty and depth of their relationship but also proceed down the path to their own joy and ultimately to their own sanctification. "In the context of a culture which seriously distorts or entirely misinterprets the true meaning of human sexuality",[13] the Church cannot refrain from urging spouses down such a path. Thus, Pope John Paul II summarizes the position of the Church:

> The Church knows the path by which the family can reach the heart of the deepest truth about itself. The Church has learned this path at the school of Christ and the school of history interpreted in the light of the Spirit. She does not impose it but feels an urgent need to propose it to everyone without fear and indeed with great confidence and hope, although she knows that the Good News includes the subject of the Cross. But it is through the Cross that the family can attain the fullness of its being and the perfection of its love.[14]

[13] FC 31.

[14] FC 86.

ABBREVIATIONS

AAS	*Acta Apostolicae Sedis*
CCC	*Catechism of the Catholic Church*
DV	Congregation for the Doctrine of the Faith, instruction *Donum vitae* (February 22, 1987)
FC	John Paul II, apostolic exhortation *Familiaris consortio* (November 2, 1981)
GS	Vatican Council II, Pastoral Constitution on the Church in the Modern World, *Gaudium et spes* (December 7, 1965)
HV	Paul VI, encyclical *Humanae vitae* (July 25, 1968)
LF	John Paul II, *Letter to Families* (February 2, 1994)
LG	Vatican Council II, Dogmatic Constitution of the Church, *Lumen Gentium* (November 21, 1964)
PH	Congregation for the Doctrine of the Faith, declaration *Personae humanae* (December 29, 1975)
RH	John Paul II, encyclical *Redemptor Hominis* (March 4, 1979)
VS	John Paul II, encyclical *Veritatis splendor* (August 6, 1993)

SELECTED BIBLIOGRAPHY

Magisterial Documents

Catechism of the Catholic Church (Vatican City: Libreria Editrice Vaticana, 1994).

Congregation for Catholic Education. "Educational Guidance in Human Love". *L'Osservatore Romano*, English ed. December 5, 1983.

Congregation for the Doctrine of the Faith. *Persona humana. AAS* 68 (1975).

Congregation for the Doctrine of the Faith. *Donum vitae*. Vatican translation. Boston: St. Paul Books, 1987.

Flannery, Austin, ed. *Vatican Council II: The Counciliar and Post Counciliar Documents*. New York: Costello Publishing, 1980.

John Paul II. *Redemptor hominis*. Vatican translation. Boston: St. Paul Books, 1980.

John Paul II. *Familiaris consortio*. Vatican translation. Boston: St. Paul Books, 1982.

John Paul II. *Discourse to the Members of the 35th General Assembly of the World Medical Association, October 29, 1983. AAS* 76 (1984).

John Paul II. *Discourse to Priests Participating in a Seminar on "Responsible Parenthood"*. In *Insegnamenti di Giovanni Paolo II*, 6, 2 (1983).

JOHN PAUL II. *Veritatis splendor.* Vatican translation. Boston: St. Paul Books, 1993.

JOHN PAUL II. *Letter to Families.* Vatican translation. Boston: St. Paul Books, 1994.

JOHN PAUL II. General Audiences from September 5, 1979, to November 28, 1984. In *The Theology of the Body*. Boston: Pauline Books and Media, 1997.

JOHN PAUL II. "Families, God Calls You to Holiness!" *L'Osservatore Romano*, English ed. October 8, 1997.

JOHN PAUL II. "Message to the Centre for Research and Study on the Natural Regulation of Fertility". *L'Osservatore Romano*, English ed. March 11, 1998.

JOHN PAUL II. "Human Life Must Originate in the Conjugal Act". *L'Osservatore Romano*, English ed. September 1, 1999.

PAUL VI. *Humanae vitae.* Translated by NCB News Service. Boston: St. Paul Books, 1991.

PIUS XI. *Casti connubii*, *AAS* 22 (1930).

PIUS XII. *Selected Discourses*. In *The Teachings of Pius XII.* New York: Pantheon Books, 1957.

PIUS XII. *Major Addresses of Pope Pius XII.* St. Paul: North Central Publishing, 1961.

PONTIFICAL COUNCIL FOR THE FAMILY. *The Truth and Meaning of Human Sexuality*. November 21, 1995. Translated by Catholic World News. Internet: New Advent, 1999.

SACRA ROMANA ROTA. *AAS* 36 (1944).

NON-MAGISTERIAL BOOKS AND ARTICLES

ALVIRA, TOMÁS, LUIS CLAVELL, AND TOMÁS MELENDO. *Metaphysics*. Translated by Luis Supan. Manila: Sinag-Tala, 1991.

ARISTOTLE. *Nicomachean Ethics*. Translated by David Ross. Oxford: Oxford University Press, 1980.

ASHLEY, BENEDICT. "The Use of Moral Theory in the Church". In *Human Sexuality and Personhood*. St. Louis: Pope John Center, 1981.

AUGUSTINE OF HIPPO. *City of God*. Translated by Henry Bettenson. London: Penguin Books, 1984.

AUGUSTINE OF HIPPO. *On the Good of Marriage*. In *Nicene and Post-Nicene Fathers*, edited by Alexander Roberts and James Donaldson. Oak Harbor: Logos Research, 1997.

AUGUSTINE OF HIPPO. *On the Grace of Christ and Original Sin*. In *Nicene and Post-Nicene Fathers*, edited by Alexander Roberts and James Donaldson. Oak Harbor: Logos Research, 1997.

AUGUSTINE OF HIPPO. *On the Morals of the Manicheans*. In *Nicene and Post-Nicene Fathers*, edited by Alexander Roberts and James Donaldson. Oak Harbor: Logos Research, 1997.

BOYLE, JOHN, ed. *Creative Love: The Ethics of Human Reproduction*. Front Royal, Va.: Christendom Press, 1989.

BROCK, STEPHEN. *Action and Conduct: Thomas Aquinas and the Theory of Action*. Edinburgh: T&T Clark, 1998.

BURKE, CORMAC. *Covenanted Happiness*. Princeton: Scepter Press, 1999.

BURKE, CORMAC. "Marriage and Contraception". In *Why "Humanae Vitae" Was Right*, edited by Janet E. Smith. San Francisco: Ignatius Press, 1993.

BUTTIGLIONE, ROCCO. *Il pensiero di Karol Wojtyla*. Milan: Jaca Book, 1982.

CAFFARRA, CARLO. "L'autonomia della coscienza e la sottomissione all verità". In *La coscienza*, edited by Graziano Borgonovo. Vatican City: Libreria Editrice Vaticana, 1996.

CAFFARRA, CARLO. *Etica generale della sessualità*. Milan: Edizioni Ares, 1992.

CAFFARRA, CARLO. *Living in Christ: Fundamental Principles of Catholic Moral Theology*. San Francisco: Ignatius Press, 1987.

CAFFARRA, CARLO. *Sessualità*. Milan: Edizioni San Paolo, 1994.

CAFFARRA, CARLO. "Who Is Like the Lord, Our God?" In *Why "Humanae Vitae" Was Right*, edited by Janet E. Smith. San Francisco: Ignatius Press, 1993.

CICCONE, LINO, *Uomo-Donna: L'amore umano nel piano divino*. Turin: Elle Di Ci, 1986.

CONCETTI, GINO. *Sessualità, amore, procreazione*. Milan: Edizioni Ares, 1990.

CROSBY, JOHN. "The Personalism of John Paul II as the Basis of His Approach to *Humanae Vitae*". *Anthropotes,* vol. 5, no. 1 (May 1989).

DINOIA, J. A. AND ROMANUS CESSARIO, eds. *"Veritatis Splendor" and the Renewal of Moral Theology*. Chicago: Midwest Theological Forum, 1999.

Escrivá, Josémaría. "In Joseph's Workshop". In *Christ Is Passing By*. New Rochelle: Scepter Press, 1974.

Fedoryka, Damian. "Man: The Creature of God". In *Creative Love: The Ethics of Human Reproduction*, edited by John Boyle. Front Royal, Va.: Christendom Press, 1989.

Franquet Casas, María José. *Persona, Acción y Libertad: Las Clavas de la Antropología de Karol Wojtyla*. Pamplona: Ediciones Universidad de Navarra, 1996.

Gallagher, John. "Magisterial Teaching from 1918 to the Present". In *Human Sexuality and Personhood*. St. Louis: Pope John Center, 1981.

García de Haro, Ramón. "Fondamenti antropologica ed etica della procreazione umana". *Rivista Rosminiana di filosofia ed cultura* 83 (1989).

García de Haro, Ramón. *Legge, coscienza, & libertà*. Milan: Edizione Ares, 1990.

García de Haro, Ramón. *Marriage and Family in the Documents of the Magisterium*. Translated by William May. San Francisco: Ignatius Press, 1993.

García de Haro, Ramón. *La vita cristiana*. Milan: Edizione Ares, 1995.

Gasparro, Guila, et al. *The Human Couple in the Fathers*. Translated by Thomas Halton. Boston: Pauline Books and Media, 1999.

Gil Hellín, Francisco. "Aspetti untivo e procreativo dell'essere del matrimonio e della vita coniugale". In *Matrimonio e Famiglia*, edited by the Pontifical Council for the Family. Turin: Elle Di Ci, 1987.

GIL HELLÍN, FRANCISCO. "Los *bona matrimonii* en la Costitución pastoral *Gaudium et spes* del Concilio Vaticano II". *Scripta Theologica* 11 (1979).

GIL HELLÍN, FRANCISCO. *Il Matrimonio e la Vita Coniugale.* Vatican City: Libreria Editrice Vaticano, 1996.

GIL HELLÍN, FRANCISCO, AND ANGEL RODRÍGUEZ LUÑO. "Il fondamento antropologico della *Humanae vitae* nel Magistero di Giovanni Paolo II". In *"Humanae vitae": 20 anni dopo. Atti del II Congresso Internazionale di Teologia Morale.* Milan: Edizioni Ares, 1989.

HAAS, JOHN. "The Inseparability of the Two Meanings of the Marriage Act". In *Reproductive Technologies, Marriage and the Church.* Braintree, Mass.: Pope John Center, 1988.

HANIGAN, JAMES P. *What Are They Saying about Sexual Morality?* New York: Paulist Press, 1982.

HÄRING, BERNARD. "The Inseparability of the Unitive-Procreative Functions of the Marital Act". In *Contraception, Authority, and Dissent*, edited by Charles Curran. New York: Paulist Press, 1971.

HEALY, MICHAEL. "Man: A Unity of Body and Soul". In *Creative Love: The Ethics of Human Reproduction*, edited by John Boyle. Front Royal, Va.: Christendom Press, 1989.

HOGAN, RICHARD. "A Theology of the Body". *Fidelity* 1 (December 1981).

HONINGS, BONIFACIO. "Il principio di inscindibilità". *Lateranum* 44 (1978).

IBÁÑEZ LANGLOIS, JOSÉ MIGUEL. "The Theological Argument at the Basis of *Humanae Vitae*". In *"Humanae vitae": 20 anni dopo. Atti del II Congresso Internazionale di Teologia Morale.* Milan: Edizione Ares, 1989.

Jimenez Hernández, Emiliano. *Uomo e donna, immagine di Dio.* Naples: Grafite Editrice, 1998.

Kiely, Bartholomew, "Contraception, In Vitro Fertilization and the Principle of Inseparability". In *"Humanae vitae": 20 anni dopo. Atti del II Congresso Internazionale di Teologia Morale.* Milan: Edizione Ares, 1989.

Kosnik, Anthony, et al. *Human Sexuality, New Directions in American Catholic Thought: A Study.* Commissioned by the Catholic Theological Society of America. New York: Paulist Press, 1977.

Lawler, Ronald. *The Christian Personalism of John Paul II.* Chicago: Franciscan Herald Press, 1982.

Lawler, Ronald, Joseph Boyle, Jr., and William May, *Catholic Sexual Ethics.* Huntington, Ind.: Our Sunday Visitor, 1985.

Leies, John, ed. *Human Sexuality and Personhood.* Braintree, Mass.: Pope John Center, 1990.

Liptak, David Q. *The Gift of Life.* Lakeforth: Liturgical Press, 1988.

Lucas Lucas, Ramón. *L'uomo spirito incarnato.* Cinisello Balsamo: Edizione Paoline, 1993.

Lucas Lucas, Ramón, ed. *"Veritatis splendor": Testo Integrale e Commento Filosofico-Teologico.* Milan: Edizione San Paolo, 1994.

MATTHEEUWS, ALAIN. *Union et procréation*. Paris: Les Éditions du Cerf, 1989.

MAY, WILLIAM. "Anthropological Advances in *Humanae Vitae*". In *"Humanae vitae": Servizio profetico per l'uomo*. Rome: Editrice Ave, 1995.

MAY, WILLIAM. "An Integrist Understanding". In *Dimensions of Sexuality*, edited by Dennis Doherty. New York: Doubleday, 1979.

MAY, WILLIAM. *An Introduction to Moral Theology*. Huntington, Ind.: Our Sunday Visitor, 1994.

MAY, WILLIAM. "Marriage and the Complementarity of Male and Female". *Anthropotes* vol. 7, no.1 (June 1992).

MAY, WILLIAM. *Marriage: The Rock on Which the Family Is Built*. San Francisco: Ignatius Press, 1995.

MAY, WILLIAM. "The Sanctity of Human Life, Marriage and Family in the Thought of Pope John Paul II". *Annales Theologici* 2:1 (1988).

MAY, WILLIAM. *Sex, Marriage and Chastity*. Chicago: Franciscan Herald Press, 1981.

MCCORMICK, RICHARD. "Notes on Moral Theology". *Theological Studies*, vol. 29, no. 4 (December 1968).

MELINA, LIVIO. *Corso di Bioetica: Il Vangelo della vita*. Casale Monferrato: Edizioni Piemme, 1996.

MIRALLES, ANTONIO. "Chiavi teologiche di lettura dei significati unitivo e procreativo dell'atto coniugale". In *"Humanae vitae": 20 anni dopo. Atti del Congresso Internazionale di Teologia Morale*. Edizione Ares, 1989.

MIRALLES, ANTONIO. *Il Matrimonio*. Cinisello Balsamo, Milan: Edizione San Paolo, 1996.

MODRAS, RONALD. "Pope John Paul II's Theology of the Body". In *John Paul II and Moral Theology*, edited by Charles Curran and Richard McCormick. New York: Paulist Press, 1998.

PINCKAERS, SERVAIS. "Coscienza, verità e prudenza". In *Coscienza*, edited by Graziano Borgonovo. Vatican City: Libreria Editrice Vaticana, 1996.

PINCKAERS, SERVAIS. *Pour une lecture de "Veritatis splendor"*. Paris: Editions Mance, 1995.

PINCKAERS, SERVAIS. *The Sources of Christian Ethics*. Translated by Mary Thomas Noble. Washington, D.C.: Catholic University of America Press, 1995.

QUAY, PAUL. *The Christian Meaning of Human Sexuality*. San Francisco: Ignatius Press, 1985.

RATZINGER, JOSEPH CARDINAL. "Man between Reproduction and Creation: Theological Questions on the Origin of Human Life". In *Trust the Truth*, edited by Russell Smith. Braintree, Mass.: Pope John Center, 1991.

RHONHEIMER, MARTIN. "Contraception, Sexual Behavior, and Natural Law: Philosophical Foundations of the Norm of *Humanae Vitae*". In *"Humanae vitae": 20 anni dopo. Atti del Congresso Internazionale di Teologia Morale*. Edizione Ares, 1989.

RHONHEIMER, MARTIN. *Natural Law and Practical Reason: A Thomist View of Moral Autonomy*. Translated by Gerald Malsbary. New York: Fordham University Press, 2000.

RODRÍGUEZ LUÑO, ANGEL. *Etica.* Milan: Le Monnier, 1992.

RODRÍGUEZ LUÑO, ANGEL. "Etica della sessualità e della procreazione". *Annales Theologici* 2 (1988).

RODRÍGUEZ LUÑO, ANGEL. *La scelta etica.* Milan: Edizioni Ares, 1988.

RUSSO, GIOVANNI, ed. *"Veritatis splendor": Genesi, elaborazione, significato.* 2d ed. Rome: Edizioni Dehoniane, 1995.

SAWARD, JOHN. *Christ Is the Answer: The Christ-Centered Teaching of Pope John Paul II.* New York: Alba House, 1995.

SCHMITZ, KENNETH. *At the Center of the Human Drama.* Washington, D.C.: Catholic University of America Press, 1993.

SHIVANANDAN, MARY. *Crossing the Threshold of Love.* Washington, D.C.: Catholic University of America Press, 1999.

SMITH, JANET. *"Humanae Vitae", a Generation Later.* Washington, D.C.: Catholic University of America Press, 1991.

SMITH, JANET. "The Importance of the Concept of *Munus* to Understanding *Humanae Vitae*". In *Why "Humanae Vitae" Was Right.* San Francisco: Ignatius Press, 1993.

SMITH, JANET. "Natural Law and Personalism in *Veritatis Splendor*". In *John Paul II and Moral Theology*, edited by Charles Curran and Richard McCormick. New York: Paulist Press, 1998.

SMITH, JANET. "Pope John Paul II and *Humanae Vitae*". *International Review of Natural Family Planning* 10, no. 2 (summer 1986).

SMITH, JANET. "The Vocation to Marriage". In *Creative Love: The Ethics of Human Reproduction*, edited by John Boyle. Front Royal, Va.: Christendom Press, 1989.

SMITH, JANET, ed. *Why "Humanae Vitae" Was Right*. San Francisco: Ignatius Press, 1993.

SOWLE CAHILL, LISA. "Accent on the Masculine". In *Understanding "Veritatis Splendor"*, edited by John Wilkins. London: SPCK, 1994.

TETTAMANZI, DIONIGI. "La *Humanae vitae* nel decennio 1968–1978. Continuitá di magistero e riflessione teologica". *La Scuola Cattolica* 107 (1979).

TETTAMANZI, DIONIGI. *I due saranno una carne sola*. Turin: Elle Di Ci, 1986.

TETTAMANZI, DIONIGI. "Reflections on *Veritatis Splendor*: Only the Son Brings True Freedom". *L'Osservatore Romano*, English ed. October 27, 1993.

TETTAMANZI, DIONIGI. *L'uomo, immagine di Dio*. Casale Monferrato: Edizione Piemme, 1992.

THOMAS AQUINAS. *Summa contra gentiles*. Translated by Vernon Bourke. London: Notre Dame Press, 1975.

THOMAS AQUINAS. *Summa theologica*. Translated by English Dominicans. Allen: Christian Classics, 1981.

TRAPÈ, AGOSTINO. Introduzione generale. *Sant'Agostino, Matrimonio e verginità*. Rome: Nuova Biblioteca Agostiniana, 1978.

VON HILDEBRAND, DIETRICH. *Marriage: The Mystery of Faithful Love*. Manchester: Sophia Institute Press, 1997.

WOJTYLA, KAROL. *The Acting Person*. Translated by Andrzej Potocki. Boston: D. Reidel Publishing, 1979.

WOJTYLA, KAROL. *Love and Responsibility*. Translated by H. Willets. San Francisco: Ignatius Press, 1993.

WOJTYLA, KAROL. "La visione antropologica dell *Humanae vitae*". *Lateranum* 44 (1978).

WOJTYLA, KAROL. "The Teaching of *Humanae Vitae* on Love". In *Person and Community*. Translated by Theresa Sandok. New York: Peter Lang, 1993.